ADHD
Coaching

ADHD Coaching

A GUIDE FOR MENTAL HEALTH PROFESSIONALS

Frances Prevatt and Abigail Levrini

American Psychological Association • *Washington, DC*

Copyright © 2015 by the American Psychological Association. All rights reserved. Except as permitted under the United States Copyright Act of 1976, no part of this publication may be reproduced or distributed in any form or by any means, including, but not limited to, the process of scanning and digitization, or stored in a database or retrieval system, without the prior written permission of the publisher.

Published by
American Psychological Association
750 First Street, NE
Washington, DC 20002
www.apa.org

To order
APA Order Department
P.O. Box 92984
Washington, DC 20090-2984
Tel: (800) 374-2721; Direct: (202) 336-5510
Fax: (202) 336-5502; TDD/TTY: (202) 336-6123
Online: www.apa.org/pubs/books
E-mail: order@apa.org

In the U.K., Europe, Africa, and the Middle East, copies may be ordered from
American Psychological Association
3 Henrietta Street
Covent Garden, London
WC2E 8LU England

Typeset in Meridien by Circle Graphics, Inc., Columbia, MD

Printer: Bang Printing, Brainerd, MN
Cover Designer: Naylor Design, Washington, DC

The opinions and statements published are the responsibility of the authors, and such opinions and statements do not necessarily represent the policies of the American Psychological Association.

Library of Congress Cataloging-in-Publication Data

Prevatt, Frances F., 1955- , author.
  ADHD coaching : a guide for mental health professionals / Frances Prevatt and Abigail Levrini. — First edition.
    p. ; cm.
  Includes bibliographical references and index.
  ISBN 978-1-4338-2014-4 — ISBN 1-4338-2014-5
  I. Levrini, Abigail, author. II. American Psychological Association, issuing body. III. Title.
  [DNLM: 1. Attention Deficit Disorder with Hyperactivity—therapy—Case Reports. 2. Counseling—methods—Case Reports. 3. Adolescent. 4. Adult. WS 350.8.A8]

  RC394.A85
  616.85'89—dc23

                                        2014048265

British Library Cataloguing-in-Publication Data
A CIP record is available from the British Library.

Printed in the United States of America
First Edition

http://dx.doi.org/10.1037/14671-000

Contents

INTRODUCTION 3

I

ADHD Coaching: Fundamentals and Beyond 7

Chapter 1. An Overview of ADHD 9

Chapter 2. A History and Overview of ADHD Coaching Interventions 25

Chapter 3. Underlying Principles and Procedures Used in ADHD Coaching 33

Chapter 4. The Nuts and Bolts of Coaching: Getting Started 45

Chapter 5. The Nuts and Bolts of Coaching: Working Through Issues 65

Chapter 6. Specific Strategies for ADHD Coaching 83

Chapter 7. Developing a Coaching Practice 109

II

ADHD Coaching Case Studies 127

Chapter 8. Case Study: ADHD Coaching With a Middle-Aged Adult 129

Chapter 9. Case Study: ADHD Coaching With a Young Professional Adult 145

Chapter 10. Case Study: ADHD Coaching With a College Student With Executive Functioning Deficits 171

Chapter 11. Case Study: ADHD Coaching With a Young Adult With Comorbid Mood Disorders 189

Chapter 12. Case Study: ADHD Coaching With an Adolescent 207

ADDITIONAL RESOURCES *227*
REFERENCES *237*
INDEX *255*
ABOUT THE AUTHORS *267*

ADHD Coaching

Introduction

Over the years, many people have asked us, as attention-deficit/ hyperactivity disorder (ADHD) specialists, to "explain how to do ADHD coaching." Although we have conducted brief workshops or made presentations, they seemed inadequate. We have long been interested in helping others to develop their skills in this area, but outside of our training clinic and practice, this has not been possible. Our intent in writing this book was to provide a theoretical orientation, foundational knowledge, and specific strategies, forms, and procedures that will help mental health practitioners to develop or improve their ADHD coaching skills. This is not the only way to do ADHD coaching, but it is based on empirically supported research documenting its efficacy. Like any therapeutic orientation, you will adapt it to fit your orientation and style.

The ADHD coaching program we describe in these pages was developed over the past 10 years at the Adult Learning Evaluation Center (ALEC) in Tallahassee, Florida, in collaboration with Psych Ed Coaches, a private practice specializing in ADHD

---

http://dx.doi.org/10.1037/14671-001
ADHD Coaching: A Guide for Mental Health Professionals, by F. Prevatt and A. Levrini
Copyright © 2015 by the American Psychological Association. All rights reserved.

coaching, with locations in the Washington, DC, and Jacksonville, FL, metro areas. ALEC is a not-for-profit psychoeducational center at Florida State University that provides training for graduate students in school psychology and counseling psychology. The program provides diagnostic and intervention services for high school students, college students, and adults from the local community who have learning difficulties, mental health issues, and ADHD. Although the basic program described in this book refers to the original ALEC model, at times we describe modifications as being "Psych Ed Coaching."

In the decade we have spent developing our coaching program, much has changed in the field of ADHD. Prevalence rates are on the rise, a new version of the *Diagnostic and Statistical Manual of Mental Disorders* (*DSM–5*) has changed the criteria we use to diagnose ADHD, and practitioners will soon be required to use the *International Classification of Diseases* (*ICD*) criteria. Theories regarding the etiology of ADHD have advanced, and we have a better understanding of the likely brain processes involved in symptoms of ADHD. New medications are on the market that seem to have better efficacy, with fewer side effects. More students with ADHD are attending college and receiving support services to help them achieve at the same rate as their peers without ADHD. Antidiscrimination laws in the workplace are providing support and protection for employees who choose to self-disclose their diagnosis. Many interventions are being promoted to help those with ADHD, and ADHD coaching is gaining acceptance as an effective clinical tool. We hope this book will motivate you to cultivate your skills in this area. Some of you may be established coaches, some may be early-career professionals, and some may be students in training. We do not believe that this book alone will make you an expert. We hope you will use it in conjunction with conference presentations and workshops, as well as supervised clinical experience. If you are a graduate student, we hope you will find practicum and internship opportunities to expand your skills.

What to Expect in This Book

Chapter 1 is a basic overview of ADHD. It includes prevalence rates, common symptoms, and types of impairment. We cover how ADHD may manifest in childhood and adolescence but focus more on college students and adults. We explain the etiology of ADHD and how it relates to executive functioning. We discuss common comorbidities and conclude with a discussion of *DSM–5* and *ICD* diagnosis of ADHD. Chapter 2 provides a general overview of ADHD coaching, including the empirical evidence of its effectiveness. This is followed in Chapter 3 by a more specific description of the underlying theories and principles used in our ADHD coaching approach. Chapters 4 and 5 demonstrate how these principles can be applied in practice and explain the "nuts and bolts" of our coaching program. Here, the reader will learn a step-by-step approach to conducting coaching, complete with forms and rating scales. Chapter 4 focuses on the initial stages of working with a client (evaluating for suitability, doing an initial intake), and Chapter 5 discusses the middle and concluding stages of coaching and includes more samples of specific measures and techniques.

Chapter 6 goes into detail about several of our favorite coaching strategies. These include the ADHD Life Wheel, the Inspiration Toolbox, the Decision-Making Table, the Juggling Exercise, the Processing Exercise, and the Eisenhower Matrix. Other strategies involve using a planner, being more "green" in coaching, and using career-planning resources. There are so many resources available on the Internet that it is not possible to list all of them, but Chapter 6 provides some good basic strategies and techniques. The chapter concludes with a resources section that provides information on various tools you and your clients may find useful, including planners, timers, apps and technology, and graphic organizers. Chapter 7 discusses the business of coaching and how to develop one's own practice and includes a list of resources to help you get started.

The five case example chapters illustrate specific goals and objectives used in various types of cases. These cases are based on clients with whom we have worked; however, all descriptions have been altered slightly to disguise the clients' identities. Although the general principles in this book apply to clients of all ages, we focus primarily on adults and older adolescents. We do not recommend individual ADHD coaching for children; rather, we find that in the primary grades, the parents will almost always need to be involved. Parents (or teachers) will be involved in planning behavioral management plans and implementing rewards or consequences. The case examples include an adult with career issues (Chapter 8), a professional adult with a variety of concerns (Chapter 9), a college student with executive functioning deficits (Chapter 10), a young adult with mental health issues (Chapter 11), and an adolescent with academic issues (Chapter 12). Many of the forms and worksheets mentioned in this text are available online at http://pubs.apa.org/books/supp/prevatt/.

We have found that ADHD coaching is one of the most rewarding areas of clinical practice. Our clients are typically motivated, engaging, and enjoyable to work with. ADHD is a treatable condition, and we see remarkable gains over time. We hope this book facilitates your own work with this inspiring population.

ADHD COACHING: FUNDAMENTALS AND BEYOND

An Overview of ADHD

This chapter provides a broad overview of attention-deficit/ hyperactivity disorder (ADHD). Most mental health professionals who are interested in ADHD coaching will likely have a basic understanding of ADHD; however, this chapter serves as a review that provides the foundation of a good coaching program. In this chapter, we cover prevalence rates, the symptoms of ADHD, and the specific impairments associated with the condition. These sections are broken down by childhood, adolescence, and college students and adults. We discuss the etiology of ADHD, as well as common comorbidities. We then conclude with a brief discussion of the fifth edition of the *Diagnostic and Statistical Manual* (*DSM–5*, American Psychiatric Association, 2013) and the most recent *International Classification of Diseases* (*ICD*; World Health Organization, 2010) codes that are generally used by practitioners.

---

http://dx.doi.org/10.1037/14671-002
ADHD Coaching: A Guide for Mental Health Professionals, by F. Prevatt and A. Levrini
Copyright © 2015 by the American Psychological Association. All rights reserved.

Prevalence of ADHD

ADHD is the most common developmental disorder in childhood, believed to affect between 3% and 5% of children and between 2% and 5% of adults (American Psychiatric Association, 2013; Biederman & Faraone, 2006; R. C. Kessler et al., 2006). However, statistics from the Centers for Disease Control and Prevention (CDC; 2012) have estimated higher rates in U.S. community samples. The CDC reports increases of up to 3% per year, with 2011–2012 rates in children at approximately 11%. Reports have also indicated a sharp increase in the number of college students with ADHD (Gaddy, 2008). Recent news reports claim that approximately 2.6 million U.S. adults now have prescriptions for medications to treat ADHD, up by half in the past few years; additionally, the biggest increase in prescriptions, up 85%, is among women ages 26 to 34 (Wente, 2014). It is unclear why prevalence rates for ADHD are increasing. Evidence suggests this may be due to a combination of factors, including better recognition, increased awareness, increasing biological vulnerabilities, and sociological factors such as chaotic households and increased childhood stress (Anuta, 2006). Hinshaw and Scheffler (2014) also reported a significant correlation between school-based accountability laws and rising ADHD prevalence rates. They speculated that school funding based on test scores gave schools an incentive to diagnose students with ADHD because that resulted in funding for special services, which helped these students do better or even removed them from the test score statistics. In summary, the widespread and gradually increasing prevalence of ADHD in both children and adults has made ADHD coaching an increasingly important therapeutic intervention (Goldstein, 2005).

Symptoms and Impairment

SYMPTOMS AND IMPAIRMENT IN CHILDHOOD

The most definable feature of ADHD is a "persistent pattern of inattention and/or hyperactivity-impulsivity that interferes with functioning or development" (American Psychiatric Association, 2013, p. 61). However, symptoms of ADHD manifest differently in children and adults. Children with ADHD tend to exhibit distractedness, impulsivity, fidgeting, and restlessness and commonly manifest limb motions such as jiggling their feet, tapping their fingers, squirming in their seats, and constantly changing their body positions (Barkley, 2005; Teeter, 2000).

Children with ADHD may run and climb excessively or have difficulty playing or engaging quietly in leisure activities; parents may first notice what appears to be deviant behavior in the home when the child is young. By the early grades, children with ADHD are often identified as deviant or immature. All of the following school-based behaviors will be difficult for children with ADHD: sitting still, attending, inhibiting impulsive behavior, cooperating, organizing actions, following through with instructions; as well as well as sharing, playing well, and interacting pleasantly with other children (Barkley, 1998). Because of a lack of concentration and behavioral self-control in class, children with ADHD are frequently unable to learn effectively and can also disturb their teachers and classmates (Barkley, 2005). Those with poor social skills may not be tolerated in group activities or may be rejected by peers (Barkley, 1998; Hoza et al., 2005; Semrud-Clikeman, 2010). Other psychosocial impairments in children include difficulties with parents compared with normal peers and problems during unstructured free time (Biederman, Faraone, & Chen, 1993). These actions often cause them problems in daily life and learning (Barkley, 2005).

As children with ADHD mature, the manifestations of their symptoms change (Adler, 2004; Loe & Feldman, 2007). During middle childhood, ADHD symptoms and the academic consequences of inattention tend to escalate. As classroom demands require sustained attention to tasks, children with ADHD begin to display more symptoms of inattention (Hart, Lahey, Loeber, Applegate, & Frick, 1995). Alternatively, the hyperactive symptomology from preschool declines somewhat (Barkley, 1998). By later childhood, patterns of academic, familial, and social conflicts have become well established, and at least 40% to 60% of these children have developed oppositional defiant disorder, and as many as 25% to 40% are likely to develop conduct disorder (Barkley, 1998).

Gender Differences in Childhood

Symptoms of ADHD appear to differ by gender. In childhood, boys tend to be diagnosed at a rate of 2 to 1 compared with girls and manifest as the predominantly hyperactivity–impulsivity type. Young girls tend to be identified more frequently as inattentive (American Psychiatric Association, 2013). Quinn (2005) speculated that females are not identified with ADHD as readily in childhood because their symptoms are often camouflaged by a higher rate of learning disorders and emotional difficulties. Furthermore, girls may manifest hyperactivity via excessive talking, rather than overt physical behaviors like those found in the male population, resulting in failure to diagnose at an early age. Early academic problems are not as obvious for young females due to pressures from authority figures to do well in school; therefore, girls may use a variety of coping skills to keep their achievement at or above average. These blinders (comorbid learning disorders, emotional difficulties, and possible high performance in early academic settings) may prevent early diagnosis for many girls with ADHD.

Specific Academic Problems in Children

Traditional school practices make academia an ordeal for many students with ADHD. Students with ADHD risk school failure at a higher rate than students without disabilities who have equivalent intelligence (Fried et al., 2013). Children with ADHD struggle with failure rates double to triple those of other children, with about one third repeating a grade by adolescence (Fried et al., 2013). Many studies have shown that younger students with ADHD may exhibit deficits in a specific academic skill, likely associated with executive functioning deficits (Raggi & Chronis, 2006). (We talk more about executive functioning in Chapter 3.) The severity of ADHD symptoms has been found to predict academic underachievement in reading, writing, and mathematics (Barry, Lyman, & Klinger, 2002). Specifically, students classified as having ADHD are reported to have problems with oral language (Sciberras et al., 2014), spelling (e.g., August & Garfinkel, 1990), and handwriting (Langmaid, Papadopoulos, Johnson, Phillips, & Rinehart, 2012). Furthermore, approximately 15% of children and adolescents classified as having ADHD present with profiles similar to students classified as having reading disorders (Aaron, Joshi, Palmer, Smith, & Kirby, 2002). It has been suggested that students with ADHD learn well when they are highly interested in material being taught and have shown improved behavior or performance when tasks are made salient, novel, or interesting (Carlson, Booth, Shin, & Canu, 2002). It appears that much of the difficulty encountered by children is related to impaired response inhibition (Bledsoe, Semrud-Clikeman, & Pliszka, 2010). Negative self-perceptions also worsen academic performance (Eisenberg & Schneider, 2007).

SYMPTOMS AND IMPAIRMENT IN ADOLESCENCE

The expression of ADHD changes qualitatively in adolescence (Sibley, Kuriyan, Evans, Waxmonsky, & Smith, 2014). Puberty is characterized by a period of rapid reorganization of neural circuitry, which is thought to influence regions of the brain associated with planning, drug sensitivity, response to reward, decision making, and risk taking (Sisk & Foster, 2004). Elevated levels of inattention, hyperactivity, and impulsivity remain, compared with typically developing peers (Sibley et al., 2011). Although some types of impairment remain consistent from childhood to adolescence (Wolraich et al., 2005), the outcomes may be more severe because of the increased responsibility placed on adolescents and the decreased supervision (Steinberg, Fletcher, & Darling, 1994). For example, both children and adolescents with ADHD display poor school grades; however, adolescents also experience failure to complete assignments; increased absenteeism; higher rates of suspension, expulsion, and dropouts; more grade failures; worse scores on standardized tests; longer time to complete high school; and lower rates of high school graduation (Advokat, Lane, & Luo, 2011; Barbaresi, Katusic, Colligan, Weaver, & Jacobsen, 2007; Loe & Feldman, 2007).

Barkley, Fischer, Smallish, and Fletcher (2006) reported that 44% of high school students with ADHD receive disability support services, 42% have been retained a grade, and 60% have been suspended from school. Similar to children, adolescents with ADHD also continue to display elevated rates of poor social skills, problems with peer relationships, and family conflict (Bagwell, Molina, Pelham, & Hoza, 2001; Edwards, Barkley, Laneri, Fletcher, & Metevia, 2001). Unlike children, adolescents with ADHD are at a higher risk for developmentally specific problems such as delinquency, substance abuse, and risky driving behavior (Charach, Yeung, Climans, & Lillie, 2011; Sibley, Pelham, Mazur, Ross, & Biswas, 2012; A. L. Thompson, Molina, Pelham, & Gnagy, 2007), and these problems often persist into adulthood (Barkley, Murphy, & Fischer, 2008).

There are some interesting findings regarding grades and achievement in adolescents. On one hand, it has been found that ADHD symptoms, motivation, and overall IQ are equally weighted in terms of their impact on grades (Birchwood & Daley, 2012). On the other hand, other researchers hold that the adolescent's degree of overall cognitive impairment leads directly to the severity of impact on academic performance (Ek, Westerlund, Holmberg, & Fernell 2011). These relationships vary, however, if the adolescent uses stimulant medication; several researchers have found that psychostimulants produce improvements in test scores, attention, class behavior, accuracy of completed assignments, and teacher ratings, as well as higher scores on achievement tests and higher grade point average (Powers, Marks, Miller, Newcorn, & Halperin, 2008).

SYMPTOMS IN COLLEGE STUDENTS AND ADULTS

The general consensus is that ADHD symptoms remain well into young adulthood for about two thirds of those with a childhood diagnosis (Davidson, 2008; Marchetta, Hurks, De Sonneville, Krabbendam, & Jolles, 2008). However, the developmental course of these symptoms appears to be influenced by maturation such that hyperactive and impulsive symptoms tend to remit with age, whereas attentional symptoms remain relatively stable (Bekker et al., 2005; Dias et al., 2008; Marchetta et al., 2008). Adults with ADHD are more likely to experience inner restlessness, inability to relax, or excessive talkativeness. Hyperactivity in adulthood may be expressed as excessive fidgeting, the inability to sit still for long in situations when sitting is expected, or being "on the go" all the time. Instead of engaging in excessive running or climbing, adults with hyperactive–impulsive symptoms tend to report poor driving performance, self-medication, and risky behavior (Montano, 2004). Impulsivity may be expressed as impatience, acting without thinking, spending impulsively, starting new jobs and relationships on impulse, and sensation-seeking behaviors. Inattention often presents as distractibility, disorganization, being late, being bored, need for variation, difficulty making decisions, lack of overview, and sensitivity to stress. Rather than having trouble staying engaged in schoolwork or avoiding homework assignments, adults with inattentive symptoms tend to be forgetful; lose personal items such as their keys, wallet, or purse; or avoid menial tasks at their place of work. Additionally, an adult with ADHD may frequently forget to pay bills on time, forget appointments, and struggle with organizing and managing daily schedules (Barkley, 2011a). In a study specific to college students, our own research indicated that, with the exception of fidgeting, the college sample overwhelmingly reported symptoms of inattention; symptoms of hyperactivity and impulsivity were significantly less frequent (Prevatt, Walker, Baker, & Taylor, 2010).

Gender Differences in College Students and Adults

As in childhood, there are gender differences in ADHD in adulthood. Women frequently do not present with histories similar to those of men with ADHD, making the diagnosis difficult (R. C. Kessler et al., 2006; Quinn, 2005). In national survey results of adults with ADHD, the ratio of men to women with ADHD is less extreme than found in children with a ratio of 1.6:1 (American Psychiatric Association, 2013; R. C. Kessler et al., 2006). Research finds that both men and women exhibit predominately inattentive symptoms as adults (American Psychiatric Association, 2013).

Specific Areas of Impairment in College Students and Adults

Academic

Although high school students with ADHD are less likely than their peers without ADHD to go on to college (DuPaul, Weyandt, O'Dell, & Varejao, 2009), more of these students are attending college than in the past (Weyandt et al., 2013). Students with ADHD rank second behind students with learning disabilities as the largest group of postsecondary students served by offices for students with disabilities (Harbour, 2004); approximately one in four college students receiving university-based disability services has been diagnosed with ADHD (DuPaul, Weyandt, O'Dell, & Varejao, 2009). However, the increase in academic and environmental demands can exacerbate symptoms of ADHD, resulting in increased difficulties (A. E. Thompson, Morgan, & Urquhart, 2003).

Research documents that adults with ADHD are at an increased risk of impairment in academics (Barkley, 2004; Barkley, Murphy, & Fischer, 2008). College students are more likely to have lower grade point averages, poorer academic coping skills, poorer study skills, and a greater likelihood of being placed on academic probation (Heiligenstein, Guenther, Levy, Savino, & Fulwiler, 1999; Weyandt et al., 2013). In our own research, we found our college students to report more difficulties with specific academic skills such as time management, concentration, motivation, test-taking skills, and study strategies. They were also more likely to experience test anxiety (Reaser, Prevatt, Petscher, & Proctor, 2007). Specifically, students in our studies reported that they could not organize well or plan their time, their minds wandered when studying, they had trouble focusing in class, and they were not good at taking notes or memorizing things they needed to understand. Additionally, they were poor at determining what to study and could not use what they had studied to take a test successfully. They became anxious when studying or taking tests to such a degree that they felt they were not doing their best work.

Students with ADHD may have particular difficulty with the transition to college because of their limitations in executive functioning and self-regulation (Parker & Boutelle, 2009). Many executive functioning skills are directly related to academic competencies. Weyandt et al. (2013) evaluated college students with ADHD and found that, compared with control participants, they performed more poorly on executive functioning–related measures of metacognition, self-monitoring, initiating, working memory, planning and organization, and task management.

Employment

In general, adults with ADHD appear to have poorer work records and lower job status than adults without ADHD. Wilens, Faraone, and Biederman (2004) reported that adults with ADHD often have lower economic status, change jobs more often, and are less likely to be in a professional position. Additionally, they are much more likely to hold only part-time jobs. Faigel (1995) added that adults with ADHD are promoted less often and fired at a higher rate. Murphy and Barkley (1996) looked at the work history of adults with ADHD and found that these workers had been fired at a rate of 53% versus adults without ADHD, who had been fired at a rate of 31%. Those with ADHD were also 3 times more likely to impulsively quit a job and changed jobs significantly more often that those without ADHD. They cited common difficulties such as impulsive speech, careless errors, disorganization, lack of timely completion of paperwork, tardiness, inconsistent attendance, missing of deadlines, lack of follow through, poor time management, short temper, problems with supervisors and coworkers, inattention in meetings, and general inconsistency in performance. They may leave jobs because of an inability to tolerate what they view as a boring, repetitive, and unrewarding daily routine. In our own research (Shifrin, Proctor, & Prevatt, 2010), we looked exclusively at college students and found that those with ADHD endorsed a common pattern of work performance; they reported particular difficulty in working on assigned tasks, managing daily work responsibilities, and meeting deadlines. Our coaching clients, who are often college students, tend to be employed in restaurants or in retail stores. They frequently tell us that they get in trouble for being late to work, and cannot remember what they are supposed to be doing. They often fail to take responsibility when they are fired and many relate detailed stories of how problematic situations and occurrences "were not their fault."

As individuals with ADHD transition into more challenging jobs after graduation, their difficulties with inattention and impulsivity become much more problematic. Positions with more responsibility can strain their ways of coping. Our own research (Painter, Prevatt, & Welles, 2008) found that adults with ADHD were more dissatisfied with and conflicted about their careers, more confused about their career choice, and more anxious about their career. These employment difficulties in adults and college students with ADHD take a toll on the U.S. economy; the loss of workforce productivity resulting from ADHD was estimated to be between $67 billion and $116 billion in 2003 (Biederman & Faraone, 2006). Nadeau (1998) concluded that therapists who work with adults who have ADHD need to have at least some willingness and ability to work on vocational issues because work is such a high-stakes area and central to overall life satisfaction. Successful vocational adjustment has implications for marital and family functioning, self-esteem, stress level, and financial stability. For all of these reasons, finding a successful educational and vocational niche and developing appropriate coping strategies are important for the adult with ADHD.

Interpersonal Relationships

Research has shown that adults with ADHD have more problems with friendships than those without the disorder (Young, Gray, & Bramham, 2009). When we work with clients in coaching, we generally ask about social relationships, and many admit that their partner complains that they never listen or pay attention. Others say that they talk excessively and always interrupt their friends. Murphy (2005) explained that adults with ADHD can have difficulties understanding social cues and do not seem to attune their behavior to other people; thus, their friends can perceive them as rude or insensitive. Paulson, Buermeyer, and Nelson-Gray (2005) also suggested that adults with ADHD miss subtle interpersonal cues, which puts them at greater risk for social rejection and relationship failure. The symptoms of impulsivity associated with ADHD can also put a strain on relationships. Our clients tell us that their friends complain that they say things that unexpectedly hurt someone's feelings.

Adults with ADHD can also have frequent mood swings in which they change from happy to sad with little obvious provocation. In addition, many adults with ADHD experience lifetime mood lability with frequent highs and lows and short-fused temper outbursts (Wender, Wolf, & Wasserstein, 2001). They can be irritating and disruptive to others (Miller-Johnson, Coie, Maumary-Gremaud, Bierman, & the Conduct Problems Prevention Research Group, 2002). Some partners report that those with ADHD have low frustration tolerance and tend to anger easily. There is a fairly high co-occurrence of depression with ADHD, which can also strain social relationships (Murphy, 2005).

The research on ADHD and marriage shows that the rates of getting married are not different for those with ADHD, but those with ADHD report lower satisfaction with their marriage (Murphy & Barkley, 1996). There is also evidence that separation and divorce rates are higher. Studies show that, in general, adults with ADHD feel that they get angry more easily, have temper outbursts, break up relationships over trivial matters, and have difficulties managing finances that lead to marital troubles (Murphy & Barkley, 1996; Overbey, Snell, & Callis, 2011; Wilmshurst, Peele, & Wilmshurst, 2011).

Barkley (2002) concluded that a developmental trajectory of ADHD has emerged. Beginning in adolescence, those with ADHD do not stay in relationships for long, and their relationship difficulties continue into adulthood. Typical refrains from spouses who do not have ADHD include complaints that their partner is forgetful, unreliable, a poor listener, self-centered, messy, disorganized, chronically tardy, and never finishes anything (Nadeau, 1996). Nadeau further reported that spouses may complain that they feel overburdened, are the glue that holds the family together, and feel they have to take care of another child instead of having an equal partner. Sometimes they wonder why it seems their spouse can function reasonably well at work and then fall apart and become disorganized and inefficient at home. Often, after years of arguing and trying to induce their partner to change, they realize the futility of their efforts and reluctantly resign themselves to believing things cannot change.

The research on college students is inconclusive. Kern, Rasmussen, Byrd, and Wittschen (1999) found that college students with ADHD were not as good at accepting constructive criticism or soliciting social support from others as students without ADHD. However, Weyandt et al. (2013) found that college students with ADHD were no different from their non-ADHD peers with regard to social adjustment or relationships with immediate and extended family.

In sum, research shows that adults with ADHD report a lower quality of life and negative differences in dating patterns and in relationships with family members (Canu & Carlson, 2003; Grenwald-Mayes, 2002). As stated earlier, many adults with ADHD tend to outgrow their symptoms of hyperactivity; however, the symptoms of inattention remain, especially distractibility, inability to pay attention, forgetfulness, and difficulties with organization (Prevatt, Walker, Baker, & Taylor, 2010). These symptoms can make it difficult to have a close, intimate relationship with someone and can cause many annoyances in day-to-day life that can escalate into serious relationship issues.

Daily Life-Functioning and Mental Health Issues

The clinical literature suggests that adults with ADHD have difficulties in numerous areas of daily life functioning. As much as 80% of the adult ADHD population experiences difficulties with sleep onset, as well as disrupted sleep (Bijlenga et al., 2013; Surman et al., 2009). Adults with ADHD are more likely to smoke cigarettes, abuse alcohol or drugs, and engage in risky sexual behavior (Barkley, 2002). In our own clinical work, we frequently encounter clients who need help with finances, paying bills, keeping their home organized, doing laundry, and keeping of a routine of healthy sleep, diet, and exercise patterns. These difficulties are better reflected in the *DSM–5* (American Psychiatric Association, 2013) criteria for ADHD than they were in the previous edition of the manual. These are discussed at greater length later in this chapter. Newly added examples of symptoms include the following: is messy; loses tools, wallet, or eyeglasses; forgetful in running errands or paying bills; unable to be still for an extended time in a restaurant; and difficulty waiting in line.

Additional research has examined the reasons for life skill deficits. Barkley and Fischer (2010) examined major life domains for adults with ADHD and hypothesized that emotional impulsiveness was a contributor to many difficulties, including driving and finances. Gudjonsson, Sigurdsson, Gudmundsdottir, Sigurjonsdottir, and Smari (2010) looked at personality traits in adult college students with ADHD and found that the domain encompassing "responsibility" showed significant impairment.

In conclusion, impairment due to the core symptoms of inattention, hyperactivity, and impulsivity is pervasive in those with a diagnosis of ADHD. For young children, externalizing behaviors first cause concern to parents or day care providers. Upon entering primary school, an inability to sit still and focus on schoolwork, as well as continuing social problems, cause more children to become noticed. In middle and high school, continuing academic difficulties are often attributed to lack of motivation, and emotional difficulties may become more pronounced. By young adulthood, for the two thirds of individuals whose symptoms have not remitted, the full range of academic, work, social, emotional, and lifestyle difficulties create major life impairments.

Etiology of ADHD

There is no single, empirically supported cause of ADHD; multiple factors likely contribute to the development of the disorder, including genetic and environmental factors (Weyandt, 2007). No single biologic marker is diagnostic; however, as a group, children with ADHD display increased slow-wave EEGs, reduced total brain volume on MRIs, and possible delay in cortical maturation (American Psychiatric Association, 2013). In terms of heritability, studies on families, twins, and siblings have shown moderate to high concordance rates, ranging from 29% to 91% (Faraone & Doyle, 2001). As a result of these high concordance rates, genetic analysts have begun the search for a gene or genes that account for ADHD. Although there continues to be dispute about which genes play a role (Nikolas & Burt, 2010), there is no dispute that when a child is found to have ADHD, one or more of their parents will commonly have it as well. There is also a "slight increased risk" for behavioral disorders such as ADHD in adopted children (Keyes, Sharma, Elkins, Iacono, & McGue, 2008). Family interaction patterns in early childhood are not likely to cause ADHD but may influence its course (American Psychiatric Association, 2013)

A review by Nigg (2012) characterized ADHD as a neurodevelopmental disorder. Nigg summarized research showing that ADHD is associated with early emerging alterations in cortical development (Shaw et al., 2006). Additionally, several gene markers are now reliably identified with ADHD (e.g., Gizer, Ficks, & Waldman, 2009). Although ADHD is among the most heritable phenotypes, evidence also suggests a gene-by-environment interaction operating in ADHD (Nigg, Nikolas, & Burt, 2010). Epigenetic changes can be stimulated by experiences such as exposure to environmental toxicants, changes in dietary health, or major stressful events. According to Nigg (2012), there is a new focus on early prenatal development; on environmental sources of brain and endocrine development, such as prenatal health associated with food intake and smoking; and perinatal factors, such as lead and household pesticides. In sum, ADHD is not necessarily a genetic condition in the simplistic sense previously believed. Rather, a genetic foundation interacts with numerous environmental contributors.

Comorbidity

It is estimated that between 65% and 89% of all individuals with ADHD will have one or more additional mental health disorders, and more than 45% of adults with ADHD will have two or more comorbid mental health disorders. As reported in the *DSM–5* (American Psychiatric Association, 2013), in children, oppositional-defiant disorder co-occurs in 25% of children with inattentive presentation and 50% of children with combined presentation. Conduct disorder co-occurs in about 25% of children with combined presentation. Most adolescents who meet criteria for disruptive mood dysregulation disorder also meet criteria for ADHD. The most common comorbidities for adults with ADHD are anxiety disorder (47%) and depression or bipolar disorder (38%) (McGough et al., 2005; Schatz & Rostain, 2006). Other comorbidities include, but are not limited to, learning and language disorders, tic disorders, and personality disorders (McGough et al., 2005). Weyandt et al. (2013) found that college students with ADHD, compared with control participants without the disorder, exhibited more symptoms of obsessive-compulsive disorder, depression, anxiety, and hostility. Alternately, they did not find differential rates of symptoms of somatization, phobic anxiety, paranoia, or psychosis. Alexander and Harrison (2013) found college students with ADHD to have higher levels of depression, anxiety, and stress.

In a review of ADHD-associated impairment in teens and adults, Murphy (2005) explained that ADHD is sometimes referred to as an invisible disability because others perceive the person as capable, intelligent, and otherwise normal, yet there is nothing obviously wrong that would explain the negative or inconsistent behavior pattern. For this reason, these individuals' behavior is frequently attributed to bad character, low motivation, or willful misconduct. Those living with ADHD have often endured a litany of negative messages about them from teachers, parents, peers, or supervisors. For example, they may be directly or indirectly told they are lazy, unmotivated, irresponsible, immature, self-centered, inconsiderate, or dumb (Murphy, 2005). As a result, those with ADHD are often forced to live with chronic feelings of demoralization, discouragement, ineffectiveness, and intense frustration caused by their persistent shortcomings.

Comorbid symptoms are especially relevant with regard to ADHD coaching. Our research (Prevatt & Yelland, 2013) evaluated the degree of self-reported anxiety and depression among college student coaching clients; many of them rated themselves as having high levels of anxiety and depression. After 8 weeks of coaching, those clients with more mental health symptoms made significantly fewer gains in coaching in the areas of study skills, time management, and test-taking strategies, compared with clients who had fewer mental health symptoms.

Comorbidity may be especially likely in college students. Many students with ADHD are unprepared for their transition to college and do not use the resources offered on campus or have appropriate strategies to cope with their symptoms (Morgan, 2012). Often students are first exposed to an independent and unstructured lifestyle during their first years in higher education. Many students no longer receive the external structure and support that was once provided by their teachers, parents, and school programs (Parker & Boutelle, 2009; Swartz, Prevatt, & Proctor, 2005). As a result, these students are particularly vulnerable to developing new mental health concerns (Troller, 2010). Rabiner, Anastopoulos, Costello, Hoyle, and Swartzwelder (2008) found that college students with ADHD demonstrated more academic concerns and depressive symptoms than students without ADHD.

DSM *and* ICD *Diagnostic Criteria*

The *DSM–5*, developed by the American Psychiatric Association (2013), provides diagnostic criteria for mental disorders. Many mental health professionals, especially those in the United States, currently use the *DSM* to diagnose ADHD. The *ICD*, developed by the World Health Organization (2010), is the medical classification and research standard for physical and mental disorders throughout most of the world. Practitioners will need to use *ICD* diagnostic criteria for insurance reimbursement purposes beginning in October 2015. (The *ICD* is now in its 10th revision, and the 11th revision is due in 2017.) We discuss both of these with regard to a coaching practice.

DSM–5

The *DSM–5* can be useful in your work with clients because it gives updated information on the following: associated features, prevalence, development and course, risk and prognostic factors, culture-related diagnostic issues, gender-related diagnostic issues, suicide risk, functional consequences, differential diagnosis, and comorbidity. The *DSM–5* uses a single axis system that combines the axes in previous versions of the *DSM* for mental disorders, medical disorders, and V codes (other conditions that may be the focus of clinical attention). Specific changes to the criteria for ADHD include the following: at least six symptoms of inattention and/or six symptoms of hyperactivity-impulsivity are required, and these must have lasted at least 6 months. However, if the client is age 17 or older, only five symptoms in either area are required; the age of onset requires several symptoms before age 12. The former subtypes have been replaced by presentations, which are also coded: combined, predominantly inattentive, or predominantly hyperactive-impulsive presentation. Severity ratings of mild, moderate, or severe are added, as well as the option of *in partial remission*. The *DSM–5* also includes the Clinical Modifications (CMs) of both the ninth and tenth revisions of the *ICD* (*ICD–9–CM* and *ICD–10–CM*) codes corresponding to each ADHD diagnosis. There are only three *ICD* codes, one for each of the three presentations (inattentive, hyperactive-impulsive, and combined). The CMs are discussed further later in the chapter.

As an example, a *DSM–5* diagnosis (with *ICD–10* in parentheses) might look like this:

> 314.00 (F90.0) attention deficit/hyperactivity disorder, predominantly inattentive presentation, moderate severity.

In addition, the *DSM–5* allows for a diagnosis of *specified ADHD* when not all criteria are met, and the clinician states which criteria are lacking (e.g., insufficient inattention symptoms or symptoms not demonstrated before age 12). *Unspecified ADHD* can be diagnosed when the clinician chooses not to state the specific criteria that are not met.

If the client has a diagnosis of ADHD with comorbid disorders, it is helpful to list the diagnoses in order of their clinical importance. Although not empirically documented, there is a general belief that the most serious disorders should be treated first. For example, if a client presents with ADHD but is primarily suffering from major depression, coaching might be delayed and a referral made to explore possible suicidal ideation. Once the client is stabilized, his or her mood lifts, and motivation to handle daily tasks increases, coaching can be resumed. A client with comorbid disorders will also need careful psychiatric planning to determine a combination of medications (if medications are used) that treat both ADHD and the other disorder(s).

Recent changes to the *DSM* allow ADHD to be diagnosed in conjunction with autism spectrum disorder. In the previous edition of the *DSM*, ADHD would have been ruled out on the assumption that ADHD symptoms were always better explained by the person's autism. This change could mean that ADHD specialists will see many more clients with a comorbid autism spectrum diagnosis and will need to have skills in this area. According to the *DSM–5*, ADHD symptoms must not occur exclusively during the course of schizophrenia or another psychotic disorder and must not be better explained by another mental disorder, such as a depressive or bipolar disorder, anxiety disorder, dissociative disorder, personality disorder, or substance intoxication or withdrawal. This does not mean that your client may not have a condition on this list in addition to ADHD, just that it is important to know that these disorders can also affect executive functioning and give the appearance of ADHD-like symptoms and may need different or additional treatment.

THE ICD–10–CM

The *ICD–10–CM* is a modified version of the *ICD* created by the U.S. National Center for Health Statistics (NCHS) and Centers for Medicare and Medicaid Services (CMS). The CM version of the *ICD* provides additional morbidity detail and is specifically used for medical coding and reporting in the United States. As noted earlier, all entities, including health care providers, covered by the Health Insurance Portability and Accountability Act must convert to using the *ICD–10–CM* diagnosis code sets beginning October 1, 2015. The mandate represents a fundamental shift for many psychologists and other mental health professionals who are far more attuned to the *DSM* system.

The *ICD–10–CM* codes are already in the *DSM–5*. As noted earlier, there are three codes relevant to ADHD, so this transition should be fairly easy for those who are primarily doing ADHD coaching. The American Psychological Association (APA) Practice Directorate recommends that psychologists use the criteria as outlined in the *DSM–5* to arrive at diagnostic conclusions and then use the appropriate *ICD* code set for billing purposes (Nordal, 2014). APA concludes that most psychologists have been trained using the *DSM* to aid diagnostic decision making. However, many practitioners also consult other sources of diagnostic information, such as guidelines and international documents. Psychologists need to have a rationale for how they determined a diagnosis and will want their rationale to be supported by the professional literature.

ICD–10–CM codes are alphanumeric, and mental health codes begin with the letter F. For example, the first three characters for ADHD are F90. F is the chapter on mental and behavioral disorders, and F90 refers to the ADHD disorders. Each character afterward adds to the specificity of the diagnosis: F90.0 is inattentive presentation, F90.01 is hyperactive-impulsive presentation, and F90.02 is combined presentation. The *ICD–10–CM* code set is free and downloadable from the Centers for Disease Control and Prevention website (http://www.cdc.gov/nchs/icd.htm). Additionally, *ICD–10–CM* implementation handbooks are located on the CMS website. The guide most useful to ADHD coaches is that for small and medium provider practices. The guide contains information on suggested business processes, communication avenues and training, and potential difficulties to expect when making the transition. It can be accessed from the following website: http://www.cms.gov/icd10/downloads/icd10smallandmediumpractices508.pdf.

Summary

1. ADHD is the most common developmental disorder in childhood, once thought to affect up to 5% of children and adults.
2. Newer statistics show that prevalence rates are increasing due to many factors, including better recognition, increased awareness, increasing biological vulnerabilities, and sociological factors such as chaotic households and increased childhood stress.
3. The severity of ADHD symptoms in children has been found to predict academic underachievement in reading, writing, and mathematics.
4. Symptoms of ADHD manifest differently in children and adults. The hyperactivity and impulsivity of childhood may give way to more inattentiveness in adults.
5. In childhood, boys tend to be diagnosed at a rate of 2:1 compared with girls. In adults, this rate drops to about 1.6:1.
6. Adolescents experience failure to complete assignments; increased absenteeism; higher rates of suspension, expulsion, and dropouts; more grade failures; worse scores on standardized tests; longer time to complete high school; and lower rates of high school graduation.
7. ADHD symptoms remain well into young adulthood for approximately two thirds of those with a childhood diagnosis.
8. In adulthood, symptoms tend to be associated with impairment in academics, work, social and interpersonal functioning, and lifestyle.
9. There is no single, empirically supported cause of ADHD; multiple factors likely contribute to the development of the disorder. It is likely that a genetic foundation interacts with numerous environmental contributors.
10. It is estimated that between 65% and 89% of all individuals with ADHD will have one or more additional mental health disorders, and more than 45% of adults with ADHD will have two or more comorbid mental health disorders.
11. Common comorbidities in children include oppositional defiant disorder and conduct disorder, whereas it is common for adults to experience depression and anxiety.
12. The new *ICD–10–CM* diagnostic codes will be required by mental health providers beginning in October 2015. However, these codes are being integrated into the *DSM–5*.

A History and Overview of ADHD Coaching Interventions

2

Interventions for individuals with attention-deficit/ hyperactivity disorder (ADHD) are important in ameliorating the negative outcomes associated with the disorder. A first-line treatment for adult ADHD is psychopharmacological intervention. Pharmacological agents have been studied extensively with regard to this disorder; however, they may not be sufficient because many adults do not respond well to medication (Chandler, 2013). The National Institute of Mental Health Multimodal Treatment of ADHD Study (The MTA Cooperative Group, 1999) found that psychosocial treatments, in combination with medication, resulted in the best outcomes for individuals with ADHD. Among the psychosocial treatments, positive results have been found for cognitive behavior therapy (CBT)–oriented treatment with regard to attention and related functions of time management, organization, and planning (Antshel, Faraone, & Gordon, 2012; Mongia & Hechtman, 2012; Ramsay & Rostain, 2006; Safren, Perlman, Sprich, & Otto, 2005; Solanto et al., 2010; Torrente

---

http://dx.doi.org/10.1037/14671-003
ADHD Coaching: A Guide for Mental Health Professionals, by F. Prevatt and A. Levrini
Copyright © 2015 by the American Psychological Association. All rights reserved.

et al., 2012). In children, behavior modification programs tend to be the most effective of the nonpharmacological treatments (Hodgson, Hutchinson, & Denson, 2014). ADHD coaching is a variant of CBT that focuses specifically on impairments related to the core symptoms of ADHD. In this chapter, we first provide an overview of ADHD coaching and then discuss how this differs from standard CBT. In the next chapter, we offer more details about how the theoretical aspects of CBT are specifically integrated into a coaching program.

What Is ADHD Coaching?

ADHD coaching has grown significantly and gained popularity in recent years (DuPaul, Weyandt, O'Dell, & Varejao, 2009; Goldstein, 2005; Murphy, 2005; Murphy, Ratey, Maynard, Sussman, & Wright, 2010; Quinn, 2001). ADHD coaching is an intervention that complements medication and other nonpharmacological alternatives. Most programs are based primarily on a CBT approach, specifically targeting the core impairments of ADHD such as planning, time management, goal setting, organization, and problem solving. Although some authors have suggested that ADHD coaching refers primarily to academic support (Ramsay & Rostain, 2006), coaching has evolved to encompass a wide range of CBT techniques that focus on all ADHD symptoms and associated impairments (Levrini & Prevatt, 2012). Most current ADHD coaching programs acknowledge the biological underpinnings of the disorder in addressing the core symptoms of ADHD (inattention, hyperactivity, and impulsivity); however, the programs address the academic, vocational, emotional, and interpersonal life difficulties that are a result of these symptoms. Kubik (2010) described coaching as focusing on behavioral, emotional, and cognitive outcomes and building life skills to change negative outcomes and beliefs. She stated that ADHD coaching "educates adults with ADHD on the outcomes of living with ADHD over a lifetime, making a logical connection to their current cognitive, emotional, and behavioral responses" (p. 443).

Empirical Support for ADHD Coaching

Although ADHD coaching is gaining popularity, the research in this area is somewhat limited (Murphy et al., 2010). This is especially so for children and adolescents. Coaching programs for children and adolescents appear more likely to involve their parents. For example, Evans, Schultz, and DeMars (2014) implemented a yearlong, school-based coaching program for high school students with ADHD. Parents attended weekly parent meetings, and adolescents attended additional group sessions targeting social functioning for 10 weeks. Effect sizes indicated moderate improvements in parent ratings of inattention, relationships with peers, academic impairment, and family functioning. Tamm, Nakonezny, and Hughes (2012) developed an 8-week program in which parents were coached to administer a metacognitive executive function intervention with their children. Parents were coached to promote positive interactions during activities, and the activities themselves were designed to improve attention and self-regulation. Results indicated improvements in executive functions (visual/auditory attention, working memory, and cognitive flexibility) and reduced inattention symptoms. Wentz, Nydén, and Krevers (2012) developed an 8-week Internet-based chat support and coaching model for teens and young adults with autism spectrum disorder, ADHD, or both. Results showed improvements in sense of coherence, self-esteem, subjective quality of life, and fulfillment.

Two additional coaching-based interventions for children with ADHD involved parents only. Friendship Coaching groups were developed by Lerner, Mikami, and McLeod (2011) to improve social competency among children with ADHD. Parents were coached, over 8 weeks, to provide the intervention to their children. Results showed improvements in several parenting behaviors and child social outcomes. Also, Fabiano et al. (2012) investigated the efficacy of a behavioral parent-training program in which fathers of elementary school children were coached to increase positive parenting skills used with their children with ADHD. Results indicated reductions in the intensity of problem behaviors, relative to the wait-list condition. All of these programs had small sample sizes (range: 10–55 participants), and only the two parenting groups used randomized controls. Nonetheless, it appears that coaching programs for children are more likely to focus on working with the parents to better understand, cope with, and modify the behaviors of their children.

There are also limited empirical studies of individualized coaching programs for college students and adults. Two studies of ADHD coaching in college students by Parker and colleagues (Parker & Boutelle, 2009; Parker, Hoffman, Sawilowsky, & Rolands, 2013) found that participants engaged in more positive thoughts and behaviors, such as taking greater responsibility for one's actions, using goal-attainment skills, modulating emotions, and increasing positive expectations for performance. They also reported improved study skills and learning strategies. A study by Field, Parker, Sawilowsky, and Rolands (2013) utilized a large college-age sample with a no-treatment comparison group and found that 6 months of ADHD coaching resulted in higher scores on study skills and learning strategies. Additionally, Richman, Rademacher, and Maitland (2014) evaluated 24 college students using a nonrandomized control group, with 12 to 24 sessions over a two-semester period. Their qualitative analysis of survey data revealed positive results for the coaching group on measures of self-awareness, self-management of skills, and subjective well-being.

Our early work (Swartz, Prevatt, & Proctor, 2005) described a single case study of a college student engaged in a structured 8-week coaching program. At that time, we concentrated on long-term goals, weekly objectives, and rewards and consequences for short-term gains. Our primary outcome measure was the Learning and Study Strategies Inventory (Weinstein & Palmer, 2002). Results indicated that after 8 weeks of coaching, study skills and learning strategies improved, study time increased, and personal course-related goals were achieved. We followed that study with a multisubject analysis of the coaching model (Reaser, 2008) that also resulted in improvements in work and academic functioning. Since that time, we have refined our methodology; our most recent empirical treatment study (Prevatt & Yelland, 2013) spanned a 5-year period and evaluated 148 coaching clients seen by 26 coaches-in-training. We put a heavy emphasis on executive functioning deficits and included between-session assignments as a primary technique. All of the coaches were doctoral students just learning the process and working with their first coaching clients. Despite this, our results were uniformly positive, with significant 8-week gains on 10 learning and study strategies, self-esteem, satisfaction with school and work, and a reduction in emotional distress. The largest effect sizes were found for time management and concentration.

ADHD coaching using a group (rather than individual) format has also been evaluated. These studies show generally favorable results, with improvements in a variety of areas. Kubik (2010) reported positive results with a six-session group-coaching intervention for 45 adults (ages 40–59) that focused on education, anxiety, homework, interpersonal interactions, planning, organization, and assertiveness. Zwart and Kallemeyn (2001) used peers to do group coaching of college students with ADHD, learning disabilities, or the two combined. Gains were found on self-efficacy, motivation, time management, anxiety, and test-taking strategies after two to 10 sessions.

In summary, the empirical studies of ADHD coaching for children and adults have been positive, yet sample sizes are small and outcome measures limited. Compared with the empirical studies of CBT treatments, coaching outcomes appear to be more directly related to academic concerns. However, the empirical studies of ADHD coaching have not yet determined whether treatment results in a direct relationship to school grades or graduation rates.

How Is Coaching Different From CBT?

Coaching has more similarities than differences with traditional CBT counseling (Thomas, Rostain, & Prevatt, 2013). As can be seen in Exhibit 2.1, the overlapping elements are extensive. In particular, both approaches target similar areas of impairment.

The exhibit also indicates major areas of difference. Although ADHD coaches vary, in general coaching is a bit more pragmatic and focuses on specific goals and objectives rather than insight and cognitive

EXHIBIT 2.1

Common Elements of ADHD Coaching and CBT

Both ADHD coaching and CBT	ADHD coaching only	CBT only
▪ Case conceptualization ▪ Information and psychoeducation ▪ Goal setting ▪ Prioritizing ▪ Motivation ▪ Organizational skills ▪ Planning and scheduling ▪ Problem solving ▪ Maintaining attention and reducing distractibility ▪ Changing procrastination to persistence at tasks ▪ Stress management and relaxation techniques ▪ Impulse control and anger and frustration management ▪ Confidence and self-esteem building ▪ Relationships and communication skills ▪ Memory improvement ▪ Between session homework activities ▪ Medication management as adjunctive to treatment	▪ Academic skills ▪ Life management and healthy lifestyle (finances, maintaining a home, nutrition, exercise, sleep) ▪ Referral for additional treatment of comorbidities (depression, anxiety, substance abuse)	▪ Behavior analysis ▪ Mindfulness training ▪ Cognitive restructuring ▪ Emotional regulation ▪ Direct treatment of comorbidities (depression, anxiety, substance abuse) ▪ Family dynamics

Note. ADHD = attention-deficit/hyperactivity disorder; CBT = cognitive behavior therapy. From *Adolescent Medicine: State of the Art Reviews* (p. 671), by A. Joffee (Ed.), 2013, Elk Grove Village, IL: American Academy of Pediatrics. Copyright 2013 by the American Academy of Pediatrics. Adapted with permission.

restructuring. Both coaching and traditional counseling establish helping relationships that are supportive, respectful, and confidential; work on setting goals and assessing priorities; and require a client who is willing to make changes in his or her behaviors. However, most therapists also help to guide clients toward insight, or a deeper understanding of behavior, whereas coaches may not do this (Levrini & Prevatt, 2012). According to Favorite (1995), therapy is about insight; coaching is about action and getting things done. It is a pragmatic, behavioral, results-oriented, "just do it" approach, as opposed to a process, insight-oriented, intellectual approach (Murphy, 2005). According to Ratey (2002), coaching focuses on what, how, and when, rather than why. Knouse, Cooper-Vince, Sprich, and Safren (2008) agreed with these distinctions. They concluded that coaching tends to focus on more specific goals, whereas CBT attempts to train general coping skills; furthermore, CBT is targeted more to mediational thoughts or beliefs, whereas coaching is not concerned with the underlying reason for behaviors.

The structure of coaching also tends to be more open and flexible. Face-to-face meetings are preferred; however, the meetings can be of various time lengths, and telephone or Internet sessions can be useful as a backup. Text or e-mail reminders by the coach to accomplish planned tasks are common. In our more recent work, we are more likely to use between-session communications in coaching. It is quite common to send clients texts or e-mails between sessions to help them achieve their weekly objectives. These communications are phased out over the course of coaching but are relied on heavily in early stages, when self-regulation of motivation may be underdeveloped.

As explained by Murphy (2005), lack of motivation is common in adolescents and adults with ADHD. This makes it difficult for them to persist in an effort over an extended period of time without frequent reinforcement. A coach, as opposed to a therapist, is more likely to help clients stay the course. This may require ongoing support, encouragement, structure, accountability, and sometimes gentle but firm confrontation (Murphy, 2005).

Goals tend to be more focused on specific behaviors in coaching than in therapy. Because of age-related differences, many young coaching clients center their goals on academics and other school-related issues. However, peer relationships and family functioning may also be targeted when parents or teachers are in charge of setting goals (e.g., Evans et al., 2014; Lerner et al., 2011). Adults, in contrast, come to coaching with a wide array of problems and desired outcomes. This can include concerns such as managing finances, losing weight or eating healthfully, finding or maintaining employment, improving work or academic skills, improving social relationships (at work or at home), or addressing emotional barriers.

In summary, there appear to be more similarities than differences between "pure" CBT-oriented work with ADHD clients and coaching, and this will vary based on the practitioner. Most programs that label themselves as ADHD coaching tend to use a CBT orientation and rely on psychoeducation as a component. Most programs also tend to be results oriented, with specific behavioral goals. If your practice meets these criteria, if you are working on issues related to the core symptoms of ADHD (inattention, impulsivity, and hyperactivity), and if you are focusing on the primary impairments associated with those symptoms (time management, organization, planning, and problem solving), then we would contend that your practice can be described as ADHD coaching.

Summary

1. ADHD coaching is a variant of CBT that focuses specifically on impairments related to the core symptoms of ADHD.
2. Most coaching programs target the core impairments of ADHD such as planning, time management, goal setting, organization, and problem solving.
3. Most ADHD coaching programs acknowledge the biological underpinnings of the disorder in addressing the core symptoms of ADHD (inattention, hyperactivity, and impulsivity); however, the programs address the academic, vocational, emotional, and interpersonal life difficulties that are a result of these symptoms.
4. Coaching programs for children are more likely to focus on working with the parents to better understand, cope with, and modify the behaviors of their children.
5. There are limited empirical investigations of ADHD coaching programs for both children and adults.
6. There appear to be more similarities than differences between "pure" CBT-oriented treatment with ADHD clients and ADHD coaching.
7. Most programs that label themselves as ADHD coaching tend to use a CBT orientation and rely on psychoeducation as a component. Most programs also tend to be results oriented, with specific behavioral goals.

Underlying Principles and Procedures Used in ADHD Coaching

Three underlying principles guide our ADHD coaching. First, as we noted in the previous chapter, cognitive behavior therapy (CBT) provides a theoretical foundation for our treatment approach. Second, psychoeducation provides a framework for explaining and implementing many of our specific interventions. Third, executive functioning (EF) is a way of understanding client difficulties and formulating coaching goals; we believe that many of the work-related, academic, and motivational impairments associated with ADHD may, in part, be related to executive dysfunction. The following sections provide an overview of these three key components of our coaching work. Next is a discussion of some specific factors that are relevant to coaching: evaluating whether a client is suitable for coaching, dealing with motivational issues, and understanding comorbidity of other mental health issues. Finally, we discuss some specific procedures related to coaching, such as determining the number of sessions, and the use of medication.

Cognitive Behavior Therapy

CBT has been shown to be an efficacious form of psychosocial treatment for individuals with ADHD, especially adolescents and adults (Antshel, Faraone, & Gordon, 2012). Previous research has demonstrated that individual- and group-administered CBT interventions have significantly improved core symptoms of ADHD (Knouse & Safren, 2010; Safren et al., 2005; Solanto, 2013). CBT focuses on problematic thoughts and negative beliefs to create change in emotions and behaviors (Kubik, 2010) and can be specifically tailored to treat many mental health disorders. Dittner, Rimes, Russell, and Chalder (2014) formulated a specific protocol for using CBT to treat symptoms of ADHD. In their approach, the client and therapist develop an individual formulation, which is a "shared hypothesis about the client's predisposition (e.g., cognitive strengths and weaknesses, personality attributes), their experiences, and how these have contributed to the development of certain beliefs, behaviours, emotions and physical reactions" (p. 3). This new, shared story about the client specifies how those beliefs and behaviors may be maintaining impairments in daily functioning. Treatment is then tailored to the individual and focuses on teaching specific skills and strategies. The therapist uses education, environmental adaptations, and repetition of adaptive skills. CBT also allows for identification and modification of irrational beliefs (e.g., "I can't do anything unless I wait until midnight of the day before it is due"), which leads to changes in the specific behaviors tied to those beliefs.

Such negative thoughts and beliefs may be the result of repeated experiences of failure and underachievement, as well as negative social feedback from peers, family, and teachers. Consequently, these negative thoughts and beliefs can often contribute to a decrease in motivation, avoidance behaviors, procrastination, and attentional problems (Knouse & Safren, 2010). Therefore, changing these thought patterns into more positive, healthy, and realistic cognitions is critical in the treatment of ADHD symptoms. Murphy (2005) gave the example of preparing clients with ADHD for the expected and inevitable feelings of disappointment when they experience a setback. Rather than viewing setbacks as catastrophic failures or evidence of incompetence, the patient can be helped to conceptualize setbacks as normal, expected, and even desirable because they represent opportunities for learning and personal growth. According to Murphy, this mind-set can help patients better tolerate frustration and maintain a positive attitude.

CBT techniques are useful in dealing with ADHD symptoms that lead to difficulties such as procrastination, lack of concentration, ineffective self-regulation, poor planning, anxiety, social incompetence, or time management (Prevatt & Yelland, 2013). Other elements consistent with CBT that are used in ADHD coaching include Socratic questioning, psychoeducation, time-limited treatment, focus on specific problems, modeling, and practicing strategies learned in sessions outside of the therapy or coaching room. As a result, cognitive changes are expected to occur as a result of beneficial changes in behaviors (Prevatt & Yelland, 2013).

Psychoeducation

Whereas CBT provides a theoretical foundation for our treatment approach, psychoeducation provides a framework for explaining and implementing many of our specific interventions. Psychoeducation can begin immediately but often continues over the entire course of treatment. The main goal of psychoeducation is to improve the client's understanding and awareness of ADHD (Estrada et al., 2013). Previous work (Bramham et al., 2009; Young, Bramham, Gray, & Rose, 2008) and the Consensus of the European Network Adult ADHD (Kooij et al., 2010) all concur that psychoeducation can offer insights into past difficulties, decrease feelings of guilt, and improve the general functioning of the patient. Additionally, as Murphy (2005) explained, the more clients understand how ADHD affects them, the better prepared they will be to identify their highest priority goals and make realistic decisions about their treatment.

UNDERSTANDING THE ETIOLOGY OF ADHD

Clients' knowledge about ADHD varies widely. A basic understanding of the biological underpinnings of ADHD will be especially helpful. Some clients have been told that they are "stupid" or "lazy." It may be the case that some individual clients have lower than average IQs or are unmotivated, and these issues would certainly need to be taken into account during coaching. However, it is not helpful if clients believe this is the cause of their symptoms and behaviors. Education regarding the cause of ADHD can be enlightening for many clients and motivate them to make connections between lifestyle and subsequent outcomes. And education can help them to realize that change is possible. The fact sheet "What Influences ADHD?" (see Figure 3.1) provides a useful summary. The sources listed on that fact sheet,

FIGURE 3.1

What Influences ADHD?

Attention-deficit/hyperactivity disorder (ADHD) is a brain-based disorder. There is no single, known cause. However, ADHD is influenced by a combination of factors.

Genes. Results of numerous studies of twins show that ADHD often runs in families, and it is likely that heredity makes a large contribution to the expression of the disorder in the population. Researchers are looking at several genes that may make people more likely to develop the disorder. ADHD is a complex disorder, which is undoubtedly the result of multiple interacting genes.

Biochemistry. Neurological studies suggest that individuals with ADHD have imbalances in the neurotransmission of dopamine, serotonin, and noradrenaline.

Environmental factors. In instances in which heredity does not seem to be a factor, difficulties during and after pregnancy may be associated with ADHD. These include prenatal exposure to alcohol and tobacco, premature delivery, significantly low birth weight, and postnatal injury to the prefrontal regions of the brain. In addition, preschoolers who are exposed to high levels of lead, which can sometimes be found in plumbing fixtures or paint in old buildings, may have a higher risk of developing ADHD.

Brain injuries. Children who have suffered a brain injury may show some behaviors similar to those of ADHD. However, only a small percentage of children with ADHD have suffered a traumatic brain injury.

Food additives. Recent British research indicates a possible link between consumption of certain food additives like artificial colors or preservatives, and an increase in activity. Research is under way to confirm the findings and to learn more about how food additives may affect hyperactivity.

Myths. Research does not support the popularly held views that ADHD arises from excessive sugar intake, excessive television viewing, parents' poor child management, or social and environmental factors such as poverty or family chaos. Problems in parenting or parenting styles may make ADHD better or worse, but these do not cause the disorder.

Sources

Children and Adults With Attention-Deficit/Hyperactivity Disorder (CHADD), http://www.chadd.org

Johns Hopkins Center for Mendelian Genomics, http://mendelian.org

National Institute of Mental Health (NIMH), http://www.nimh.nih.gov/health/topics/attention-deficit-hyperactivity-disorder-adhd/index.shtml

National Resource Center on ADHD (NRCA), http://www.help4adhd.org/en/about/what/WWK1

Attention-deficit/hyperactivity disorder fact sheet.

especially Children and Adults With Attention-Deficit/Hyperactivity Disorder (CHADD), are excellent resources for information on the causes of ADHD.

UNDERSTANDING DISABILITY RIGHTS

Psychoeducation can also be important for students or employees with regard to being evaluated for and accessing disability services (Connor, 2012). For primary and secondary students, the Individuals With Disabilities Education Improvement Act of 2004 and Section 504 of the Rehabilitation Act of 1973 mandate the consideration and use of needed accommodations to "level the playing field" between students with disabilities and those without. Both regulations mandate the consideration and use of reasonable interventions, accommodations, and modifications. For college students and working adults, the Americans With Disabilities Act of 2008 will be more relevant. A variety of modifications (e.g., shortened assignments), accommodations (e.g., having a test read out loud), and interventions (e.g., remedial reading classes) have been used for individuals with ADHD, but not all of these have been shown to be effective (Harrison, Bunford, Evans, & Owens, 2013). Therefore, it is important for the coach to help clients understand the empirically supported benefits of different accommodations. Finally, in working with younger coaching clients, the coach can be helpful in educating parents about relevant case law regarding eligibility for services, proper identification and diagnosis, intervention plans, and accommodations for high-stakes testing (Martin & Zirkel, 2011). The Additional Resources section lists a full range of resources for both coaches and clients that can be helpful for psychoeducation.

EMPIRICAL SUPPORT FOR PSYCHOEDUCATION

The empirical literature on the benefits of ADHD psychoeducation has been positive for parents of children with ADHD (Montoya, Colom, & Ferrin, 2011) and suggests that it leads to an improvement in behavior (McCleary & Ridley, 1999), ADHD symptoms (Sonuga-Barke, Daley, Thompson, Laver-Bradbury, & Weeks, 2001), adherence to psychopharmacological treatment (Monastra, 2005), and parent and child satisfaction. Estrada et al. (2013) found that a psychoeducational group for adults resulted in significant improvements in inattention, hyperactivity, impulsivity, self-esteem, and quality of life, as well as a reduction in depression. They speculated that a primary causal agent was that the new understanding of ADHD helped individuals to change their attributions, especially regarding self-blame, which led to increased motivation to change.

Executive Functioning

WHAT IS EXECUTIVE FUNCTIONING?

Impairment in EF is thought to have an influence on ADHD symptoms (Field, Parker, Sawilowsky, & Rolands, 2013); therefore, we selected this construct as important in developing our coaching program. *Executive functions* can be described as the capacities needed for individuals to manage the goal-oriented and purposeful tasks of daily life (Suchy, 2009). There are a variety of ways to define or categorize executive functions. Weyandt (2005) described EF as a complex construct that can be broadly defined as higher order cognitive abilities that allow for strategic planning, cognitive flexibility, self-regulation, and goal-directed behavior. Brown (2008) stated that ADHD is not a behavioral disorder but rather a cognitive disorder due to developmental impairment of executive functions. He identified the following six components of EF: activation, focus, effort, emotion, memory, and action. These descriptions of EF identify the underlying cognitive processes that are believed to comprise EF. However, executive dysfunction, as measured by specific tests of neuropsychological function, is not universally seen in children and adults with ADHD (Willcutt, Doyle, Nigg, Faraone, & Pennington, 2005). These neuropsychological tests tend to measure specific cognitive domains, such as inhibition, set-shifting, working memory, verbal fluency, or selective attention. There is a growing belief that EF related to ADHD might be better measured by identifying specific behavioral, emotional, and social impairment (Barkley, 2011b). As such, researchers are beginning to focus more on the actual behaviors that are problematic in individuals with EF deficits. For example, deficits in EF can affect time management, organizational skills, problem-solving abilities, motivation, sustained attention, and regulation of emotions and behaviors (DuPaul, Weyandt, O'Dell, & Varejao, 2009; Parker & Boutelle, 2009). Consequently, EF deficits commonly affect academic, social, occupational, and psychological functioning (DuPaul et al., 2009; Swartz, Prevatt, & Proctor, 2005; Weyandt et al., 2013). Evaluating these areas may be a more productive way of using the EF construct.

Barkley and Murphy (2011) developed a theory of EF that is based on behavioral impairment, rather than underlying cognitive function. Their work is based on factor analytic studies of actual behaviors exhibited by individuals with ADHD. Their findings resulted in five subdomains of EF: self-management of time, self-organization and problem solving, self-restraint, self-motivation, and self-regulation of emotions. According to Barkley and Murphy, EF deficits create an inability to regulate one's behavior over time. As a consequence, those with ADHD are unable to organize behavior effectively to anticipate the future or pursue long-term goals and self-interests. Barkley (2010) suggested that it is not an *attention*-deficit disorder, but an *intention*-deficit disorder, meaning that people with ADHD are deficient in their ability to plan for the future in an intentional way. The problem is not a poor attention span but an inability to do what is intended—not a deficit in knowledge but a deficit in performance. In fact, Barkley believes that ADHD and EF deficits are synonymous, and he has stated that ADHD should be renamed executive functioning–deficit disorder.

ETIOLOGY OF EF DEFICITS

What causes these EF deficits? There is no single, established cause; however, most researchers agree that EF dysfunction is influenced by a combination of genetic and environmental influences. Genes are thought to give us a range of possibilities, and experiences shape that genetic expression (Tuckman, 2012). A large body of evidence from direct neuroimaging studies indicates that persons with ADHD demonstrate patterns of hypoactivation in the areas of the brain responsible for EF (Cortese et al., 2012). It is also believed that EF development is not complete until later in the life span.

HOW TO MEASURE EF DEFICITS

Barkley (2011b) developed the Barkley Deficits in Executive Functioning Scale (BDEFS) to measure the specific behaviors that define EF. Empirical studies have shown that the BDEFS is a more ecologically valid measure in predicting ADHD symptomatology compared with cognitive tests of EF (Dehili, Prevatt, & Coffman, 2013; Kamradt, Ullsperger, & Nikolas, 2014). Consequently, the BDEFS can be useful as a pre–post outcome measure, as well as a way of understanding client difficulties and formulating coaching goals. The schema developed by Barkley for categorizing EF domains is a useful platform for implementing a coaching program. The behaviors described in the five BDEFS domains are areas of impairment commonly targeted in work with individuals with ADHD (e.g., self-management of time, self-organization and problem solving, self-restraint, self-motivation, self-regulation of emotions). For example, the following items depict behaviors often endorsed by clients (these are paraphrased from the actual items and include one item from each of the five domains):

- I procrastinate or put off doing things until the last minute.
- I have trouble organizing my thoughts.
- I find it difficult to tolerate waiting; I'm impatient.
- I do not have the willpower or determination that others seem to have.
- I overreact emotionally.

According to Barkley, ADHD is not a skill deficit but a difficulty with behavioral execution and self-regulation. People with ADHD can identify the behaviors just described as being areas of difficulty. They can also explain what they might need to do to rectify these and even describe some specific coping techniques. They may try out these techniques; however, because of EF deficits, those with ADHD will have significant difficulty implementing and persisting with coping techniques. They find it difficult to sacrifice an immediate reward either to gain some longer term reward or to avoid some later harm (Levrini & Prevatt, 2012). It can be useful to look at clients' functioning in each of these domains to see exactly what sort of impairments they are experiencing and to help them formulate specific goals.

Specific Procedures Used in ADHD Coaching

Before accepting a client for coaching, the therapist is encouraged to evaluate the client's suitability with regard to three issues. First, are the client's concerns and objectives compatible with coaching? Second, does the client present with mental health issues that might delay or contraindicate coaching? Third, does he or she exhibit sufficient motivation to engage in coaching? Taking the time to consider these questions will help the therapist determine which clients are more likely to benefit from ADHD coaching.

SUITABILITY OF THE CLIENT FOR ADHD COACHING

An initial screening is recommended to determine the suitability of the client for ADHD coaching. This can be done with a brief interview or a written questionnaire (see, e.g., the discussion of using an Application for Services in Chapter 4). It is not actually necessary that the client have a diagnosis of ADHD. Many individuals can benefit from coaching if their impairments are consistent with ADHD. Clients who primarily want to work on time management, procrastination, organization, lack of focus, impulsivity, or motivation are likely to benefit from ADHD coaching.

MENTAL HEALTH ISSUES

The coach should probe to determine whether there are significant mental health concerns. Issues such as anxiety and depression do not rule out ADHD coaching; however, the mental health issue should not be so severe as to overwhelm the ability of the client to work on issues primarily related to ADHD symptoms. Many adults with ADHD have anxiety or depression directly related to their symptoms. If they are not doing well at work, are feeling overwhelmed, struggling academically, or having difficulties with a spouse or partner due to symptoms of ADHD, then this can lead to frustration, anxiety, or depression. Helping them manage their symptoms of ADHD can lessen their anxiety or depression. Alternatively, a client may have mental health issues so severe that ADHD coaching needs to be delayed until his or her condition stabilizes. We have accepted clients in the past only to find that each session was dominated by a personal crisis, mental health counseling was needed, and the standard ADHD coaching procedures were rarely used because the client needed to process an ongoing crisis. Sometimes the extent of the mental health issue is not fully revealed until coaching has progressed to the second or third session. If it becomes apparent that the mental health issue is undermining the effectiveness of coaching, the coach may want to recommend that the client temporarily halt coaching. The coach might help the client seek out a licensed psychologist or mental health counselor who will deal specifically with the mental health issues or refer the client to a psychiatrist who can prescribe medication (or perhaps both interventions may be necessary). Once the mental health issue is better controlled, the client can resume coaching with the anticipation that treatment will be much more effective. Alternatively, it may be appropriate for a client to be engaged simultaneously in ADHD coaching and mental health counseling. In this case, it is important for the coach to clearly delineate the boundaries and specific objectives of the two processes. This issue is discussed further in the case study in Chapter 11.

MOTIVATION

The motivation of the client should be evaluated before she or he is accepted for ADHD coaching. In our early work at the Adult Learning Evaluation Center (ALEC), we would occasionally receive calls from parents of college students or spouses of adult clients requesting help for a student or spouse. The person making the referral indicated that the potential client was ready and willing to engage in coaching. However, it was often the case that several weeks might go by before the intended client returned phone calls to set up an appointment. Cancellations were common. Weekly objectives were frequently not completed. We were able to document empirically that clients' low motivation was correlated with poor progress in coaching (Prevatt, Lampropoulos, Bowles, & Garrett, 2011).

Currently, we inform parents or spouses of adult clients that the client must make contact with us before we will accept them into coaching. We encourage the parents to require the student to pay some or all of the fee. We accept the client only if it is clear that she or he has specific goals in mind and has at least minimal motivation to attend. With younger clients, it can be helpful for the coach to meet privately with the client to assess whether they are ready and willing to engage in coaching. If at any time it becomes clear that the client is not actively participating in the coaching process, parents can be brought back in to explore other options. For adult clients who contact us on their own initially, motivation remains an important issue. It can be useful to ask why the client has decided to seek coaching at this time and get a general sense of the client's expectations for coaching.

MEDICATION

Whether to use medication needs to be the client's decision. However, it is common to discuss this issue and help the client to make an informed choice. The evidence in favor of medication is positive: Psychostimulants such as methylphenidate and amphetamine are associated with 70% response rates, which increase to 90% when nonresponders are switched to an alternative stimulant (Wigal, 2009). Psychostimulants appear to reduce the core symptoms of ADHD and also to improve academic task performance and increase productivity (Powers, Marks, Miller, Newcorn, & Halperin, 2008; Wigal et al., 2011). In a study of undergraduate students with ADHD, 92% believed that medication helped them academically (Advokat et al., 2011), whereas other work with undergraduates has suggested that the use of an amphetamine improved study habits and the chances for academic success (DuPaul et al., 2012).

The coach should present a balanced picture regarding the pros and cons of medication. Clients treated with psychostimulants are most likely to achieve improvements in academic and work-related performance because of alleviation of ADHD symptoms and not because psychostimulants directly improve their skills. The client will still need to change some behaviors to accomplish goals. Medication may not work initially, side effects can be problematic, and this can be frustrating for clients. Clients should be encouraged to carefully monitor their medication because it may take several months to achieve the best dosage and type of medication. For more detailed information on medication, the reader is referred to Thomas, Rostain, and Prevatt (2013) and Prevatt and Young (2014).

NUMBER OF SESSIONS

One of the first decisions will be to determine the number of sessions in a coaching program. In reviewing the literature, wide time frames are used, from 2 weeks to an entire semester. However, this has not been empirically studied, so there is no evidence tying number of sessions to effectiveness of coaching. When working with students, schedules are likely to be affected by specific time constraints, such as midterm and final examinations or semester breaks; therefore, scheduling of coaching around a semester schedule can be advantageous. When working with other non–college student adults, start and end times can be more flexible. The ALEC program uses an 8-week format. In our experience, coaching programs of fewer than 8 weeks do not allow adequate time to cover a sufficient number of content areas, practice new skills, and monitor progress and make adaptations. Within an 8-week framework, clients are generally able to work on two to three major goals. Clients frequently sign up for additional sessions after the initial 8 weeks. This can involve an additional 8-week program, a few single sessions, or booster sessions during critical time periods. Alternately, Psych Ed Coaching does not determine the number of sessions a priori. Rather, sessions are tied to goals, and coaching continues until long-term goals have been successfully completed. The average number of sessions is approximately 16 (4 months). Some clients remain in coaching for several years, continuously using the help of their coach to reach and maintain new goals.

Summary

1. Research has demonstrated that individual- and group-administered interventions based on CBT have significantly improved core symptoms of ADHD.
2. CBT focuses on problematic thoughts and negative beliefs to create change in emotions and behaviors.
3. CBT techniques are useful in dealing with ADHD symptoms that lead to difficulties such as procrastination, lack of concentration, ineffective self-regulation, poor planning, anxiety, social incompetence, or time management.
4. The main goal of psychoeducation is to improve the client's understanding and awareness of ADHD.
5. A basic understanding of the biological underpinnings of ADHD can give clients insight into their actions, help them make better choices about a healthy lifestyle (sleep, diet, exercise), and motivate them to make connections between lifestyle and subsequent outcomes.
6. Psychoeducation can be useful in helping clients and their parents understand their rights with regard to disability laws and regulations.

7. Executive functions were traditionally defined based on cognitive domains, such as inhibition, set-shifting, working memory, verbal fluency, or selective attention. However, researchers are beginning to focus more on the actual behaviors that are problematic in individuals with EF deficits.
8. The BDEFS can help determine which areas show impairments in EF: self-management of time, self-organization and problem solving, self-restraint, self-motivation, or self-regulation of emotions.
9. To determine whether a client is suitable for ADHD coaching, his or her motivation and possible mental health issues should be evaluated.
10. Psychostimulants lead to positive improvements in the majority of clients with ADHD; they appear to reduce the core symptoms of ADHD and also improve academic task performance and increase productivity.
11. There is great variability in the typical duration of ADHD coaching; however, a minimum of eight sessions is recommended.

The Nuts and Bolts of Coaching
Getting Started

4

In this chapter, we describe specific details of our coaching program. We start with a general overview of some important aspects related to coaching and preparation for seeing a client. We then describe the initial session and intake interview, including basic rules of coaching, determining coaching topics, and goal setting. We explain the general format for weekly sessions, with an emphasis on weekly goals and objectives. All of the forms we use are included in the chapter. Some forms, such as the Client Intake and the Client Symptom Checklist, are placed at the end of this chapter. Other forms are spread throughout the chapter and appear in the order in which they would be used. These include the Coaching Topics Survey (used to determine goals) and the Client Goals and Objectives (used to track weekly progress). Chapter 5 follows with more specific details about how to coach, as well as some additional forms. Figure 4.1 gives an overview of the steps we describe in the next three chapters.

http://dx.doi.org/10.1037/14671-005
ADHD Coaching: A Guide for Mental Health Professionals, by F. Prevatt and A. Levrini
Copyright © 2015 by the American Psychological Association. All rights reserved.

FIGURE 4.1

GETTING STARTED

Application and Precoaching Paperwork
(May use the intake interview in lieu of paperwork)

Intake Interview
Determine suitability for coaching (motivation, comorbid disorders)
Discuss informed consent and confidentiality
Gather background information
Establish long-term goals using Coaching Topics Survey
Determine one or more between-session assignments (BSAs)
Fill out Client Goals and Objectives Worksheet

MIDDLE SESSIONS

Administer BDEFS or ASICS if appropriate
Use specific strategies (Chapter 6)
Continue with weekly BSAs, develop incentives or consequences
Discuss barriers and successes using problem-solving approach
Continue to refine goals and objectives

CONCLUDING COACHING

Review skills learned, successes and barriers
Complete posttest measures, if applicable
Complete client evaluation

Conducting attention-deficit/hyperactivity disorder coaching. ASICS = Academic Success Inventory for College Students; BDEFS = Barkley Deficits in Executive Functioning Scale.

Preparation for Seeing a Client

Paperwork can be filled out before the first session or during intake. Some coaches prefer to put less emphasis on paperwork because clients with attention-deficit/hyperactivity disorder (ADHD) often have difficulty with paperwork. Rather, information can be generated via interview and discussion. When coaching is conducted in research or training centers, there is a greater need for standardization and data collection. Additional information obtained from paperwork can be used in planning the initial coaching session and determining client motivation and goals, as well as for ongoing research on the effectiveness of coaching. Table 4.1 gives a brief description of the precoaching paperwork used at the Adult Learning Evaluation Center (ALEC).

The ALEC coach will score and review these measures before conducting the first session. Many times, the client has already undergone an evaluation for ADHD, and that report will also offer useful background information. Clients with ADHD may not do well when expected to relate a great deal of information and details verbally during a single session. It is helpful if the coach has gathered much of this information before the first session because it decreases the burden on clients and allows for faster progress toward areas that they will find motivating (e.g., why they are there and what they can get started on right away). After scoring these measures, the coach gathers information from an application that is completed before coaching. The coach summarizes key features of the client's history and functioning and uses this information to determine areas to discuss during the first session. Finally, the coach conducts the initial session and further clarifies client issues. This process is elaborated in the next section.

The Initial Session

Before beginning the intake, the coach discusses confidentiality with the client and the client signs an Informed Consent form. This document will vary depending on the type of clinic you work in, the age of your clients, and the laws in your state. Figure 4.2 is an excerpt from the ALEC Informed Consent document for adults. You can find more information about informed consent documents in Chapter 7. Notice that the example in Figure 4.2 refers specifically to suicide or homicide. Some practitioners may wish to change this to the more generic "harm to self or others."

TABLE 4.1
Precoaching Paperwork

Measure	Description
Application for services	This varies by practitioner but will generally ask for basic demographic and referral information
Academic Success Inventory for College Students (Prevatt, Li, et al., 2011)	Includes 50 items that measure academic functioning in 10 domains: general academic skills, career decidedness, internal and external motivation, anxiety, concentration, socializing, personal adjustment, and perceived efficacy of the instructor. (This scale is described in detail in Chapter 5 and in the case study in Chapter 10.)
Barkley Deficits in Executive Functioning Scale (Barkley, 2011b)	Includes 89 items with five domain scores: self-management to time, self-organization/problem solving, self-restraint, self-motivation, and self-regulation of emotions. Additionally, a total executive functioning (EF) summary score and an ADHD–EF Index are produced. (This scale is described in detail in Chapter 5 and in the case study in Chapter 10.)
Client Symptom Checklist (see Appendix 4.1)	Includes 24 items using *DSM* terminology to rate symptoms of depression, anxiety, panic, and ADHD. The following symptoms screen for depression: depressed mood, feeling hopeless, fatigued, poor concentration, difficulty sleeping, and irritable. The symptoms that screen for anxiety include restless, poor concentration, anxious, worried, difficulty sleeping, and feeling irritable.
Coaching Topics Survey	Includes 27 items asking clients what they need to work on, such as time management, establishing routines, and healthy lifestyle.
Barkley Adult ADHD Rating Scale—IV (Barkley, 2011a).	Includes 18 items based on *DSM* rating symptoms of inattention, hyperactivity, and impulsivity.
The Outcome Questionnaire—45 (Lambert & Finch, 1999)	Includes 45 items that measure functioning in three areas: Symptom Distress (heavily loaded for depression and anxiety), Interpersonal Functioning (e.g., getting along with others, satisfaction with relationships), and Social Role (e.g., find school or work satisfying).
Rosenberg Self-Esteem Scale (Rosenberg, 1965)	Includes 10 items that measure global self-esteem.

Note. ADHD = attention-deficit/hyperactivity disorder; *DSM* = *Diagnostic and Statistical Manual of Mental Disorders.*

FIGURE 4.2

Staff members will safeguard your confidentiality, and your relationship with ALEC will not be revealed to anyone without your prior written consent. However, under certain conditions, ALEC is legally and ethically obligated to release information about a client whether or not the client approves. These conditions are as follows:

1. Suspected abuse (physical, sexual, neglect) of children, the aged, and the disabled: As counselors and psychologists we are required by law to report suspected abuse to the Department of Children and Families.

2. Potential suicide or homicide: In instances in which a client threatens homicide, we may have to notify the intended victim and police. Likewise, if a client is thought to be at high risk for suicide, family, the authorities, or both may need to be notified to protect the client.

3. Court order: We must release a client's records if a judge issues a court order compelling us to do so.

Informed consent document from the Adult Learning Evaluation Center (ALEC).

If you see clients who are minors, you need to be aware that minors can give assent, but their parents must give informed consent. The informed consent should cover, if applicable, permission to videotape, permission to use client data in research projects, payment policies (including missed sessions), and how and under what circumstances records will be released. If video or distance coaching is conducted, or if information is transmitted over the Internet, the informed consent needs to address this. One platform for doing this is VSee (http://www.vsee.com) for online face-to-face video chats. This program is compliant with the Health Insurance Portability and Accountability Act; however, there is inherent risk with regard to confidentiality in any Internet transmission.

The initial session is structured around an intake interview. Much needed information will have already been gathered and recorded, so the coach will begin by inquiring about information that is missing or needs elaboration. Appendix 4.2 gives examples of some questions that might be helpful during the first session. In standard therapy or counseling, the therapist and client may be seated in couches or armchairs. In coaching, it can be more effective to be seated at a working distance from a table or desk. The coach and client will spend a great deal of time going over papers, writing plans, and examining planners and calendars. You might want to consider putting all paperwork on a cloud-based platform so that the coach and client can simultaneously view and work on documents.

In the initial session, the coach might also engage in some brief psychoeducation about ADHD. That information can come in the first session, a later session, or be spread over several sessions as the need arises (Chapter 3 provides information on psychoeducation). The coach explains the basic concept and format used in coaching, noting that a cognitive behavioral theory is used, that psychoeducation about ADHD will be presented, and that executive functioning skills will be emphasized, for example. The differences between coaching and mental health counseling are discussed, and the coach reiterates that if the client has significant anxiety, depression, or other mental health issues, counseling may be a better alternative. Several basic rules are stressed in the following section.

Basic Rules of Coaching

1. The coach is not a teacher or a parent. The coach will not tell the client what to do. It is important that individuals with ADHD learn how to manage their life with strategies that work for them. Something that works for other individuals may not work for a given client. The coach might make suggestions and give options, but he or she will primarily help clients determine their own effective strategies and solutions.
2. Coaching helps clients learn how to manage their life by using a problem-solving approach. Most issues or goals that the client deals with can be addressed with the problem-solving approach. Figure 4.3 is a schematic of the problem-solving approach.
3. Motivation is a critical part of coaching. Incentives and consequences are routinely used in coaching. Initially, the coach may provide external motivation (reminders, text messages) and play a major role in helping clients manage their incentives and consequences. However, as coaching progresses, clients are encouraged to manage their own incentives and consequences and work toward using more internal motivation.

FIGURE 4.3

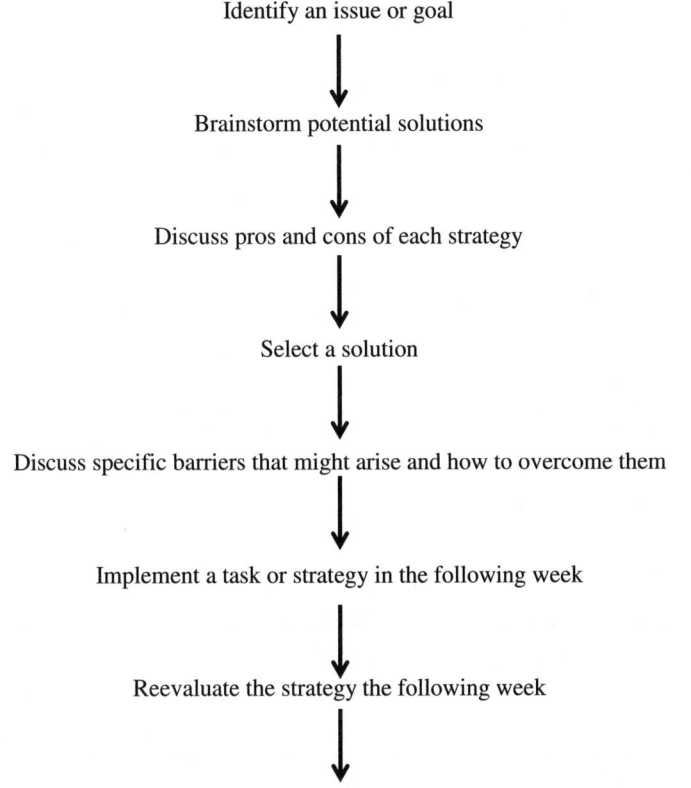

Schematic of the problem-solving approach.

Long-Term Goals

On the basis of the information gathered during the initial session, the coach helps the client develop some long-term goals. Generally, two to four goals are adequate. A *long-term goal* is defined as a desired result in an area that can be accomplished within a reasonable time frame. It is more general in nature but will be tied to weekly short-term objectives that require specific behaviors. Clients will have already completed the Coaching Topics Survey (Figure 4.4), where they rate the need to work on a variety of areas; this is used to help them identify long-term goals. The Coaching Topics Survey is useful in helping clients

FIGURE 4.4

Coaching Topics Survey

For each of the following items, circle the number from 1 to 5 that indicates the degree to which you need to work on that area, with 1 = *definitely need to work on* and 2 = *don't need to work on*.

	Definitely need to work on				Don't need to work on
Improving time management	1	2	3	4	5
Establishing routines and good habits	1	2	3	4	5
Organizing school or work	1	2	3	4	5
Organizing personal space	1	2	3	4	5
Getting to class on time	1	2	3	4	5
Studying	1	2	3	4	5
Scheduling classes	1	2	3	4	5
Paying attention in class and taking good notes	1	2	3	4	5
Managing long-term assignments	1	2	3	4	5

Coaching topics survey. ADHD = attention-deficit/hyperactivity disorder.

FIGURE 4.4

Planning and prioritizing	1	2	3	4	5
Making decisions and solving problems	1	2	3	4	5
Keeping track of things	1	2	3	4	5
Doing laundry	1	2	3	4	5
Exercising	1	2	3	4	5
Eating healthfully	1	2	3	4	5
Waking up and staying up	1	2	3	4	5
Getting to bed	1	2	3	4	5
Taking medication	1	2	3	4	5
Making friends	1	2	3	4	5
Keeping friends	1	2	3	4	5
Getting along with roommates	1	2	3	4	5
Getting along in group situations	1	2	3	4	5
Decreasing negative self-talk	1	2	3	4	5

Coaching topics survey. ADHD = attention-deficit/hyperactivity disorder.

(continues)

FIGURE 4.4 (*Continued*)

Managing stress and anxiety	1	2	3	4	5
Establishing realistic goals	1	2	3	4	5
Understand more about ADHD	1	2	3	4	5
Explaining ADHD to professors (requesting accommodations)	1	2	3	4	5
Figuring out the next step in my career or job	1	2	3	4	5

Coaching topics survey. ADHD = attention-deficit/hyperactivity disorder.

think about a variety of concerns in advance, be more thoughtful in considering each area, and prioritize needs. After reviewing the areas checked as a 1 (*definitely need to work on*) or a 2 on the Coaching Topics Survey, the coach helps the client prioritize and select two to four topics and turn them into long-term goals. The Parent-Child Version of the Coaching Topics Survey can also be used. For adolescents, it can be helpful for both the client and the parent to fill this out independently and then compare their responses. It can be useful to discuss differences in perceptions. The Parent-Child version of the Coaching Topics Survey can be seen in Appendix 4.3.

There are some important general principles used in creating long-term goals (Levrini & Prevatt, 2012). First, they need to be *measurable*.

This can generally be accomplished by using specific phrases in the goal's wording. For example, "to be better organized" is not specific, and it would be difficult to know whether the client has accomplished this. However, the phrase "to be more organized with my finances" adds a quantifiable aspect. Second, goals should be *process based*. This is the *how* part of the goal. We can modify the previous goal with a process: "to be more organized with my finances by putting all my bills in folders." Finally, the goal should be *time sensitive by creating a deadline*. A final modification of our example would be "to be more organized with my finances by putting all my bills into folders each week, and doing this for the next 3 months." It is also important that the goals be *realistic*. Setting a goal that is not likely to be accomplished will often lead to discouragement and the client wanting to give up. We discuss more about how to work through goals and identify potential barriers as a way to ensure goals are realistic later in the chapter.

At ALEC, the most common long-term goals (in order of frequency of selection) have been in the following general areas:

- time management;
- establishing good habits and routines;
- planning and prioritizing;
- managing long-term assignments;
- organizing schoolwork, managing stress and anxiety;
- establishing realistic goals;
- keeping track of things, organizing personal space;
- paying attention and taking good notes;
- making decisions and problem solving; and
- establishing better sleep routines (getting to bed, waking up, and staying up).

These goals tend to be more academically focused because ALEC serves a predominantly college student population. Psych Ed coaches tend to encounter more diverse goals because their clients may or may not be in an academic setting. Some of these additional general goal areas include

- exercising, eating healthfully;
- getting to bed or waking up;
- figuring out the next step in a career or job;
- improving relationships with spouse and family;
- improving parenting skills;
- decreasing negative self-talk; and
- managing stress or anxiety.

The long-term goal areas are broad in scope and general in nature. After they have been selected, the client and coach further refine them using the Client Goals and Objectives form (see Figure 4.5).

Turning Long-Term Goals Into Weekly Objectives

After determining the long-term goals, the coach helps the client complete the Client Goals and Objectives form (Figure 4.5). Coaching is centered on this form; it is used weekly to guide the coaching, and it provides structure for each session. Each of the case studies featured later in this book shows examples of how this form is used. In this process, the two to four broad long-term goals are broken down into their component parts. Individuals with ADHD have a difficult time knowing where to get started and how to complete the many small steps that result in a completed task. Therefore, a major component of coaching is to help clients learn how to make continual progress toward reaching their objectives. The Client Goals and Objectives form may or may not be completed during the initial session, depending on how long it takes to complete the intake, engage in psychoeducation about ADHD, and select long-term goals. Before completing the form, we generally inquire about the client's use of a planner, calendar, or organizer. It is common that clients with ADHD do not use a consistent method for remembering details and planning their life. If this is the case, we encourage them to master this skill immediately because coaching will be difficult without this basic ability. This is often the first weekly objective created for the client. This is also the first of many times that we use one of our basic coaching premises: We can provide clients with ideas about what might work, but it is up to them to determine what will work best in their particular circumstance.

Again, throughout coaching, it is important to emphasize that the coach is not a teacher or parent who will instruct the client. Rather, the coach will guide, advise, and collaborate with the client to help the individual determine how to manage his or her life. With regard to a planner, the coach will advise the client that not a single client in 10 years has been successful without some form of planner (one of the few times we exaggerate!). We then discuss a variety of options: Some clients prefer large, notebook style planners with each day on a separate page. Others prefer small, checkbook size planners that can fit in a pocket. Increasingly popular are online systems that can be synced to smart phone and laptop or tablet. Our high school and college age clients tend to prefer newer technology, whereas older clients may prefer the physical options. A general Week 1 objective is to decide on a planner or calendar, purchase or download it, and enter some upcoming dates or assignments.

FIGURE 4.5

CLIENT GOALS AND OBJECTIVES

NAME _____ WEEK _____ DATE _____ NEXT SESSION _____

GOAL 1:
GOAL 2:
GOAL 3:
GOAL 4:

Objective A (Goal)	Objective B (Goal)	Objective C (Goal)
What is your level of motivation to do this objective? 0 1 2 3 4 not at all somewhat moderately very completely motivated motivated motivated motivated motivated	**What is your level of motivation to do this objective?** 0 1 2 3 4 not at all somewhat moderately very completely motivated motivated motivated motivated motivated	**What is your level of motivation to do this objective?** 0 1 2 3 4 not at all somewhat moderately very completely motivated motivated motivated motivated motivated
How well does this objective match with a goal? 0 1 2 3 4 not at all somewhat moderately very much completely a match a match a match a match a match	**How well does this objective match with a goal?** 0 1 2 3 4 not at all somewhat moderately very much completely a match a match a match a match a match	**How well does this objective match with a goal?** 0 1 2 3 4 not at all somewhat moderately very much completely a match a match a match a match a match
In general, I enjoy this activity. 0 1 2 3 4 strongly disagree neutral agree strongly disagree agree	**In general, I enjoy this activity.** 0 1 2 3 4 strongly disagree neutral agree strongly disagree agree	**In general, I enjoy this activity.** 0 1 2 3 4 strongly disagree neutral agree strongly disagree agree

Client goals and objectives form.

(continues)

FIGURE 4.5 (Continued)

FOLLOW-UP	FOLLOW-UP	FOLLOW-UP
How easy was it to complete this objective? 0 1 2 3 4 Not at all somewhat moderately very completely easy easy easy easy easy	**How easy was it to complete this objective?** 0 1 2 3 4 Not at all somewhat moderately very completely easy easy easy easy easy	**How easy was it to complete this objective?** 0 1 2 3 4 Not at all somewhat moderately very completely easy easy easy easy easy
How much of this objective did you complete? 0 1 2 3 4 None 25% about half 75% totally completed	**How much of this objective did you complete?** 0 1 2 3 4 None a little bit about half most totally completed	**How much of this objective did you complete?** 0 1 2 3 4 None a little bit about half most totally completed
Regardless of how much of the objective you completed, what was the quality of the work that you did do? 0 1 2 3 4 Not good at all okay really good work	**Regardless of how much of the objective you completed, what was the quality of the work that you did do?** 0 1 2 3 4 Not good at all okay really good work	**Regardless of how much of the objective you completed, what was the quality of the work that you did do?** 0 1 2 3 4 Not good at all okay really good work
Barriers to not completing objective (check all that apply): ___forgot, ___lack of ability or didn't know how, ___confused about how to do it, ___fear or avoidance of task, ___just not motivated, other →	**Barriers to not completing objective (check all that apply):** ___forgot, ___lack of ability or didn't know how, ___confused about how to do it, ___fear or avoidance of task, ___just not motivated, other →	**Barriers to not completing objective (check all that apply):** ___forgot, ___lack of ability or didn't know how, ___confused about how to do it, ___fear or avoidance of task, ___just not motivated, other →

Client goals and objectives form.

FIGURE 4.6

GOAL 1: Create and follow through with a weekly assignment schedule for the entire semester
GOAL 2: Become better organized in my home life with regard to putting up my things and organizing my papers each week, for at least 3 months
GOAL 3: Create a space for my phone, keys, and glasses and use this space consistently for 8 weeks
GOAL 4:

Select overarching client goals.

Client Goals and Objectives

As we have just covered, for many clients, the first week's objective will be to develop a planner or calendar. If they have already mastered this skill, other objectives can be tackled. Regardless, the Client Goals and Objectives form will be used. This form is easy to follow and is used weekly. The following steps explain how to use this form. For each step, that specific portion of the form has been duplicated, with a case example provided.

1. Fill in up to four overarching client goals. These are generally determined in the first session and maintained throughout the coaching program (see Figure 4.6).
2. Decide on one or two of those goals to work on immediately.
3. Select up to three objectives for the coming week that will help the client reach his or her long-term goals. Fill in these objectives on the form (see Figure 4.7).
4. Discuss how the client will implement these objectives. Be specific. Brainstorm ideas for how to accomplish each objective.

FIGURE 4.7

Objective A (Goal 1)	Objective B (Goal 2)	Objective C (Goal 3)
Read syllabi for all classes. Make an hour-by-hour homework schedule for the week. Complete at least 2 hours of homework every day except Sunday.	Clean room tomorrow (Thursday). Hang up all clothes, empty all trash, file all papers.	

Determine objectives for the upcoming week.

What behaviors or tasks might the client engage in that will accomplish each objective? Come up with a variety of possibilities and help the client evaluate each one. How likely is it to work? What might get in the way? Does the client have the skills to accomplish the task? What barriers exist? When will the client perform the task or behavior?

5. Discuss how the client will be motivated to complete the objective during the week. Will the client use an incentive, or would a consequence work better in this situation? Discuss the difference between internal and external motivators. Decide on the incentive or consequence and determine who will help to implement it. Will the coach be involved in sending reminders?

6. Ask the client to rate the three items on the form for the objective he or she has just selected. If client gives a rating of 0 or 1 (*not* or *only somewhat*) for the item regarding motivation or enjoyment of the activity, discuss these as possible barriers to completing the objective, and brainstorm ways to overcome this. If client gives a rating of 0 or 1 for the item regarding how well the objective matches his or her goals, discuss this. Consider revising the objective so that it is more congruent with what the client hopes to accomplish (see Figure 4.8).

FIGURE 4.8

Objective A (Goal 1)				
What is your level of motivation to do this objective?				
0	1	2	3	4
Not at all motivated	Somewhat motivated	Moderately motivated	Very motivated	Completely motivated
How well does this objective match with a goal?				
0	1	2	3	4
Not at all a match	Somewhat a match	Moderate match	Good match	Complete match
In general, I enjoy this activity.				
0	1	2	3	4
Strongly disagree	Disagree	Neutral	Agree	Strongly agree

Client rates the objectives selected on a scale of 0 to 4.

7. Repeat Steps 4, 5, and 6 for each objective. Copy the Client Goals and Objectives form (Figure 4.5); give one copy to the client, and put the other copy in the client file. (Some clients appreciate having a coaching binder in which to keep their coaching forms.)
8. Confirm the time the client will be coming in for his or her next session, and write this information in the space at the top of the form.
9. This process is repeated every week during the coaching program.

Summary

1. The client's background history and current functioning can be assessed via structured paperwork or through extensive interviewing.
2. Coaches should create informed consent documents consistent with the laws and regulations in their state and in accordance with the age of their clients.
3. The Coaching Topics Survey can be useful in creating long-term goals.
4. Long-term goals should be measurable, process based, time sensitive, and realistic.
5. Weekly objectives are used to complement the long-term goals.
6. Clients should be made aware that the coach is not a teacher or parent who will instruct them. Rather, the coach will guide, advise, and collaborate with clients to help them determine how to manage their life.
7. The Client Goals and Objectives form is used weekly to monitor progress.

APPENDIX 4.1

Symptom Checklist

Please indicate which of the following is currently or has been a problem:

Symptom	In general		When studying, taking tests, or thinking about academics	
	Yes	No	Yes	No
Nausea or stomachaches	___	___	___	___
Difficulty following instructions	___	___	___	___
Depressed mood	___	___	___	___
Easily distracted	___	___	___	___
Restless	___	___	___	___
Careless	___	___	___	___
Feeling of losing control	___	___	___	___
Poor concentration	___	___	___	___
Anxious or worried	___	___	___	___
Cannot sit still, fidgets	___	___	___	___
Feeling hopeless	___	___	___	___
Poor organizational skills	___	___	___	___
Palpitations, increased heart rate	___	___	___	___
Act as if "driven by a motor"/have nonstop energy	___	___	___	___
Irritable	___	___	___	___
Trembling or shaking	___	___	___	___
Forgetful	___	___	___	___
Difficulty sleeping	___	___	___	___
Act without thinking, impulsive	___	___	___	___
Fail to finish tasks	___	___	___	___
Talk excessively	___	___	___	___
Shortness of breath, dizziness	___	___	___	___
Feel sluggish, low energy, or fatigued	___	___	___	___
Difficulty sustaining attention	___	___	___	___

APPENDIX 4.2

The Intake Interview

If the coach is using standardized forms, such as those recommended in Table 4.1, they should be scored, patterns noted, and briefly summarized, as follows.

Academic Success Inventory for College Students (ASICS): Note any subscale scores below the 25th percentile.
Barkley Deficits in Executive Functioning Scales (BDEFS): List all items that were rated a 3 (*very often*).
Client Symptom Checklist (includes items related to depression and anxiety): List all items endorsed as *yes*.
Coaching Topics Survey: List all the 1s (*definitely need to work on*).
Current ADHD Symptoms Scale: List all the scores that were rated a 3 (*very often*).
Outcome Questionnaire (OQ–45): Note any of the questions with scores of *almost always*. Especially take note of the following items: *I feel worthless, I feel hopeless about the future, disturbing thoughts come to my mind that I cannot get rid of, I feel angry enough at school/ work to do something I might regret,* or *I have thoughts or feelings of ending my life.*
Rosenberg Self-Esteem Scale: List overall range and any items of concern.

On the basis of this summary, the coach can develop a set of questions that he or she feels would be important for the initial session. If standardized forms are not used, the coach will inquire about the areas covered above in their interview, as needed.

Specific Intake Questions
(Remember to first go over and obtain signature on the informed consent.)

Why is the client seeking coaching services?

If the client has received coaching services before, what worked well, and what would he or she like to do differently?

Is the client currently receiving counseling services?

What are the current medications (with dosages) that the client is taking?

- When did the client start taking medication? _____
- Does the client have any problems with the medication (e.g., sleep, effectiveness, dosage, eating, forgetting to take the medication)?

Is the client having any difficulty with:

- Sleep? _____ How many hours of sleep do they average per night? _____ (# of hours)
- Eating? _____ Does the client eat breakfast? _____

Example of what the client eats for breakfast_____

If a student, discuss current coursework, grades, GPA, academic strengths and difficulties.
If working, discuss current employment strengths and difficulties.
Discuss relationships.
What does the client feel are the biggest obstacles or barriers he or she faces when trying to accomplish goals?
What current coping strategies does the client use when dealing with these obstacles?
What are the client's strengths?

(continues)

APPENDIX 4.2 (Continued)

What does the client like to do for fun?
What type of social support does the client have from family and friends?
How does the client view himself or herself?
Does client have current mental health diagnosis?
Is there a family history of attention-deficit/hyperactivity disorder or learning disabilities or other mental health disorders?
Discuss the Coaching Topics Survey to determine three long-term goals.
Determine planned day and time of weekly coaching sessions.
Does the client prefer text messages, e-mail, or phone call reminders?

APPENDIX 4.3

Coaching Topics Survey—Child

For each of the following items, circle the number from 1 to 5 that indicates the degree to which your child needs to work on that area.

	Does need to work on				Doesn't need to work on
Improving time management	1	2	3	4	5
Establishing routines and good habits	1	2	3	4	5
Organizing schoolwork	1	2	3	4	5
Organizing personal space	1	2	3	4	5
Getting to class on time	1	2	3	4	5
Studying	1	2	3	4	5
Scheduling classes	1	2	3	4	5
Paying attention in class and taking good notes	1	2	3	4	5
Managing long-term assignments and projects	1	2	3	4	5
Planning and prioritizing	1	2	3	4	5
Making decisions and solving problems	1	2	3	4	5
Keeping track of things	1	2	3	4	5
Doing laundry	1	2	3	4	5
Exercising	1	2	3	4	5
Eating healthfully	1	2	3	4	5
Waking up and staying up	1	2	3	4	5
Getting to bed	1	2	3	4	5
Taking medication	1	2	3	4	5
Making friends	1	2	3	4	5
Keeping friends	1	2	3	4	5
Getting along with classmates or siblings	1	2	3	4	5
Getting along in group situations	1	2	3	4	5
Decreasing negative self-talk	1	2	3	4	5
Managing stress and anxiety	1	2	3	4	5
Establishing realistic goals	1	2	3	4	5
Understanding more about his or her disorder(s)	1	2	3	4	5
Using accommodations	1	2	3	4	5

The Nuts and Bolts of Coaching
Working Through Issues

5

In this chapter, we discuss more specific details of coaching. We describe how to incorporate the Barkley Deficits in Executive Functioning Scales (BDEFS; Barkley, 2011b) and the Academic Success Inventory for College Students (ASICS; Prevatt, Li, et al., 2011) into the coaching program. We discuss and provide samples of progress notes and between-session assignments. Finally, we give more details on the middle and ending phases of the 8-week coaching program.

Executive Functioning

As mentioned in Chapter 3, we use two primary theories to guide our coaching program: cognitive behavioral theory and psychoeducation. In addition, we use executive functioning (EF) as a way of understanding client difficulties and formulating coaching goals. EF deficits can have an impact on

http://dx.doi.org/10.1037/14671-006
ADHD Coaching: A Guide for Mental Health Professionals, by F. Prevatt and A. Levrini
Copyright © 2015 by the American Psychological Association. All rights reserved.

academic, social, occupational, and psychological functioning (DuPaul, Weyandt, O'Dell, & Varejao, 2009; Swartz, Prevatt, & Proctor, 2005; Weyandt et al., 2013). At the beginning of coaching, we often have adult clients fill out the BDEFS (Barkley, 2011b). The BDEFS allows us to determine which of five areas may show primary impairment: self-management of time, self-organization and problem solving, self-restraint, self-motivation, and self-regulation of emotions. The goals the client selects should be consistent with his or her ratings on the BDEFS. For example, if the client indicates primary impairment in self-management of time yet does not select any goal that is consistent with this area of functioning, we inquire about that discrepancy. We might go over the specific items on the scale that the client has endorsed and help determine whether he or she might wish to add that area as a goal. The ultimate decision needs to come from the client; however, the coach ensures that clients consider multiple areas.

Clients with attention-deficit/hyperactivity disorder (ADHD) who are in school might be particularly susceptible to difficulties because the rigors of academic life require strong EF. In a recent research project, we tested the 89 BDEFS items to determine which are most descriptive of college students with ADHD who have academic difficulties (Coffman, 2014). We discovered that 14 of the 89 items were highly prevalent in a college student sample. All of the items were from domains that measure time management, self-organization, and problem solving. The following list gives a description of those items.

- Forgetting to do things
- Not able to accomplish goals
- Unable to remember things that need to be done
- Difficulty judging how much time it will take to do something or get somewhere
- Difficulty with motivation to do work
- Trouble finishing one thing before starting another
- Unable to prioritize well
- Hard getting started on work
- Difficulty organizing thoughts
- Difficulty concentrating and not getting distracted
- Difficulty understanding what has been read and needing to reread material
- Difficulty focusing on work
- Easily confused
- Difficulty concentrating on work or lectures or paperwork

Difficulties with these tasks will be particularly problematic for a college student who needs to be reading, paying attention in class, taking notes, working on projects and papers, and studying for exams. In fact, it is difficult to imagine a set of skills that are more essential to do well in college courses. College is particularly difficult for students who are suddenly away from home for the first time and in charge of making all their own decisions about time, effort, and workload. Most beginning college students (particularly those with ADHD) are used to the support they received from parents and teachers in high school. They may have had someone who made sure they got up in the morning, fixed their breakfast, and drove them to school. They may have had someone come to school during the day to bring the book or paper they left at home. They may have had a strict after-school schedule of studying and someone to ensure that they started on projects and had the materials they needed to accomplish school-related tasks. In college, students are suddenly in a situation in which time management and organization are critical; however, they no longer have the support system of parents or teachers to help keep them organized and on track.

EF deficits may also help us understand the motivational deficits seen in many of our clients, whether they are students or employed. EF skills are especially crucial for college students due to the demands of academic coursework (e.g., using study skills, prioritizing coursework, completing assignments) and managing independence (e.g., paying bills, incorporating diet and exercise, maintenance of medication). Likewise, EF skills will be critical in many jobs because of demands to be on time, prioritize tasks, remember things that need to be done, stay organized, problem solve when difficulties arise, focus on work tasks without distraction, and complete tasks in a timely manner. How does this relate to motivation? It is believed that the behavior of individuals with ADHD may be under the control of immediate sources of reinforcement because of an inability to bridge the delay between goal-directed behavior and its long-term consequences (Barkley, 1997). Because individuals with ADHD have a deficit of intention, they do not appreciate the payoff later for hard work now. Working on ways to increase motivation will be a key part of ADHD coaching. The case study in Chapter 10 shows how motivation and other EF deficits can be integrated into the ADHD coaching framework.

Characteristics Associated With Academic Success

When working with college students, we often use the ASICS (Prevatt, Li, et al., 2011) as a tool to understand areas of positive functioning and help in setting objectives. The ASICS provides a measure of a student's

TABLE 5.1

Sample of Client Feedback After Completion of the Academic Success Inventory for College Students

Domain	Student's score	25th percentile cutoff	X indicates student's score is less than cutoff
Academic skills	73	45	
Internal motivation and confidence	77	45	
Instructor efficacy	77	46	
Concentration	25	29	X
External motivation (future)	96	36	
Socializing	71	57	
Career decidedness	100	57	
Anxiety	48	29	
Personal adjustment	33	43	X
External motivation (current)	90	52	

thoughts and behaviors in 10 domains. These domains help determine if the student's difficulty in college may be affected by poor academic and study skills, a lack of internal or external motivation, a belief that instructors are not helpful, a poor ability to focus or concentrate, an excess of time spent in social activities, a lack of career goals, an excessive amount of anxiety, or poor personal adjustment. A domain is considered to be of significant concern if the student scores lower than 75% of college students in the normative sample (that is, in the bottom 25th percentile). The chart in Table 5.1 shows a sample of the feedback a client might receive after completing this measure.

Similar to the BDEFS, the coach reviews this measure to ensure that domains highlighted as problematic are considered when determining goals and objectives. Depending on which domains are low, we might offer specific suggestions about career counseling, learning different study skills, engaging in some stress-reduction techniques, or discussing motivational issues. This measure might also lead us to consider whether concurrent mental health counseling with a licensed practitioner might be needed.

Between-Session Assignments

Between-session assignments (BSAs), or homework assignments, are frequently used with both cognitive behavioral therapy and other therapeutic orientations for a variety of clinical problems (Kazantzis, Lampropoulos, & Deane, 2005; Prevatt, Lampropoulos, et al., 2011).

BSAs help clients to engage in self-help tasks between sessions. Meta-analytic research has shown that the use of BSAs improves treatment outcome and that client compliance with BSAs is also related to benefits from treatment (Kazantzis, Deane, & Ronan, 2000). In our own research, clients who believed the BSAs matched well with their personal coaching goals showed improvement on test taking strategies, and clients who indicated willingness to try BSAs showed an improvement in attention and a decrease in anxiety. Additionally, the coach's ratings of client BSA use (in terms of both quality and quantity) were associated with client improvement on concentration and test-taking strategies and with a decrease in anxiety (Prevatt & Yelland, 2013). BSAs seem to work because they affect two primary areas of EF: problem solving and motivation (Prevatt & Yelland, 2013).

Each week, clients determine two to four specific objectives that will help them reach their long-term goals. For each objective, an associated BSA is created. For example, a long-term goal might be to become more organized. A weekly objective for this goal might be to organize the client's homework space. A relevant BSA for the week would be to create file folders for different paperwork. The client and coach mutually decide on the BSA, and a standard problem-solving approach is used (see Figure 4.3 in Chapter 4 to review the problem-solving approach). In the earlier example, the coach would ask the client about any possible barriers to achieving the BSA (remembering to go to the store to buy folders, finding time to go to the store, or following through on labeling the folders). The coach and client strategize to overcome barriers (set phone reminder to go to the store, create an incentive after going to the store, and label folders).

Incentives or consequences are an important part of the BSAs. These tend to fall into three categories: internally motivated incentives, externally motivated incentives, and consequences.

1. An example of an *internally motivated incentive* might be to study for an exam based on the inherent satisfaction of getting an A in a class.
2. An example of an *externally motivated incentive* might be to study for an exam and reward oneself with double mocha frozen latte for each day in which an hour was spent studying.
3. An example of a *consequence* might be to put a dollar in a jar for each day in which no studying was accomplished.

It is important that the objective be specific and measurable (1 hour of studying for a math test, three times per week). In our experience, incentives (both internally and externally motivated) and consequences work equally well. However, clients tend to use incentives over consequences (Smith et al., 2014). The key is that the client selects them and

TABLE 5.2

Examples of Long-Term Goals, Weekly BSAs, and Incentives and Consequences

Long-term goal	BSA	Incentive or consequence
Obtain *As* and *Bs* in all classes	Schedule study times in planner	Go to a movie with friends
	Put a whiteboard in bedroom with due dates for papers	Ride skateboard for 30 minutes
	Start term paper 5 weeks before due date by doing an outline (by October 14)	No television until this is accomplished
Engage in healthier lifestyle	Go to gym three times per week	Will be self-motivating because will feel better
	Eat protein for breakfast each morning	Cannot put on makeup until breakfast is eaten (so will look "awful" if don't do this)
	Go to bed by 11 p.m. each night	Will be self-motivating because will feel better
Better communication with friends	Call a friend at least one time this week (no later than Wednesday) to schedule an activity	No Internet at night until phone call is made
Be on time for appointments	Pick one appointment for this week and make a detailed schedule of time needed to arrive on time (e.g., shower, dress, eat, drive, park, walk to meeting)	Employer will not be exasperated

Note. BSA = between-session assignment.

believes that they are workable. If the client fails to meet the objective for the week, the process of analyzing the client's behaviors becomes a learning opportunity. The chart in Table 5.2 gives examples of long-term goals, weekly BSAs, and incentives and consequences that our clients have used.

Weekly Progress Notes

At the Adult Learning Evaluation Center (ALEC), we complete weekly progress notes and send a copy of these to the client. These notes follow a structured format. Each progress note summarizes the background information regarding the client and states his or her long-term goals; these two things remain the same each week. Next, the progress note summarizes what the client did the previous week with regard to the planned objectives. If he or she was successful, the reasons for this are iterated; likewise, if the client encountered some obstacles, these are listed. Incentives or consequences used in the previous week are listed. Finally, plans for the upcoming week are summarized: New objectives, incentives and consequences, as well as potential obstacles, are detailed. Figure 5.1 is a template with instructions for writing progress notes, followed by a sample progress note in Figure 5.2.

The progress notes serve several purposes. Adults with ADHD tend to have memory difficulties. In our earlier work, we found that a common reason clients give for not completing objectives during the week is that they had forgotten what they were supposed to do. Part of the difficulty with remembering tasks is that the adult with ADHD may be distracted when first hearing information, and so it is likely the information never makes it into short-term memory. We e-mail the client written progress notes (password protected). Most clients pull these up on their smartphones and so can easily access their weekly tasks.

The progress notes also serve as an ongoing blueprint for how to engage the problem-solving process and cope with ADHD. The notes list goals, short-term steps to accomplish those goals, incentives to motivate the client to engage in weekly goal-directed behaviors, and an analysis of what works. Additionally, we note potential barriers that may get in the way of accomplishing tasks. We explain to the client that this process is how adults without ADHD subconsciously manage their lives. This type of meta-thinking occurs constantly for many individuals. By engaging in this verbally each week in session, and seeing it in writing, we hope that the client internalizes the process of planning, problem solving, analyzing, revising, and behaving.

Finally, we think the progress notes help to engage the client in the coaching process. Clients report that they enjoy reading about themselves and find the specific tasks to be motivating. A great deal of thought and effort goes into creating the progress notes, and clients seem to be aware of this and enjoy the implication that they are valued by the coach. Many adults with ADHD have low self-esteem, and we believe that progress notes are a small part of why our coaching program can increase self-esteem (Prevatt & Yelland, 2013).

Between Sessions

Clients with ADHD may have difficulty remaining enthusiastic and motivated from week to week. They can be quite animated during sessions, with good intentions and plans for the coming week. However, the very symptoms that brought them to coaching may well undermine their

FIGURE 5.1

General Template and Instructions for Progress Notes

Session # ____ Date: _____ Coach: _____

Client Name is a xx-year-old (include relevant demographic characteristics)

Provide one to two paragraphs that include the following information (once you write this section, it will likely remain the same throughout the course of coaching, unless something changes):

- Difficulties the client is experiencing, such as time management, organization, inattention, procrastination, sleep difficulties, or eating concerns
- Diagnoses client may have, such as ADHD, depression, or anxiety
- Medication information (type, dosage, whether taking consistently)
- Counseling information, if applicable (how often, where he or she attends, whether it is helpful)
- Any other important information that would be useful to know, such as whether the client is on academic probation or has been fired from a job
- What the client hopes to improve over course of coaching

Long-Term Goals: (these are the long-term goals established in session one)

- _____
- _____
- _____

Prior Week's Progress:

Progress Toward Last Week's Objectives: (How much of each objective did the client complete? If he or she modified the objective during the week, include that information.)

- Objective A: _____
- Objective B: _____
- Objective C: _____

Weekly Successes and What Contributed to Successes: (Include anything that helped the client reach his or her objectives, such as social support, having a plan for accomplishing the objective, writing down steps to complete objective)

- _____
- _____
- _____

Obstacles: (What obstacles did the client face? If the client overcame the obstacle, how did he or she overcome it?)

- _____
- _____
- _____

General template and instructions for progress notes.

FIGURE 5.1

Plans for Upcoming Week

Weekly Objectives:

1. _____
2. _____
3. _____

Incentives and Consequences:

- Objective A: (State the incentive/consequence)
- Objective B: (State the incentive/consequence)
- Objective C: (State the incentive/consequence)

Potential Obstacles: (What obstacles might the client face this week in accomplishing his or her objectives? What are the plans if the client faces this obstacle?)

_____
_____
_____
_____

Plan for Next Session: We will meet next _____ (date) at _____. Throughout the week, coach will _____ (could state that you will send the client text or e-mail reminders, or anything else you might do throughout the week to help the client). During our next session, we will _____ (plan for next session).

General template and instructions for progress notes.

FIGURE 5.2

Session #3   10/25/2013   Coach: John Smith

Name Jane Doe is a 19-year-old African American woman pursuing a bachelor of science degree in political science at Florida State University. She reported difficulties with organization, time management, inattention, starting assignments, and anxiety. Additionally, she finds that she often misplaces her phone, keys, and glasses. Jane has not been formally evaluated for ADHD; however, she exhibits significant symptoms of ADHD. She is not currently taking medication or receiving counseling services; however, she received services last semester and found it somewhat helpful. She feels that coaching services would better fulfill the help she needs. Jane hopes to improve her organizational skills, punctuality, and academic performance.

Long-Term Goals:
- Obtain *As* and *Bs* in all of her classes.
- Become better organized.
- Always know the location of her phone, keys, and glasses.

Prior Week's Progress:

Progress Toward Last Week's Objectives:
- Objective A: Jane completed the objective of making a schedule for her studying and homework. While the initial objective was to do this on an hour-by-hour scheduling sheet, she decided that doing this on a large white board at home would be more effective. She thought it would be easier to see and remind her to follow through. Moreover, things could be more easily changed on the white board.
- Objective B: Jane began studying for her two tests on October 31. However, she was frustrated that she didn't study more than she actually did.
- Objective C: Jane successfully cleaned her room. However, she had a difficult time keeping her room clean, which interfered with her ability to complete work at home.

Weekly Successes and What Contributed to Successes:
- Jane reported that she found the Client Goals and Objectives sheet helpful because it was like a "recipe" for what she had to do for the week.
- Jane found that talking with her friends about coaching and her objectives was helpful because they were able to follow up with her and see how she was doing. Additionally, they provided positive encouragement for the things she did. Even when she would "beat herself up" for not studying as much as she would have liked, her friends reminded her of the positive successes she had for the week.

Obstacles:
- Jane had a difficult time studying. She found that one assignment required more work than originally anticipated, resulting in more time dedicated to the assignment and less dedicated to studying. Jane also found that she had a hard time getting started and staying on task. She would often say, "In 30 minutes, I'll start studying." However, an hour would pass, and she would not have started.
- Jane had a difficult time keeping her room clean.

Sample progress note.

FIGURE 5.2

- Jane found it difficult to use a paper hour-by-hour calendar to schedule study times because things would sometimes change and she would need to readjust. However, she overcame this obstacle by using a white-board system at home, and she has found it to be helpful thus far.
- Jane reported that she has been "beating herself up" if she doesn't complete an objective to the highest quality. Although the objectives have been helpful at getting her to do things, if she has difficulties with objective, she engages in negative self-talk.

Upcoming Week

Weekly Objectives:
1. Jane will clean her room over the course of 3 days. She'll conquer one of three sections each day.
2. Every day at lunch and once on Sunday (at the completion of the week), Jane will tell herself "I did a good job." If she adds a "but I didn't do X," she will add either "But it's OK," or "But it's not the end of the world" to the sentence. Therefore, she might say, "I did a good job starting to study, but I didn't study the whole 3 hours at the library, but it's okay."
3. Jane will follow through on her study schedule by using alarms on her telephone to remind her of study times.

Incentives and Consequences:
- Objective A: Incentive—Have a snack each time she cleans her room
- Objective B: Incentive—Ride her skateboard around campus
- Objective C: Incentive—Go to Halloween party with friends on Thursday night

Potential Obstacles:
- Getting started on studying. Jane will attempt to use alarms to remind her of study times. However, she may become distracted after the alarm. If this occurs, we will troubleshoot in next session.
- Restructuring her thoughts may prove to be difficult because it is a difficult task to combat those thoughts. It may also take some time for this to be helpful. Jane will try writing down two or three negative thoughts and then positive additions to those thoughts.

Plan for Next Session: We will meet next Friday (11/1/13) at 10:30 a.m. I will send her intermittent reminders via e-mail and text messages to remind her to continue to place her phone or keys on the nightstand and to schedule her study times. During our next session, we will review her objectives and any challenges and/or obstacles to completing them. As needed, we will modify the strategies and techniques. We will also discuss whether the incentives and consequences were motivating.

Sample progress note.

weekly progress. Between-session communications can be useful in coaching. Specifically, sending clients texts or e-mails between sessions can facilitate achievement of weekly objectives. These between-session communications are phased out over the course of coaching but are relied on heavily in the early stages.

This contact is discussed during the session, and clients determine what type of contact would be beneficial. The most frequent request is for e-mail or text reminders to engage in specific activities associated with the BSAs. We explain to the client that we will use these communications more frequently in the early sessions of coaching. However, over time, we will decrease the number of communications as the client learns ways to remind himself or herself and to engage in self-motivation. Some clients will use a portion of each session to set several reminders on their phone for the coming week, consistent with that week's planned objectives.

The Middle Phases of Coaching

Each week of coaching follows the same basic format. The coach usually begins by asking how the week has gone, focusing on the Client Goals and Objectives Worksheet. The coach asks about each individual objective from the prior week (there should be two to three of these). The client completes the Follow-Up Questions on the worksheet (Figure 5.3).

Successes

If a client has been successful in meeting an objective, the coach inquires about what strategies the client used to be successful. Did the motivators work? Were there barriers that the client had to overcome? How was the client able to accomplish his or her goals? This discussion helps solidify the problem-solving approach to accomplishing tasks by encouraging the client to mentally rehearse the steps taken to overcome barriers. It boosts confidence by encouraging the client to talk about success at a task. It serves as a motivator that clients can overcome difficulties and helps change their internal belief into a positive, I-can-do-it schema. Each weekly objective is just one step toward accomplishing the overarching long-term goal. Each weekly success will be followed by discussing the next weekly objective; this is a logical building block toward

FIGURE 5.3

Follow-Up
How easy was it to complete this objective?   0   1   2   3   4   Not at all   somewhat   moderately   very   completely   easy   easy   easy   easy   easy
How much of this objective did you complete?   0   1   2   3   4   None   25%   About half   75%   Totally completed
Regardless of how much of the objective you completed, what was the quality of the work that you did do?   0   1   2   3   4   Not good at all   OK   Really good work
Barriers to not completing objective (check all that apply):   ___forgot ___lack of ability or didn't know how ___confused about how to do it ___fear or avoidance of task ___just not motivated   other → _____

Follow-up questions for the client to complete.

that long-term goal. The next week's objective is discussed, entered on the Client Goals and Objectives Worksheet, and the problem-solving approach is repeated (refer back to Chapter 4). To summarize those steps, the coach and client brainstorm ideas for accomplishing the objective (specific behaviors, likelihood of success, possible barriers, specific timing). The coach and client discuss motivators for completing the objective (incentive vs. consequence, internal vs. external, how implemented). Finally, the client completes the ratings on the worksheet regarding motivation, difficulty, enjoyment, and congruence with goals. If low ratings are given, possible revisions to next week's objectives are discussed.

Barriers

When clients have not been successful in meeting their objectives, these are discussed in a manner similar to successes. What happened? Were the motivators insufficient? Did the client not have the skill to complete the task? The coach and client dissect the unsuccessful attempt and use this as a learning experience. Generally, the same objective is set for the upcoming week; however, either the specific plan or the motivators are revised. Unsuccessful objectives are not seen as failures but as ways to learn how to overcome obstacles. Many clients are used to failure, and they respond by quitting, thus reinforcing their cognitive belief that they are lazy or inept. We frame this in a positive light and help clients to view themselves as people who can persevere and be ultimately successful.

New Goals

Once a long-term goal has been successfully met, a client may choose a new goal. Sometimes goals are quite substantial and take the entire 8 weeks to accomplish (e.g., develop better interpersonal skills in my relationship with my wife, get an *A* in my accounting class). Other goals may take only a few weeks to accomplish and will be replaced several times in the 8-week program (e.g., organize my bills, set up a study schedule). At Psych Ed Coaches, clients continually add new goals as old goals are accomplished, and coaching usually lasts much longer than 8 weeks. Throughout the process, the client is learning how to accomplish goal setting and task completion on his or her own after the end of coaching. The coach teaches the following skills:

- identify goals,
- break goals down into manageable objectives,
- use a problem-solving approach to develop a plan for accomplishing objectives,
- identify motivators to help themselves to complete objectives,
- learn from successes,
- use lack of success to identify barriers and persevere with new plan, and
- develop an "I-can-do-it" attitude.

Specific Strategies

The weekly coaching sessions revolve around the client goals and objectives. Within that framework, the coach works with the client to develop numerous specific skills. Chapter 6 goes into detail about several of our favorite coaching strategies. These include the ADHD Life Wheel, the Inspiration Toolbox, the Decision-Making Table, the Juggling Exercise, the Processing Exercise, and the Eisenhower Grid. Other strategies involve using a planner, being more "green" in coaching, and using career planning resources. There are so many resources available on the Internet that it is not possible to list all of them, but Chapter 6 offers some good basic strategies and techniques. Also, coaches will be familiar with specific resources available in their own communities. For example, we routinely recommend that clients take advantage of local college and university tutoring, career advising, study groups, and library resources. Institutions in your own town will likely have similar resources.

Concluding Coaching

At the end of the 8 weeks, the coach and client review the progress made during the program. The coach helps the client consider what skills he or she has learned that can be generalized to daily life. Successes and barriers are reviewed. The coach encourages the client to determine some new goals that he or she can work on independently. Some clients sign up for an additional 8-week coaching program, whereas others request one or more booster sessions in a few months' time. We use the feedback form in Figure 5.4 to evaluate our coaching program. Many clients say that coaching helps them learn new ways of being organized and new ways of thinking about how to accomplish objectives.

Because of our ongoing research program, we also ask clients to complete the following posttest measures (these were previously completed at intake): ASICS, BDEFS, the Client Symptom Checklist, the Coaching Topics Survey, the Current ADHD Symptoms Scale, the OQ-45, and the Rosenberg Self-Esteem Inventory. Please refer back to Chapter 4 for a description of these measures (Table 4.1). For those clients who have previously signed an informed consent to allow their data to be evaluated, we calculate pre–post difference scores to determine which area of coaching have been most effective and which may need to be modified.

In Chapters 8 through 12, we describe several case studies that give additional details for conducting ADHD coaching. These cases describe working with an adult with career indecision (Chapter 8), a professional adult with work and daily living difficulties (Chapter 9), a college student with EF deficits (Chapter 10), a postbaccalaureate student with comorbid anxiety and depression (Chapter 11), and a younger high school student with learning and family issues (Chapter 12).

FIGURE 5.4

ADHD COACHING EVALUATION FORM

1. What has changed for you as a result of coaching?
   _____
   _____
   _____
   _____

2. What aspect of coaching was the most helpful?
   _____
   _____
   _____
   _____

3. What aspect of coaching was the least helpful?
   _____
   _____
   _____
   _____

4. What suggestions do you have to improve coaching?
   _____
   _____
   _____
   _____

Coaching evaluation form.

Summary

1. The BDEFS can help to determine which areas show impairments in EF: self-management of time, self-organization and problem solving, self-restraint, self-motivation, or self-regulation of emotions.
2. The ASICS can help to determine whether the client might have impairment in motivation, academic skills, or other thoughts or behaviors.
3. BSAs are used to help clients achieve their weekly objectives.
4. There are three primary types of incentives: internally motivated incentives, externally motivated incentives, and consequences.
5. Progress notes help clients remember their weekly assignments, remain motivated, and learn problem-solving skills.
6. Between-session text messages or e-mails can be appropriate to use in coaching.
7. Both successes and failures can be learning experiences.
8. Coaching can be concluded by looking at pre–post gains on specific measures of perceptions and behavior, as well as client satisfaction surveys.

Specific Strategies for ADHD Coaching 6

To achieve successful outcomes with your clients, it is important that you maintain consistency in your approach and use the empirically supported outline set forth in the previous chapters. However, while working within the coaching framework, particular strategies should be individualized for each client and his or her particular needs, strengths, and goals. Undoubtedly, as a trained mental health practitioner, you have already developed a wide variety of counseling skills and know many useful interventions that can be applied within the coaching setting, such as journaling, desensitization, cognitive restructuring, or role-playing exercises. These strategies will be of particular use when working with clients struggling with coexisting mood disorders or other conditions.

In addition to these eclectic counseling skills, there are several specific strategies that may lead to positive outcomes with coaching clients. It is important that coaches become familiar with specific resources available in their own communities, such as professionals who conduct psychoeducational

http://dx.doi.org/10.1037/14671-007
ADHD Coaching: A Guide for Mental Health Professionals, by F. Prevatt and A. Levrini
Copyright © 2015 by the American Psychological Association. All rights reserved.

evaluations, attention-deficit/hyperactivity disorder (ADHD) support groups, or programs designed to help students with specific learning disabilities, such as reading or writing.

The following is a list of strategies you may find helpful when working with clients. Consider this your coach's toolbox. It is up to you to choose the right tool for your client and to work it into the coaching framework so that it makes sense. We start by describing strategies that are most helpful during the psychoeducational phase of coaching, most commonly at the outset or within the first few sessions, but sometimes throughout the coaching process. We then break down strategies as they pertain to particular goals, commonly set by clients, that can be introduced as needs arise or as between-session assignments (BSAs) during the middle phase of coaching. At the beginning of each set of strategies, we present some of the items clients may have rated positively on the Coaching Topics Survey (see Chapter 4) or goals they may have set that relate to those particular strategies.

Strategies for the Beginning (Psychoeducational) Phase of Coaching

All coaching clients will need, to varying degrees, psychoeducation about ADHD or other mental health issues despite their perceived level of knowledge. Sometimes this phase is about dispelling myths; other times it is about building up clients to believe that they can be successful despite previous setbacks, or maybe it is simply reinforcing what they already know in a new way. Some clients may even have a goal relating to psychoeducation or give a rating on the Coaching Topics Survey that indicates they want to understand more about their disorder.

This section includes methods for educating and encouraging your client through psychoeducation, setting the stage for a successful coaching program.

LEARNING STYLE

Often individuals with ADHD are seen as a problem to be fixed, rather than viewing the problem as lying within our educational or workplace environments. However, despite problems in academia and the world of work, it is now widely known that most individuals with ADHD do not lack the intellectual ability to learn or make valuable contributions to the workplace. Studies have shown that college students with ADHD do not differ significantly from their peers without ADHD with regard to cognitive ability (Reaser, Prevatt, Petscher, & Proctor, 2007). ADHD coaching clients may be intelligent in ways not typically demonstrated in schools or in most jobs.

Many clients with ADHD may possess what's called *naturalist intelligence*, or sensitivity to the natural world and living things, an ability that was of great value in our evolutionary past as hunters, gatherers, and farmers and in today's society as scientists, chefs, or artists. Others might display *spatial intelligence*, which relates to the ability to visualize or imagine, a trait that comes in handy in professions such as architecture, design, or art. Some other types of intelligence common to those with ADHD, but not as valued in our schools or jobs, includes *musical*, *bodily kinesthetic* (or the capacity to handle and manipulate objects), *intrapersonal* (self-reflection), and *interpersonal* (interaction with others; Schirduan, Case, & Faryniarz, 2002).

Individuals with ADHD learn well when they are highly interested in the material being taught and have shown improved behavior or performance when tasks are made salient, novel, or interesting. Therefore, before you begin to try different learning techniques or coping strategies with your client, it is imperative that you get to understand the ways in which he or she learns best. For example, it would be a waste of time, money, and resources if you implemented a flashcard study program with a student who is best at auditory processing. Much of this can only be learned through conversation (i.e., naturalist intelligence, intrapersonal intelligence) or through a simple question on your intake form; however, psychoeducational assessment can tell us about many areas of relative strength and weakness when it comes to learning (i.e., visuospatial, auditory processing). For adults or other clients who have not had psychoeducational assessment and have little insight into how they learn best, there are many online learning-style quizzes. See the Resources section at the end of the chapter for some websites to try.

ADHD Life Wheel

The life wheel is a fairly common exercise in general life coaching, and it can be used to help clients gain perspective on the different facets of their life in a visual and creative way. In ADHD coaching, clients can create an ADHD Life Wheel, which is more specific to their ADHD symptoms and behaviors than a general life wheel. The *ADHD Life Wheel*, like more general forms of the exercise, allows clients to look at the larger picture of their life to determine whether they are addressing key areas and giving enough attention to issues of importance. The exercise is fairly quick and simple, but it can be quite powerful for clients and can be done at different points throughout coaching to visually depict changes in attention and behavior. To establish a baseline and better understand his or her needs, you will want to have your client complete one life wheel early on in the coaching process. This will also give additional information and aid in the creation of your client's long-term goals.

Here are the steps to creating an ADHD Life Wheel:

1. On a piece of paper, have your client draw a large circle. This will be the "wheel." Include the client's name, date, and coaching session number (i.e., Session 2) at the top of the paper. (You may also want to create copies of a blank wheel so that clients can skip Steps 1 and 2.)
2. Draw two perpendicular lines, like a cross, through the center and outer edges (perimeter) of the circle. Like four "spokes" on a wheel, this will divide the circle into four quarters. Draw two more perpendicular lines, dividing each of the four quarters in half. You will end up with a diagram looking like a wheel with eight spokes or like a pie with eight slices.
3. At each point at which a line, or "spoke," intersects the circle, or "wheel," have clients write one area that is important to them in terms of life in general or that is specific to their ADHD behaviors. Have clients take some time to consider the most important areas, because there is only room for eight. See Figure 6.1 for an example of an ADHD Life Wheel.

FIGURE 6.1

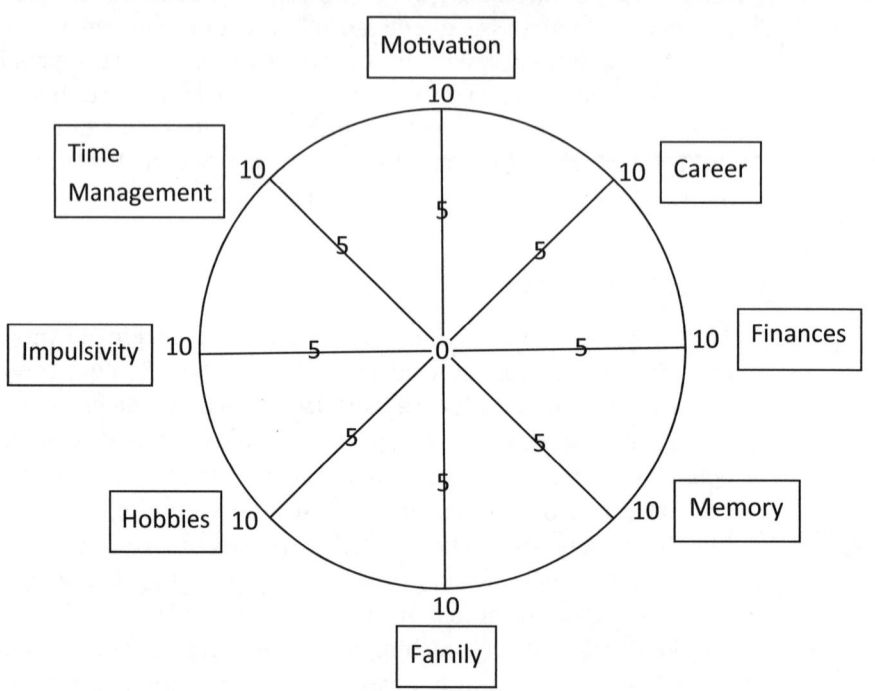

An ADHD Life Wheel.

The following are some common life categories that clients may want to consider:

- school, work, career
- relationship, family, friendships
- recreation, hobbies
- finances
- exercise, fitness, health
- religion, spirituality

Here are some ADHD categories clients may want to consider:

- motivation
- organization
- time management
- memory
- completing tasks
- paying attention
- impulsivity
- social skills

4. Once the eight points are labeled, have the client mark the center point of the circle with a zero. Next, he or she can label the point where each spoke meets the perimeter of the circle with a 10. (This step can also be included on your copies.)
5. From here you can choose among several questions to invoke insight from your client. See the following for example:
    a. "If zero stands for no satisfaction, and 10 stands for full satisfaction, how satisfied do you feel with each of these areas of your life?"
    b. "If zero is stands for something that is very easy for you, and 10 stands for something that is very challenging for you, how successful do you feel in each of these areas of your life?"
    c. "If zero stands for nowhere near where you want to be and 10 stands for being perfectly fulfilled, where do you think is realistic and acceptable in each of these areas of your life?"
6. Have clients write their number along the relevant spoke and draw a line across that piece of the pie, estimating where that number may fall. You and your clients can now use the ADHD Life Wheel to consider balance and direction in life and to help guide the coaching process. You can do this by looking at the rating numbers given to each life dimension individually as well as by comparing the numbers for each dimension to see how similar or different they are (see Figure 6.2).

FIGURE 6.2

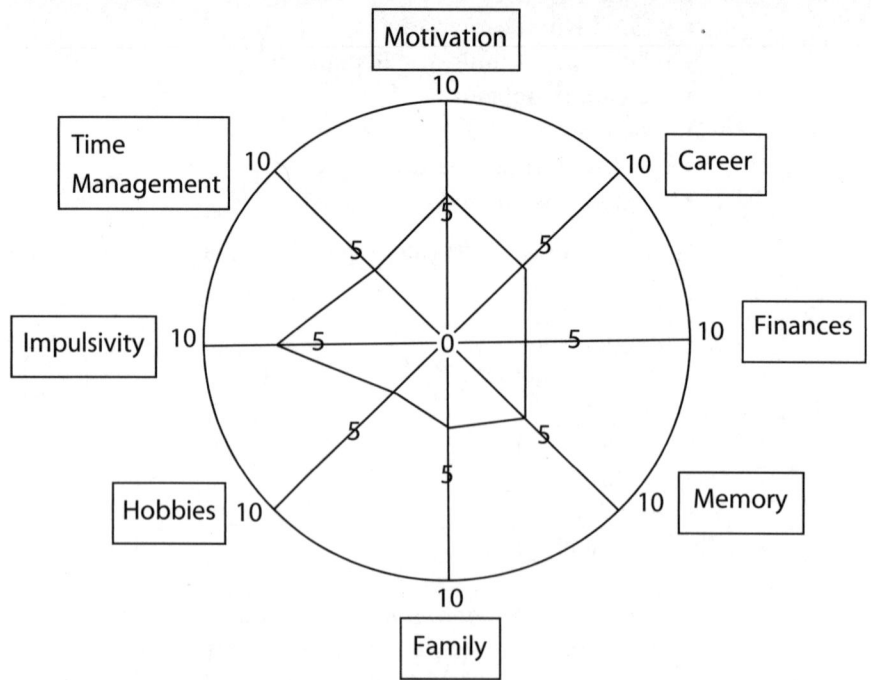

An ADHD Life Wheel completed by a client.

Here are just some of the questions your client may consider when reviewing his or her completed wheel:

a. Are the results what I expected, or is there anything surprising to me about the way my wheel looks? What stands out? Why?
b. What areas need the most attention? Least? Why?
c. What does the wheel show about my values, strengths, choices, coping skills, and interests?
d. Which ADHD symptoms are causing me the most trouble? In which areas of my life are they a factor?
e. In the areas I am strong, are there skills I can use and apply in other areas to increase satisfaction in those?

An ADHD Life Wheel is a simple way for clients to create a snapshot of life as they see it in that moment. Although this tool is most commonly used at the outset of treatment, consider putting the wheel away toward the end of coaching and have clients re-create their wheel to see if and how much they have changed. It can be emotional and uplifting for clients to see solid proof of their growth from coaching and can make for a great parting gift. The ADHD Life Wheel will be used in action later in one of the case study chapters.

Inspiration Toolbox

As mentioned earlier in reference to learning style, many individuals with ADHD enjoy learning kinesthetically, or being hands-on. Therefore, having multiple ways of making the learning process active for your clients is an important part of being an effective coach. Having your client create and use an *Inspiration Toolbox* (Levrini, 2012) is just one way to make coaching a creative and unique learning experience for your client. Metaphorically, coaching is about filling your client's "inner toolbox" so that he or she has many ways to approach a situation or particular challenge. When routine and consistency start to fail or become mundane, clients will need additional strategies to try throughout their life. Some studies have shown that the benefits of behavioral interventions are often limited to those settings in which treatment is occurring and do not generalize to other settings that are not included in the management program (Barkley, 2004; MTA Cooperative Group, 1999). With this in mind, it is important to not only focus on helping clients achieve their goals during coaching but also to attempt to help transfer those skills beyond coaching. There is no silver bullet for these clients, and even if something works for a while, it does not mean that it will always work. However, it did work once, and could possibly work again in a new situation. Hence, the idea of a toolbox—a box to carry, organize, and protect the owner's tools. Coaches need to clearly communicate to their clients that the idea is to complete the coaching process with a plethora of options in terms of effectively addressing their goals going forward, and the Inspiration Toolbox helps to teach this idea in a hands-on, tactile way.

To create an Inspiration Toolbox, clients can use an old shoebox or any small box that can be opened (we like colorful party favor boxes, which can be purchased inexpensively online). Depending on clients' artistic nature, they may or may not choose to decorate the box with inspirational pictures or words. Some just write their names on the box; others like to personalize their box. During each coaching session, keep a stack of blank index cards available so that clients can record ideas they find helpful, phrases they find inspirational (e.g., a metaphor or mantra, discussed in the next two subsections), pitfalls they identify, or any other "tools" they would like to hold on to for future use. They can write or draw the idea on a card and put it into their box. Our clients enjoy opening the box from time to time to review ideas they may have otherwise forgotten. These toolboxes also give clients something tangible to take with them once coaching is done, filled with the short-but-sweet invaluable lessons they took from the coaching process and that now fill their metaphorical toolbox going forward.

Metaphors

A *metaphor* (from the Greek word meaning "transference") is a figure of speech in which a word or phrase is used to describe something it does not denote literally. We find metaphors useful in coaching. Specifically, they accomplish the following:

1. Make ideas more vivid and entertaining, thus helping people focus and process an idea more easily, as well as store and retrieve it from memory.
2. Increase understanding between coach and client. If you say something is a "gem" or "his eyes lit up," the client knows exactly what you mean.
3. Say what can't be said. Maybe your client is not ready for the literal interpretation but can comfortably speak on an issue under the guise of metaphor. We once had a client who would refer to "ice cream" (a tasty, delicious treat that really isn't that good for you) when talking about smoking.
4. Describe a concept. Maybe we cannot find the exact words to explain an experience or a thing, but a metaphor comes close for us. For example, "It was like I was waiting for the other shoe to drop."
5. Explain difficult or scientific concepts. Even in explaining the neurobiology of ADHD, almost all of us use metaphors: Neurons "fire" along "pathways." "Impulses" cross at "junctions." There are no pathways or junctions, but we explain what is going on based on what we know about our world.

Here are some favorite metaphors that we use, many of which are helpful when educating your client on ADHD and coaching during the beginning sessions. You are likely to have others based on your own experience that will work well with your clients.

1. Setting long-term goals at the outset of coaching is like *building the foundation of a house.* Your foundation must be strong, or the whole house falls apart; likewise, without clearly and effectively written long-term goals, most attempts to change behavior will end in failure. Most clients who come to coaching have tried to put up walls before building a solid foundation. In other words, they have attempted many strategies in a piecemeal way, without a larger, measurable goal in mind and without a well-thought-out, well-laid plan as to how and when to engage these strategies. The impulsive nature of ADHD is to blame for this, and by bringing this idea to your client's attention, you can start to shift her or his behavior toward a more deliberate, goal-oriented approach—and ultimately more favorable outcomes.

2. Coaching is like *adding tools to a metaphorical toolbox.* Sometimes you use a nail gun, and sometimes you use a hammer. You should acquire various tools that you can pull out when needed. (This idea was discussed in detail earlier but is worth mentioning as a metaphor as well.)
3. Having ADHD and taking medication is a little bit *like having dyslexia and turning a light on while you read.* It will help the words look clearer and crisper, but it can only do so much. Medication can help with focus and impulse control, but it won't teach clients the strategies to overcome weaknesses in executive functioning. To better understand ADHD behavior and learn strategies that will ultimately help clients to overcome areas of weakness such as time management, organization, or social skills, behavioral interventions such as coaching offer far more than medication ever can.
4. The pathways of your brain are *like a college campus.* Have clients first picture a campus, scattered with different buildings that they need to get to at different times throughout the day. Between each building are paved sidewalks. Most students use these without giving it much thought and get to class in plenty of time. Others students, like those with ADHD, create alternate paths to get to the same place. Instead of sticking to the paved sidewalks, they cross between them, wearing the grass down as they repeatedly use the same pathways over and over. This is much like what happens inside your brain as you go through coaching and begin to develop strategies that you did not previously have and use your brain in ways you did not previously use it. Most important, clients need to understand that like most things, you "use it or lose it"—you need to keep walking those alternate pathways or the grass grows back on the college campus just like you need to continue to use the strategies you learn in coaching or they will be forgotten.
5. The process of coaching is *like hiking up a mountain.* Ask your clients what they might do if they were hiking up a mountain and slipped off the trail momentarily when they were three quarters of the way up. Most people would answer that they would simply regain their footing, dust themselves off, and find their way back to the path. However, when progressing toward a goal, many clients with ADHD will not see a momentary lapse as just that but rather as a complete failure. They metaphorically roll down to the bottom of the mountain at the first slip-up and erroneously believe that they need to create an entirely new plan to get to the top. It is important that you, as the coach, are not swayed if a client is insistent that something "didn't work." Instead, you must help the client see that a brief lapse in forward

momentum does not undo everything he or she has already done, then find a way to proceed together.
6. This final metaphor has to do with anxiety rather than ADHD or coaching specifically, but we find it to be a simple and helpful image for anxious clients: When dealing with anxiety, you have to *dive into the wave* rather than run from it. As a mental health professional, you most likely already know this idea is the basis of treating any specific phobia with desensitization intervention. Any client who has had experience swimming in the ocean as a child can recall being tossed through a wave and landing face down in the sand. Usually, this is the result of trying to run toward the shore, away from a wave. If asked what to do to avoid getting pummeled by a wave, the common and correct response is to dive head-first into it, rather than run away from it. It's a little scary and challenges the natural flight instinct, but you come out feeling better in the end. Have your clients evoke this image when they are challenged to perform outside of their comfort zone and feel their anxiety start to rise. By facing that discomfort and not running from the anxiety-producing behavior, it will become easier and easier each time.

Mantras

Mantras are short, self-affirming statements that help clients remain encouraged and motivated throughout their day. Have your client create one or more personal statements that resonate with them and are easy to remember. If they don't already believe a mantra they have chosen (i.e., "I am bold"), tell them to start by saying it anyway. The more we tell ourselves something is true, the more we just may start to believe it and act accordingly. Clients can use sticky notes or phones to display mantras or repeat them out loud in private to gain strength from their words, and they are also useful to include in the Inspiration Toolbox. Mantras are especially useful for individuals with ADHD because of their simplicity and the ease of memorization.

Juggling Exercise

The *Juggling Exercise* (Hearn & Levrini, 2009) is another teaching method centered in kinesthetic learning and the idea that coaching should be fun and sometimes physical—it is more than just writing things down while sitting at a desk. The idea is to (literally) show clients how difficult it is to mentally juggle multiple tasks and thoughts and that the more tasks and thoughts we add, the harder it becomes to keep all of our "balls in the air." Following are the instructions to give to your client.

Instructions

- Step 1: Try to juggle two balls. Can you do it? Pretty easy, right?
- Step 2: Now, try to juggle three balls. If you can do three, try four. A little harder, right? The more balls you add, the faster they fall.

Ask yourself:

- What is your strategy as you add more balls?
- Do you go faster?
- Concentrate a little harder?
- Get a little more frustrated?

Now tell your clients to imagine those balls as information they are trying to "mentally juggle" in their mind. The more thoughts and ideas they try to process simultaneously, the harder it is to keep track and follow through without dropping something along the way. They may think faster, missing important pieces, or concentrate harder, using extra mental energy. They may also find themselves feeling overwhelmed, stressed, or frustrated when things don't go right—just like juggling balls. The trick to juggling is determining which balls are made of rubber and which are made of glass. If you drop a rubber ball, it will bounce back, but the balls made of glass will be damaged or broken if dropped. That is where learning to prioritize is key. You will see this exercise in action in the case study featured in Chapter 12.

Processing Exercise

As we have noted, simultaneous processing, or "mental juggling," requires mental energy associated with switching cognitive gears. Many people with ADHD think this way, rather than one step at a time (or sequentially), which quickly exhausts their cognitive resources. Thinking sequentially also involves a change in attention and focus, and people with ADHD struggle with this. The *Processing Exercise* (Hearn, 2009) is a quick and easy way to educate clients on these different ways of thinking (see Figure 6.3).

Instructions

The client is given a piece of paper with several dots drawn on it; the same figure appears on the flip side of the paper. Instruct the client to connect the dots in the drawing.

The client connects the dots. Often individuals with ADHD cannot interrelate separate parts into a whole by examining all the elements of the activity simultaneously. This can result in their finding a less direct

FIGURE 6.3

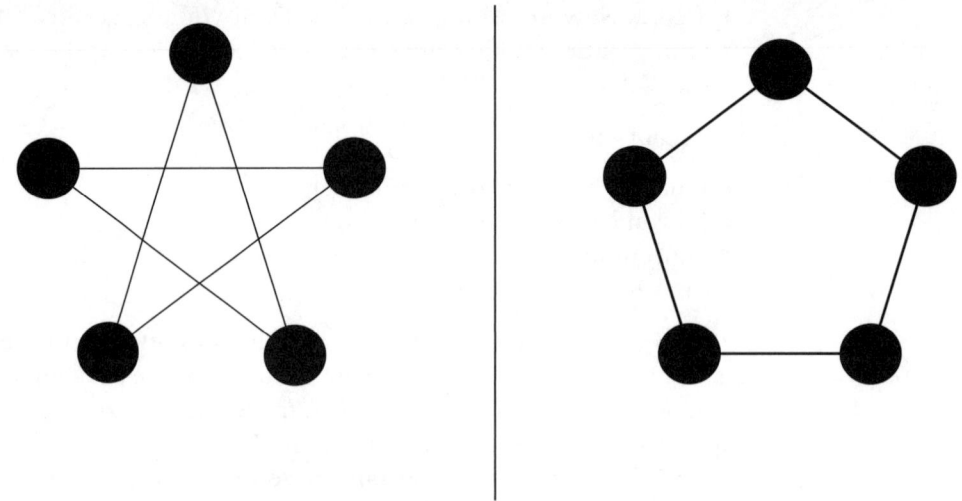

The Processing Exercise (as described by Hearn, 2009).

route to connecting the dots, as shown by the example in Figure 6.3 in which a client drew a star to connect the dots.

"Now let your coach show you another way!"

The coach flips over the page and uses a clean version of the same figure to show a simplified means of connecting the dots, creating a hexagon. Note that some clients may draw the hexagon; coaches can point out that this is positive—the client solved the exercise efficiently and expediently. For clients who do create the star, coaches can point out that even though it isn't as quick to connect the dots that way, it is creative!

Cognitive Impulsivity Exercise

Cognitive impulsivity is the tendency to perform intellectual or academic tasks too quickly and without planning, an issue that is all too common for individuals with ADHD. The *Cognitive Impulsivity Exercises* that follow can serve as quick tests to see whether a client will answer impulsively or think the question through. Consider asking your client one or more of the following questions, and follow with a discussion about impulsivity and how this symptom may have affected his or her past behavior.

Question: You have 10 pears and give all but six away. How many do you have left?

Coaches: Cover below the line while your client looks at the question.

Incorrect:	Many people would say four.
Correct:	If you take your time to think the question through, it's actually six—you gave all *but* six away.
Question:	Some months have 30 days, and some have 31. How many months have 28 days?
Coaches:	Cover below the line while your client looks at the question.
Incorrect:	Many people would say 1 month—that is, February.
Correct:	It's actually all 12 months. All months have at least 28 days.

Goal-Specific Strategies

After you and your client have established long-term goals for coaching and laid your metaphorical foundation, you will need to come up with various methods that will aid the client in long-term goal attainment. Consider these the metaphorical brick and mortar to help build your walls. The "roof" of the house will be your client's successful achievement of the once-theoretical goals, but just as important are the strategies the client learns along the way to take with him or her and use as new goals arise.

TIME MANAGEMENT

One of the most common long-term goals set by clients involves improving time management. Clients with time-management goals will rate the following items highly on the Coaching Topics Survey:

improving time management,
establishing routines and good habits,
organizing (school)work,
getting to class or work on time,
scheduling classes or meetings, and
managing long-term projects or assignments.

Timers

Almost every client with a time-management goal should consider using a timer of some sort. Timers can be helpful before planning to show clients how long a particular task will typically take or to break up a large project into smaller time segments. Free timers are all around us—on phones, computers, even microwave ovens. However, there are some specific timers you may not know about that work in unique ways that are helpful clients with ADHD. To read about these particular timing devices, see Resources at the end of this chapter.

On a related note, although many professionals who treat ADHD know the value of encouraging clients to use timers, what is often overlooked is the value of using timers in the session itself. By modeling the correct use of timers to your clients in session, you can help them increase their understanding of time management, transition more easily between parts of a session, and perhaps even appreciate that their coach can benefit from timing tools as well, thus increasing rapport between you and your client. Coaches can easily use a desktop or tablet version of a timer app to count down session minutes so that you can both see how much time remains. Additionally, timers can be set for just parts of a session or to transition from one to another (e.g., 30 minutes to discuss previous weeks' objectives and 30 minutes to plan for upcoming week).

Planners

The old-fashioned paper-and-pencil method of planning offers some advantages for time management that computers and apps cannot. Although technology is helpful in its own way, when computers do the "remembering" for us, our brains don't get the exercise they need. Paper-and-pencil weekly planners that engage the individual in the act of writing their schedule help to give perspective as well as to encode and store the information into working memory, allowing it to be more easily recalled when necessary. Plus, the act of writing things down brings information to the surface and triggers the brain to pay attention. The part of the brain that is associated with writing is also the part most affected by ADHD; therefore, by encouraging clients to think about and write out a schedule, you are helping to strengthen connections that may be lacking (Feder & Majnemer, 2007). There are even paper planners specifically designed for individuals with ADHD that integrate coaching fundamentals with time management. See the Resources section to learn about Dr. Levrini's ADHD planner, which integrates coaching goals and objectives with a weekly planner.

Although writing can offer some advantages, there are several apps and computer-based programs that can also be helpful to your clients. There is an exhaustive list of timing devices, planners, programs, and apps available for your clients' use, and certain clients will like some better than others. The Resources section also has a list of apps that was current at the time of press. There is no "best" timer or planner for everyone, and the list is growing and changing all the time. As a coach, it is up to you to stay abreast of the ever-growing list of time management products that may be helpful to clients.

LEARNING AND STUDY STRATEGIES

A second common goal in coaching is to improve learning and study strategies in the hope that this will have a positive effect on grades and outcomes in school. Clients with learning- and study-related goals will rate the following items highly on the Coaching Topics Survey:

- studying,
- taking good notes,
- managing long-term assignments or projects,
- establishing routines and good habits, and
- organizing (school)work.

The first step in helping a client with learning and study strategies is to determine how each client learns best, as discussed at the beginning of this chapter. Once you have identified your client's learning style, you can get more creative with new ways of learning material and encoding it into working memory.

Graphic organizers, also called mind maps or concept maps, are a way to organize thoughts in a creative way—and perhaps more important, in a way that makes sense to their creator. The user creates a pictorial illustration of ideas and knowledge, rather than simply writing words. Graphic organizers can help the user brainstorm, organize or learn new ideas, outline papers, problem solve, or even make decisions. They are especially helpful for individuals who have strong visual learning abilities but who might struggle with reading or writing, and they can be effective for users across all age groups. There are many websites available for downloading a multitude of graphic organizers (see Resources). Figure 6.4 is an example of just one of these.

There are also many learning tools found online or as apps. For example, you can create flashcards on your computer screen and flip them with the click of a button. Mind maps can be arranged at your desktop. Some of these kinds of technological products that help with learning are listed in the Resources section as well.

HEALTHY LIVING AND LIFE SKILLS

Many coaching clients have goals centered on improving basic housekeeping or life skills, such as doing laundry or improving overall health

FIGURE 6.4

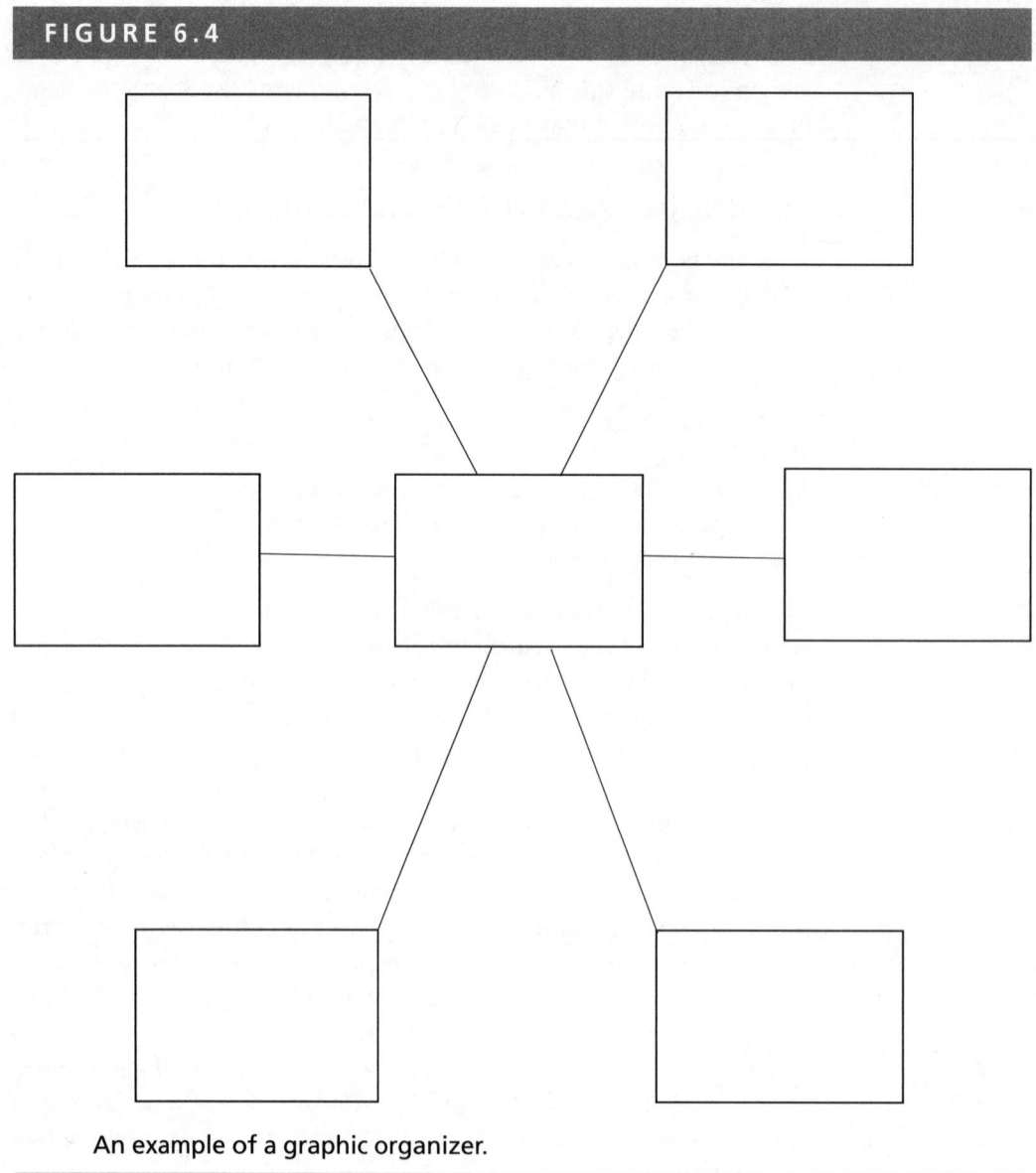

An example of a graphic organizer.

habits. Clients with healthy living or life skills–related goals will rate the following items highly on the Coaching Topics Survey:

- keeping track of things,
- doing laundry,
- exercising,
- eating healthfully,
- waking up and staying up,

- getting to bed, and
- taking medication.

For many of these items, developing a ritual or routine to make tasks seem less effortful will be important. Taking medication, for instance, becomes much easier for clients if they use a pill box, keep it out in the open, and pair it with another routine activity, such as brushing teeth. Developing a bedtime and wake-up ritual that signals to the body it is time to go to bed or time to start the day will also be helpful. For laundry, have clients do it on the same night each week, or help them break the task into smaller, more doable steps. Reminders will also be important. Have clients set watch and cell phone alarms or create online calendar pop-up notifications.

Some other counseling techniques that can be helpful for these types of goals are as follows:

- deep breathing and relaxation exercises to help restless clients toward better sleep patterns;
- exercise regimens that take little time and are easy to incorporate into one's day, such as taking the stairs at work or doing jumping jacks between study sessions; and
- Bluetooth tracking devices and apps for easily lost items such as cell phones, planners, and keys.

As with all other goal areas, you, as the coach, will want to familiarize yourself with strategies to help clients overcome common struggles as they relate to ADHD. It may be helpful to keep a running list or file that you can easily pull from as needed in sessions.

SOCIAL SKILLS

Although the best way to develop social skills is to practice them in a social setting, there are things you can do in and out of sessions as homework for a client in need of improvement in this area. Clients with social skills–related goals will rate the following items highly on the Coaching Topics Survey:

- making friends,
- keeping friends,
- getting along with others, and
- getting along in group situations.

Both children and adult clients can struggle with social skills, and it is important that you do not overlook these concerns in lieu of purely academic- or work-related goals. Most social skills goal–directed behavior in individual coaching will consist of giving your client assignments to practice at school or work, then reviewing the assignment in session.

Barkley (2013) has a home-based social skills program that parents can implement and you, the coach, can assist with. You can read about it in more detail in the Resources section. Adult clients can practice accepting compliments, thinking through decisions and refraining from impulsive behaviors, and positive listening skills. In session, your skills as a therapist will be extremely valuable when it comes to social skills goals. Therapeutic techniques such as role-playing, modeling, motivational interviewing, or drawing and games can all be helpful interventions.

CAREER

Many adult ADHD coaching clients have long-term goals centered on their job or career. These might include finding a new job, reentering the world of work after a break, deciding whether to stay in a current position, or just figuring out what "I want to be when I grow up." Clients with career-related goals will rate the following item highly on the Coaching Topics Survey:

- figuring out the next step in my career or job.

For career-related goals, several tools are available in paper format and online (see Resources) that can be helpful for your client.

DECISION MAKING, MOTIVATION, AND PRIORITIZATION TOOLS

Sometimes clients simply don't know what their goals are. Many clients end up in coaching when they are at an impasse in terms of a major life decision, whether it is looking for a new job, settling down with a partner, or going back to school after a long break, and they aren't sure what their long-term goals look like. Clients with decision-making-related goals at the outset will rate the following items highly on the Coaching Topics Survey:

- planning and prioritizing, and
- making decisions and solving problems.

However, sometimes clients present as though they know exactly what they want to do and then discover at some point during the coaching process that they feel "stuck" or unsure of their original plan. For these clients, the following tools may be brought out later in the coaching process.

Decision-Making Form

The *Decision-Making Form* (see Figure 6.5) is helpful to ADHD coaching clients who are having difficulty understanding how to make

FIGURE 6.5

Possible Choice(s)	1. What would motivate you to do this?	1. What would stop or keep you from doing this?
	2. How does it serve your goals to choose this option?	2. How does it hurt you or keep you from your goals to choose this option?
	3. What do you gain by doing it?	3. What do you stand to lose by doing it?
	4. What do your loved ones gain?	4. What do your loved ones stand to lose?

The Decision-Making Form. From *The Confidence Plan: How To Build a Stronger You* (p. 56), by T. Ursiny, 2005, Naperville, IL: Sourcebooks. Copyright 2005 by Tim Ursiny. Adapted with permission.

a decision or trusting in their decision-making abilities. In the first column of the form, have your clients write several possible choices they might have in making a particular decision, then have them answer the questions in the second and third columns. Talk through each choice and the corresponding responses with clients to help them come to a decision.

The Eisenhower Matrix

U.S. President Dwight D. Eisenhower was credited for saying, "What is important is seldom urgent and what is urgent is seldom important" and for using a quadrant-based decision principle. This idea sums up the concept of what has come to be known as the *Eisenhower Matrix*. This so-called Eisenhower Principle is said to be how Eisenhower organized his tasks. Over the years many people have modified and marketed this original idea in different ways; however, the basic principles remain the same. It can be quite helpful to any client having difficulty making a decision about where to focus his or her efforts.

The Eisenhower Matrix classifies most tasks under two headings: *urgent* or *important*. This is a powerful way of thinking about priorities. Using it can help your clients overcome the natural tendency to focus on urgent activities, so that they can make time to focus on what's really important. In other words, it can help move clients from "firefighting" into a position where they can accomplish goals, reduce stress, and more effectively manage their lives.

The following are the definitions of Important and Urgent, according to the Eisenhower Principle:

- Important activities have an outcome that leads to the *achievement of your goals*, whether these are professional or personal. (Unimportant Activities do not aid in goal completion.)
- Urgent activities *demand immediate attention* and are often associated with the achievement of someone else's goals. (Nonurgent activities do not demand immediate attention.)

Using these definitions, have your clients list several tasks in need of attention or that they value, and talk about which box they might fall into and why. Tasks can be labeled as one of the following:

1. *Urgent and Important*—a house fire, a big presentation for work, a baby crying
2. *Not Urgent and Important*—exercising, nurturing relationships, working on a project
3. *Urgent and Not Important*—donuts in the break room, Facebook updates, a solicitor calling with a "once in a lifetime" opportunity
4. *Not Urgent and Not Important*—surfing the Internet for no reason in particular, watching TV

The goal is for clients understand how to order tasks (1–4; Figure 6.6) to stop ignoring Box 2, and achieve a balance, making Important but Not Urgent activities more of a priority. The number on the quadrants is the order in which your client should be attending to tasks. Some even use the easy to remember rule of "1 = *do*; 2 = *plan*; 3 = *delegate*; 4 = *eliminate*."

MULTIMODAL APPROACH METHODS

Other ways to increase motivation and positive outcomes for your clients involve thinking outside the box. For example, ecotherapy, or treatments taking place in relatively "green" or natural settings, have been shown to significantly reduce ADHD symptoms compared with activities in other settings, even when activities were matched across settings (Brymer, Cuddihy, & Sharma-Brymer, 2010). Although most of these studies have looked at children, the same is hypothesized to

FIGURE 6.6

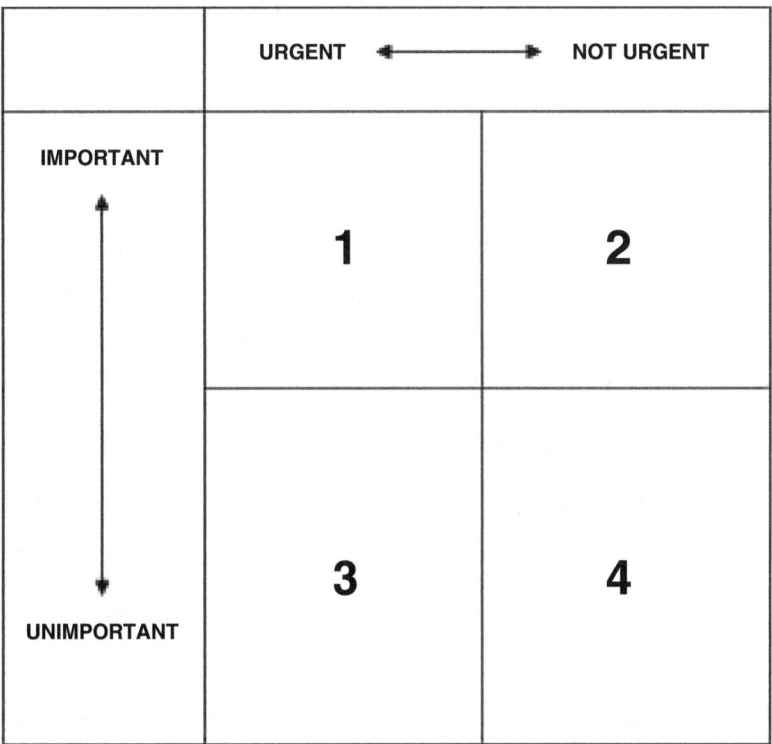

The Eisenhower Matrix.

be true for adults. Because of this research, you may want to consider holding coaching sessions as you and your client take a walk or sit outside. If you don't have the ability to conduct sessions in a green space, BSAs or homework assignments might consist of getting outdoors. Even having plants and pictures of nature in your office may have an impact on client functioning.

Apps and technology have a place in motivation and goal achievement as well. Because of the fleeting and ever-changing nature of technology, we won't list any specific programs here; however, a quick search of your app store or via an online search engine will produce a variety of games and products that help clients in fun and unique ways, from getting "unstuck" when it comes to decision making or charting progress on a goal. (We list some that were current at the time of press in the Resources.)

Ultimately, coaching strategies for ADHD clients should be viewed not just as using worksheets at a desk but as integrating multimodal aspects of treatment; from green space and technology, exercise, nutrition, meditation, and sleep, to other significant areas that can drastically improve functioning for your clients. This chapter was but a small look into the possible tools you may want to fill your own coaching toolbox with.

Summary

1. Several specific strategies may lead to positive outcomes with coaching clients. It is important that coaches become familiar with various resources available in their own communities, such as professionals who conduct psychoeducational evaluations, ADHD support groups, or programs designed to help students with specific learning disabilities, such as reading or writing.
2. It is important to understand the specific learning styles of individuals with ADHD.
3. The ADHD Life Wheel allows clients to look at the larger picture of their lives to determine whether they are addressing key areas and giving enough attention to issues of importance.
4. The Inspiration Toolbox is a way of metaphorically filling your client's "inner toolbox" so that he or she has many ways to approach a situation or particular challenge.
5. Metaphors are figures of speech in which a word or phrase is used to describe something it does not denote literally.
6. The Juggling Exercise idea is to (literally) show clients how difficult it is to mentally juggle multiple tasks and thoughts and that the more we add, the harder it becomes to keep all of our "balls in the air."
7. Some tools for time management include timers and planners.
8. Clients with learning- and study-related goals can make use of graphic organizers.
9. Various techniques can help your clients deal with healthy living goals, social skills, and decision making.
10. A variety of software apps are available to help clients in fun and unique ways, from getting "unstuck" when it comes to decision making to charting progress on a goal.

Resources

TIMERS

- Time Timer (http://www.timetimer.com) is the creator of a variety of products that create a graphic image of the passage of time. As time elapses, a red disk gradually disappears under a clear lens,

so clients gain a real understanding of how much time is left for a particular task. The desktop version has been around for more than 20 years, but more recently the company launched a watch version as well as an App for iPhones and Android phones.
- Datexx Smart Cube Timer, available at Amazon.com and various other retailers, works by simply resting the cube with the desired time facing up—5, 15, 30, or 60 minutes. When your time is up, a loud alarm will ring; simply set it back to zero at the top to silence it. This saves the user the time and effort it takes to program the amount of time needed, making it far more likely your clients with ADHD will use it.

PLANNERS

- Dr. Levrini's ADHD Planner (in collaboration with Tools4Wisdom) was specifically designed and created to help individuals with ADHD effectively manage their time and reach their goals. The planner combines the best aspects of a quarter-hour planner, monthly planner, and our Long-Term Goals and Weekly Objectives worksheets. Clients are able to organize their time and plan their activities in a way that makes sense to them, assign incentives and consequences to tasks, and even rate their performance on a weekly basis right in the planner itself. Dr. Levrini's goal in creating the planner was to eliminate the need for clients to be responsible for tracking several documents in addition to a separate agenda or planner. Instead, the planner contains several aspects of the coaching strategies outlined in this book in one well-organized calendar-notebook. You can view it on her website: http://www.psychedcoaches.com.

APPS AND TECHNOLOGY

The following is a list of apps that can help clients stay organized, manage their time, make decisions, and follow through with other ADHD-related goals. Some but not all are available currently for iPhone/iPad or Android products.

Time Management and Organization Apps

- *Planner Plus* is like a paper planner in digital form. It has monthly and weekly views, as well as task lists and notes section.
- *Wunderlist* is a list-making app that allows the user to easily share to-dos or ideas with others.
- *Cozi* is a calendar app and website designed to incorporate schedules for the entire family, integrating shopping lists, sports activities, chores, meal plans and more.

- *TaskCurrent* is an iPhone and iPad app that turns a to-do list into a list of skills to learn, motivational tricks, productivity tips to work into one's day-to-day life, and more.
- *Task Timer* allows the user to create a list of tasks, set time goals for a task, and keep track of the amount of time spent in each task. It has several options available for customization.

Especially for Kids

- *iRewardChart* is an app that brings the traditional reward chart onto a mobile device, with a customizable, interactive interface. iRewardChart helps parents (or coaches) keep track of the child's good behavior and then reward them appropriately.
- *Epic Win* is a streamlined to-do list to quickly write down everyday tasks, but with a role-playing spin. Rather than just ticking off chores and reminders, completing each one earns points to improve and develop one's character in an ongoing quest to improve statistics, gain riches, and win levels.
- *Chore Pad* is a tool for motivating kids to complete chores. Each child completes assigned chores to earn stars, which are redeemable for rewards that the parents (or coaches) can create. The user can also give bonus stars for a job well done or penalty stars to encourage the child to do better.

Miscellaneous Apps

- The *Evernote* brand is most commonly known by its original product of the same name. The Evernote app helps users remember everything across all of the devices he or she may use. It helps the individual to stay organized, save ideas, and improve productivity by managing notes, photos, to-do lists, and recorded voice reminders all in one place. In addition, Evernote makes these notes completely searchable at any time. More recently, the Evernote brand has launched some new products that are equally as creative and helpful: *Skitch* allows the user to use annotations, sketches, and shapes to develop ideas; *Web Clipper* allows the user to save ideas from the Internet with one click; and *Evernote Peek* turns notes into study materials.
- *Meditation Oasis* offers a variety of apps with guided meditations for sleep, relaxation, stress relief, energizing, and mindfulness. It is available at https://www.meditationoasis.com/smartphone-apps/iphone-ipod-touch-ipad-apps.
- *Moodtracker.com*—clients can track changes in mood and behavior online and share with their coach.

- *Lumosity* is a website and app scientifically designed and researched to train memory and attention, cognitively challenge the user in new ways, and track progress.
- *Total Recall* is a mind-mapping app. In other words, users create graphic organizers on their mobile device and can easily share their creations with others.
- *Unstuck* advertises itself as an "in-the-moment approach to personal growth for anyone who wants to live better every day." The app combines personalized digital tools with tips and know-how from a community of other people facing "stuck moments," offering on-demand coaching for the user. Through a series of questions and answers, the Unstuck app pinpoints the type of stuck moment you're in then provides suggestions on how to become "unstuck."

GRAPHIC ORGANIZERS

- http://www.ldpride.net
- http://www.educationplanner.org
- http://www.enchantedlearning.com
- http://www.edhelper.com
- http://www.eduplace.com

Remembering

- *Watchminder:* Invented by a child psychologist specifically for individuals with ADHD, the Watchminder is a wristwatch that can be set up to send the user discreet vibrating messages throughout the day. Messages can be personalized or per the user's needs with statements such as "Take Medication" or "Do Laundry." Available at http://www.watchminder.com.
- *The Tile App:* When you attach Tile to an item (such as your keys), you're tethering them to your phone. So when something gets lost, you have a buddy that knows what to do. The app automatically records the last place your phone (or any other phone with the app open) saw your Tile. If you have to retrace your steps, it's good to know where to start walking. When you begin searching for a lost item, your phone tracks the signal strength of your Tile. As you get closer, the app's tracking circle fills in, giving you a clear indication of your progress. Available at http://www.thetileapp.com.

Career

- *Self-Directed Search* (SDS) is a career interest test that asks questions about one's aspirations, activities, skills, and interests in different jobs. From the responses, the SDS produces a personal three-letter Summary Code, which can be used to find occupations and fields of study that match well with one's personality. The SDS is based on John Holland's theory that both people and working environments can be classified according to six basic types: Realistic, Investigative, Artistic, Social, Enterprising, and Conventional. These personality types are known together as RIASEC (http://www.self-directed-search.com/what-is-it-). Clients can take the SDS online and receive a comprehensive report at http://www.self-directed-search.com.

- The *Career Thoughts Inventory* (CTI) is a self-administered and objectively scored assessment designed to identify the nature of clients' career problems. The CTI was developed by a group of professors and researchers at the Florida State University Career Center (Sampson, Peterson, Lenz, Reardon, & Saunders, 1999). Accompanying the inventory is a workbook, which helps individuals to identify, challenge, and alter negative career thoughts that interfere with effective career decision making. The CTI yields a Total Score (a single global indicator of negative thinking in career problem solving and decision making), as well as scores on three construct scales: Decision-Making Confusion, Commitment Anxiety, and External Conflict. The CTI Workbook is a learning resource that includes information and exercises designed to help clients identify the number and nature of their dysfunctional career thoughts, challenge and alter these thoughts, and take concrete action to make career decisions. The CTI and CTI workbook are available on the PAR website: http://www4.parinc.com/Products/Product.aspx?ProductID=CTI.

- My Next Move (http://www.mynextmove.org) is sponsored by the U.S. Department of Labor in partnership with the American job center network and developed by the National Center for O*NET development. Clients can search careers via key words, browse careers by industry, or take an online inventory to help identify fields and jobs they may be interested in. Some of the unique characteristics of this site include an "outlook" forecast for careers reflecting growth rate, number of openings, and new and emerging fields, "green" career fields, and links to job postings, trainings, and apprenticeships.

Developing a Coaching Practice   7

Now that you have read and studied the first several chapters of this book, you are well versed in the attention-deficit/ hyperactivity disorder (ADHD) coaching framework and how to structure sessions, set goals and objectives, and use specific strategies. Perhaps you have started to think about how you would like to integrate ADHD coaching into your other work as a therapist and how your unique skill set can be complemented by the approach laid out in this text. In the coming chapters, you will get to see the coaching framework put into action with specific client examples to further your clinical knowledge. However, before presenting the case examples, the present chapter discusses a variety of issues related to the business side of an independent coaching practice.

As psychologists, therapists, and counselors, most of our education revolves around becoming skilled at our profession and learning how best to serve our clients. What is rarely taught in our graduate coursework or thought about when we embark on our journey is how to run a successful and viable

http://dx.doi.org/10.1037/14671-008
ADHD Coaching: A Guide for Mental Health Professionals, by F. Prevatt and A. Levrini
Copyright © 2015 by the American Psychological Association. All rights reserved.

independent practice. Sometimes even the most talented and educated practitioners flounder when faced with the challenges of being a "businessperson," and that professional talent can then go to waste. You may have heard that "nine out of 10 businesses fail." This isn't exactly accurate, but only about half survive the first 5 years (G. Kessler, 2014).

Whether or not you choose to think of it that way, your coaching or therapy practice is a business. Most businesses do not fail because they were poor ideas but rather because the person running the business did not have the knowledge or ability to make it successful. Good executive skills (like those we help our clients to achieve) are helpful as well.

This chapter addresses some areas you'll want to consider when developing a coaching or therapy practice. Whether you are new to independent practice or have been successfully running your practice for years, and whether you plan to advertise your services as ADHD coaching or integrate coaching techniques into a more generalized psychological practice, we hope that this chapter offers some new and helpful information so that you can optimize your success as a practitioner. The following sections discuss just some of the issues you, as a business owner of a coaching practice, will want to consider.

Coach or Therapist

As mentioned earlier, the first business matter you'll want to consider is how you'll use ADHD coaching in your specific practice. Ask yourself the following:

- Am I a newly licensed therapist, just starting my career, or am I a seasoned professional with an established reputation?
- If I am an early-career professional, do I want to identify myself as a coach or as a therapist?
- If I am a seasoned professional, do I want to change my professional identity or keep it and use coaching to enhance my techniques in session?
- Do I have enough expertise in ADHD to run an ADHD-focused practice, or should I use coaching strategies with psychotherapy clients who may occasionally come to me with an ADHD diagnosis in addition to other disorders?

To begin to answer the question about how you will identify yourself to the public, reconsider the differences between coaching and therapy. Coaching is similar to traditional counseling in several ways. Both coaching and therapy establish helping relationships that are supportive, respectful of clients' needs, confidential, and free of manipulation or abuse; work on setting goals and assessing priorities; and require a client who is willing to work toward change (Jaska & Ratey, 1999). Another way in which therapy and coaching are similar is the individualized help each client receives. Both effective therapists and effective coaches possess a wide array of strategies and tools to help their clients, knowing that one size does not fit all when it comes to producing results.

Unlike therapy, coaching is not focused on treating serious emotional, cognitive, or behavioral problems of clinical intensity, such as major depression, anxiety, or substance abuse. Instead, coaching is about increasing executive functions, client action and behavioral outcomes (Murphy, 2005). This can sometimes mean gaining insight or uncovering an emotional issue that is preventing one from reaching his or her goals (Reaser, 2008), but overall, coaching is a pragmatic, behavioral, results-oriented approach, as opposed to a process, insight-oriented, intellectual approach. Goal completion and strategy building are the most important aspects of the coaching process. The focus is on developing strategies and skills to become more effective in everyday life. The ADHD coach and client have a structured, goal-driven, strategy-oriented relationship. The bond between and coach and client is more of a partnership, whereas in some (but not all) therapeutic modalities, the therapist can be perceived more in a position of authority. It is the coach's job to help clients understand how ADHD affects their behavior and then encourage their motivation and active involvement in making changes to this behavior. The coach also elicits creative strategies to serve the needs of the client. Unlike in therapy, the coach and client may be in contact many times during a week, between sessions, to monitor the client and encourage accountability. Contact can include in-person meetings, video conferencing, texting, phone calls, and e-mails.

If you choose to position yourself as a coach (who is also a mental health professional), here are some things to consider. Because the idea of *coaching* leaves people with a different impression than the idea of *therapy*, your client's expectations will be different, and on the plus side, you may have access to some clients who wouldn't go to therapy because of the stigma associated with it. Still, it can be an assurance to clients to know that their coach has achieved a certain level of education in mental health and is being monitored by a licensing board, so your credentials are valuable to your clients. On the downside, you must be careful not to overstep your boundaries when working as a coach. All of the extra knowledge and experience can be a danger and lead you to try to take on too much with clients. Although some aspects of "therapy" can be integrated into a coaching session, serious cases of depression, anxiety, or substance abuse, for example, should still be referred to a colleague who specializes in treating these issues or can devote entire sessions to them. In this scenario, therapist–coach and therapist–therapist can work closely to integrate their treatment approaches in the appropriate manner. Another challenge is maintaining the ethical standards required by your licensing board, such as compliance with the Health Insurance Portability and Accountability Act (HIPAA), when clients may expect coaching to be a more casual relationship that includes texting and e-mail correspondence.

If you choose to position yourself as a therapist and supplement your practice with coaching strategies, this will allow you to work with a greater variety of clientele and explore psychological issues to a greater degree. Although this, too, has its advantages, such as making yourself available to a larger client pool, it comes with its own set of challenges. As mentioned earlier, you may miss out on helping clients who could really use your help, because they fear the stigma of therapy. Knowing when to pull back from insight-oriented processes and introduce behavioral goals can also be tricky. In the case study about Audrey (Chapter 11), you will see how a coach can appropriately integrate therapeutic and coaching strategies to help clients with comorbid mood disorders.

Ultimately, though, it is virtually impossible to separate one's actions–behaviors, cognitions–thoughts, and feelings–emotions. This is what is called, in therapy, the *cognitive triad*, and it is for this reason that regardless of which approach you use, coaching should be viewed as a cognitive behavioral intervention rather than a separate entity. No matter which approach you take, coach or therapist, you will end up bringing in valuable tools from both facets of your professional training. As more health care providers and professional organizations recognize coaching as a therapeutic and empirically validated approach to treating ADHD, insurance companies are more apt to reimburse for coaching as a form of psychotherapy, which is an added benefit to your clients.

One other note, if after reading and studying this book in its entirety, you feel it would be beneficial to gain additional training as a coach or add a coaching certification to your professional profile, there are several organizations that offer official training programs. See the Resources section at the end of this chapter for a list and descriptions of each.

Ethics of Coaching

Regardless of how you position yourself, you will have to take into consideration some major ethical issues because you are ultimately a mental health professional who has agreed to abide by the rules of your particular licensing board and to protect and aid your clients. We stated earlier that coaches are often in touch with clients throughout the week via texting, e-mail, and video-chat, among other modes of communication. Therefore, you'll first need to consider your compliance with the HIPAA, which requires appropriate safeguards to protect the privacy of personal health information and sets limits and conditions on the use and disclosure that may be made of such information without client authorization. We recommend using a HIPAA-compliant video and electronic information-sharing platform. Such platforms require that protocols are scrupulously followed to ensure clients are informed about all participants in a telemedicine consultation; that the privacy and confidentiality of the patient are maintained; and that the integrity of any data or images transmitted is ensured (Wachter, 2001). More and more companies produce these products, so finding one should not be difficult.

Along those lines, you'll want to think about how you will maintain professional boundaries. This concern is a big focus of our training as therapists because boundaries are a crucial element in the ethics of patient–therapist interaction. Lott (1999) explained that, first, boundaries recognize the inherent power inequity of the relationship and set limits for the therapist's expression of power. Second, they set a structure for the relationship, providing a consistent, reliable, predictable, and knowable frame for a process that remains somewhat mysterious. Lott goes on to note that most therapists agree about the broad basics. For example, a client should be able to count on a particular appointment time, which is not changed frequently or capriciously, and a set fee for sessions. Practitioners should not engage in ongoing secondary relationships with clients. Boundaries also relate to time devoted to a patient or client. Most therapists exercise their professional boundaries by meeting with their patient only in the time allotted each week, and minimize contact between sessions. You can start to see where challenges may lie for therapist–coaches. Although other coaches may casually give a client a call to check in, mental health professionals who are coaches should probably set firm guidelines and expectations about when and how they will make contact between sessions. Coaches who are not mental health providers may choose to meet a client at a coffee shop or park for a session, but mental health professionals who are coaches should probably stick to in-office visits. The climate is changing, however, when it comes to "e-therapy," or conducting therapy via the Internet or online video platforms. This is becoming more accepted as a means of therapy, and there is research to support its effectiveness (Barak, Hen, Boniel-Nissim, & Shapira, 2008). Furthermore, it is likely in the next few years that we will see state-to-state licensure for conducting e-therapy (Millan, 2014).

The American Psychological Association's (2010) "Ethical Principles of Psychologists and Code of Conduct" consists of five aspirational General Principles and 10 enforceable Standards that cover, among other concerns, Competence, Privacy and Confidentiality, and Human Relations, which includes appropriate boundaries and informed consent. Although other coaches are not bound to maintain confidentiality with their clients, mental health professionals are. Similarly, Standard 3.10 on Informed Consent states that psychologists obtain appropriate informed consent to therapy or related procedures, using language that is reasonably understandable to participants. With these concerns in mind, Exhibit 7.1 includes some points a therapist as coach should consider in creating an informed consent for her or his clients.

In terms of Boundaries of Competence (Standard 2.01), the Code maintains that psychologists provide services with populations and within areas only within the boundaries of their competence, based on their education, training, supervised experience, consultation, study, or professional experience. Therefore, although this book contains a solid foundation for conducting ADHD coaching, you may want to consider additional training before calling yourself a coach; individuals who are not bound by such standards can advertise their services as a coach at their discretion. Furthermore, as stated in the Code of Conduct, psychologists do not solicit testimonials from current psychotherapy clients or patients or other persons who because of their particular circumstances are vulnerable to undue influence. This means that for purposes of

EXHIBIT 7.1

Points to Consider When Creating an Informed Consent for Clients

_____ I understand that my coach will not use my name to discuss the details of our sessions with any outside source (i.e., friends, family, professors, etc.) unless the following circumstances are present:

1. I direct the coach to discuss my information with an outside source (e.g., a therapist), and I have signed a Release of Information form.
2. The coach determines that I am an imminent danger to myself or to others.
3. The coach is ordered by a court to provide information about our sessions.

_____ I understand that my coach complies with Health Insurance Portability and Accountability Act (HIPAA) standards. For more information on HIPAA, I can visit: www.hhs.gov/ocr/hipaa/finalreg.html.

_____ I understand that my coach may need to consult with other mental health professionals about my case and that my coach will keep my identifying information confidential if this occurs.

_____ I understand there is a possibility of a minimal level of risk involved in the coaching process. I might experience anxiety while thinking about my self-esteem or academic/work strategies. I also might experience emotional discomfort. The coach will be available to talk with me about any emotional discomfort I may experience. If the coach determines I require additional psychological support, I will be referred for further assistance.

_____ I understand that if my coach and I communicate by e-mail, text, or other electronic means, it cannot be guaranteed that what is discussed remains confidential due to the unpredictable nature of virtually transmitted information.

advertising, coaching clients cannot provide solicited reviews for therapists but can for coaches outside of the mental health industry.

The main principle to keep in mind if you are a licensed mental health practitioner who is acting as a coach is that you are a therapist first and should act in accordance to your licensing board. You do not get to behave one way when you call yourself a coach and another when you call yourself a therapist. Display your license number on all of your documents, and take all the same precautions you would take with your coaching clients as you do with your therapy clients. View coaching as an intervention rather than a separate profession. Once you have determined how to ethically unite your roles as coach and therapist, you can move on to other practice matters.

Your Coaching Practice

If you are new to the world of independent practice, next comes the task of creating a successful business from your theoretical ideas. If you have an existing practice, you'll need to fully integrate your new coaching knowledge and expertise so that it makes sense with what you already do. Starting and running a business is no easy task, regardless of one's industry or field. In this section, we tackle some of the common issues and decisions all ADHD coaches or therapists must face when building a business for themselves, including pitfalls to avoid. We start by providing a list of questions to ask yourself before making the leap into the world of entrepreneurship. If you already have, these questions may help you decide if you are missing anything important.

- Are things in your personal life organized and in order—finances and budgeting, time management, family responsibilities, for example?
- Are you prepared to handle business issues and emergencies as they come up, even if it means canceling dinner with a friend?
- If you are interested in having a group practice, do you possess leadership qualities, and do others respond well to your leadership style? Are you able to make hard decisions and deal with upset employees?
- Have you considered whether you will handle all of your own administrative duties, such as fielding phone calls and e-mails, billing, scheduling, angry customers, or even website creation and content, or will you outsource some or all of these responsibilities?
- Have you considered how lucrative a coaching or therapy practice would be in your city or town? Is the market there? Who will you market to?

- Are your loved ones supportive of this idea? What will they be giving up? What extra responsibilities might they have to take on while you focus on your practice?

These are just some of the many questions you should consider when making such a huge commitment for yourself and your loved ones. Although you can't think of everything beforehand, and circumstances will constantly change as your business evolves, the more prepared you can be, the easier the implementation process will be for you.

CREATING A BUSINESS PLAN

A *business plan* is an official document you create for your business that helps you to think through some of the tough questions and think long term. Numerous websites offer free templates for business plans. In addition to creating a written plan, there are several programs that provide business mentors, free of charge. Some organizations provide free and confidential counseling, mentoring, and advice to small business owners nationwide via a network of business executives, leaders, and volunteers. You can connect with these volunteers through in-person and online counseling.

CHOOSING YOUR COACHING BUSINESS STRUCTURE

One big decision you will have to make early on is what business structure you will choose. Your business structure will have legal and tax implications. Choices include the following:

- A *sole proprietorship* is the most basic type of business to establish. You alone own the company and are responsible for its assets and liabilities.
- A *limited liability company (LLC)* is designed to provide the limited liability feature of a corporation and the tax efficiencies and operational flexibility of a partnership. A sole practitioner can be the sole owner of an LLC.
- A *corporation* is more complex and generally suggested for larger, established companies with multiple employees.
- An *S corporation* is similar to a standard corporation, or *C corporation*, but you are taxed only on the personal level.
- Two or more practitioners may come together to form a *partnership*. There are several different types of partnerships, depending on the nature of the arrangement and partner responsibility for the business.
- People form a *cooperative* to meet a collective need or to provide a service that benefits all member–owners.

If you are going to be the only employee of your practice, as most coaches and therapists are, you are most likely going to choose between a sole proprietorship or an LLC. As a licensed mental health professional, you may also qualify as a professional LLC.

Those who are interested in running a nonprofit organization rather than a for-profit business will need to take different steps. Before starting a nonprofit, your first task is to find out whether there is already an organization (nonprofit or otherwise) in your community performing the same services. It will be more difficult to gain financial backing or be approved for nonprofit status if you are simply duplicating existing services, versus improving or adding to them. Resources that can help you identify nonprofits in your area include the following:

- GuideStar (http://www.guidestar.org): This information service features a central database that includes information for and about nonprofits.
- 211 call centers, available in many areas of the United States and Canada, provide information and referrals to health, human, and socials service organizations. Call centers in some areas also provide searchable databases of local organizations.
- Search the Internet for your area, plus keywords describing your mission, for example, "ADHD coaching Virginia."

After you determine that the work you do will meet a real need in the community, you must spend some time developing these essential ingredients of a successful nonprofit:

- a vital mission;
- high-quality, responsive, and unduplicated programs and services;
- reliable and diverse revenue streams;
- clear lines of accountability; and
- adequate facilities.

Starting a nonprofit generally also requires these steps to formalize your organization:

1. File articles of incorporation with the secretary of state or other appropriate state agency.
2. Apply for exempt status with the Internal Revenue Service (IRS). Note that it can take 3 to 12 months for the IRS to return its decision.
3. Register with the state(s) where you plan to do fundraising activities.

To learn more about starting and running a nonprofit organization, visit http://www.grantspace.org.

SOLO OR GROUP PRACTICE

If you are interested in hiring others to work with you, you will have another decision to make. As a small business owner, you may hire people as independent contractors or as employees. IRS.gov offers seven tips for business owners making this decision.

1. The IRS uses three characteristics to determine the relationship between businesses and workers:
   a. *Behavioral control* covers facts that show whether the business has a right to direct or control how the work is done through instructions, training, or other means.
   b. *Financial control* covers facts that show whether the business has a right to direct or control the financial and business aspects of the worker's job.
   c. *Type of relationship* factor relates to how the workers and the business owner perceive their relationship.
2. If you have the right to control or direct not only what is to be done but also how it is to be done, then your workers are most likely employees.
3. If you can direct or control only the result of the work done, and not the means and methods of accomplishing the result, then your workers are probably independent contractors.
4. Employers who misclassify workers as independent contractors can end up with substantial tax bills. Additionally, they can face penalties for failing to pay employment taxes and for failing to file required tax forms.
5. Workers can avoid higher tax bills and lost benefits if they know their proper status.
6. Both employers and workers can ask the IRS to make a determination on whether a specific individual is an independent contractor or an employee by filing a Form SS-8, Determination of Worker Status for Purposes of Federal Employment Taxes and Income Tax Withholding, with the IRS.
7. You can learn more about the critical determination of a worker's status as an independent contractor or employee at IRS.gov by selecting the Small Business link.

GETTING CLIENTS

One of the most important aspects of operating a coaching or therapy practice is getting clients. Without them, after all, no amount of smart planning and preparation matters. This means marketing, something in which most mental health professionals have had little to no training.

The single most important aspect of marketing today isn't necessarily who you know or how glossy and attractive your brochures are; instead, it can be summed up in two words: *web presence*. In an age in which technology and social media are changing at lightning speed, bluntly put, you will be left behind if this is not where you focus much of your time, energy, and financial resources. Furthermore, because coaching is such a unique field, many potential clients turn to the Internet to locate professionals in their area. Unlike deciding on a dentist, for example, potential clients can't simply ask a neighbor which coach he or she recommends.

There are several aspects to web presence you will want to consider:

1. *Your website*: The single most important advertising opportunity you have is your website. You can choose to hire a graphic designer. There are also companies that create websites just for mental health professionals and understand their particular needs. Or you may choose to create a professional looking website inexpensively with sites that offer customizable templates. Just as important as the look and usability of your website is the content. You may want to take a crash course in marketing by reviewing some articles online to avoid some common pitfalls and make your site stand out.
2. *Social media*: Although social media sites aren't the most important Internet products for professional service businesses such as coaching or therapy, they can certainly help. By creating pages and gaining "fans" or "followers," you can advertise your services, make viewers aware of upcoming events, or even share important information and research about the world of ADHD and coaching that will help to educate others and see you as an informed professional.
3. *Professional referral networks*: Rather than a place to gain clients directly, online professional referral networks are helpful in terms of building your referral network with other professionals. You can become a member of networks filled with other professionals who have a common interest or inform potential connections about your services.
4. *Online video sharing*: Posting videos on a video sharing website is a great place to display recordings of presentations or webinars in which you participate. Not only do viewers get to see that you are an intelligent and experienced expert in the field, they also get a sense of who you are and how well they might relate to you. Potential clients may comment that after watching a video, they felt like they "knew" you a little better and weren't so nervous or anxious walking into a first session as they might have been without this experience.

5. *Webinars, interviews, and podcasts*: In addition to all of the sites and ideas just mentioned, there are countless other avenues you can take to add to your web presence. Some ideas we have tried include webinars, podcasts, and interviews for online articles from credible sources. Of course, for some of these, you may first have to establish yourself as an expert in the field, but once you do, you may find you are approached by popular media sites wanted your input for their articles. Others you can create and distribute yourself—record a webinar or podcast, or write a blog about your thoughts on coaching. The more you put out there, the more visible you become, and the more opportunity you have to attract potential clients.
6. *Professional directories*: There are a number of sites where you can pay to belong to a professional directory so that potential clients can find you. These sites allow for you to put a photo and brief bio and sometimes even a video or voice recording. Most also enable you to link directly to your website or receive calls and e-mails through the site.
7. *Search engines*: All of the foregoing ideas and others will result in a rise in your "searchability" via popular search engines. You can pay for ads, too, but you may find it is just as effective to create a presence in the arenas we have just described. As people search and find you more often in different places, you will slowly rise in the hierarchy of the search engine. It will become easier and easier for people to find you, thus resulting in more potential clients. Last, make sure you link all the information about social media and other pages where you have a presence back to your website.

Beyond the Internet, there are many ways to get noticed as a brand in your area and connect with other professionals and potential clients. Consider doing presentations for PTA boards, libraries, mental health agencies, and similar locales. Attend conferences focusing on learning differences or special needs. Cold call or knock on the doors of local medical doctors, dentists, counselors, schools, or others who might want to know about your services. There are specific national organizations that work to support ADHD and local chapters with their own board of directors. By joining, you gain exposure as an ADHD authority. It is also a great way to give back to the community.

WHAT TO AVOID

In terms of what to avoid or at least not waste energy on, you may want to save your pennies when it comes to printed material. Although it is true that potential clients want something tangible they can hold on to,

90% of the time printed brochures and the other materials will be discarded. Keep it simple, design a business card and a one-page flyer, but keep it at that. It is not necessary to spend a lot; websites can help you to create nice looking and inexpensive products. Be sure to put your website address on all marketing materials, because that's where most people end up going for their information.

FEES, BILLING, AND INSURANCE

If you've chosen to manage a for-profit practice, you'll have several more decisions to make when it comes to finances. Here are some questions to consider:

1. How much will I charge? Will I slide my scale, or require the same payment from all clients? Will I charge extra for time spent going "above and beyond" for a client?
2. Will I take cash, check, credit card, or all three? Will I accept payment plans, bill clients after a session, or require payment up front?
3. How will I link payment to session notes? Will I use accounting software?
4. How do I document a session for clients so that they can get insurance reimbursement? Will I join any health care panels to be an in-network provider, or will I be an out-of-network provider?

To answer the first question, about fees, you will want to consider several things. First, what is your level of training, and to what degree will people value your expertise? Second, how much is charged for similar services in your area? You may be the only professional offering coaching for miles around, in which case in might be hard to know what to charge, but this could also place you in high demand. However, keep in mind that despite your credentials, some people might expect to pay less for "coaching" than for "therapy." However, if you are able to offer a receipt for insurance purposes, people might be willing to pay a little bit more knowing they are receiving the services of a licensed professional and may receive reimbursement for those services.

We recommend accepting as many forms of payment as possible. These days, taking credit cards is as simple as a swipe on your laptop, smartphone, or tablet. Although credit card processing companies will usually take between 1.5% to 3% of your profits for the service, the ease of use and keeping track of payments makes up for the slight loss. This is also helpful to clients with ADHD who tend to be forgetful. Taking credit cards at time of service also means knowing right away whether a payment has gone through rather than depositing a check and waiting 10 days only to find out it bounced and you are out that payment plus $10 for the bounced check fee.

We also recommend using some sort of accounting software to keep track of all of your business expenses, including client payments. In addition, a variety of integrated systems (see this chapter's Resources section), both currently available and in development, are available help professionals keep track of client notes via electronic health records as well as receive payment, linking it to a specific session. (Some of these systems are free of charge.) You will also want to make sure you open a separate bank account for all of your business transactions and link that account to whatever accounting software you choose.

We do not go into depth here about joining insurance panels as a mental health professional, but regardless of what you choose to do, the Current Procedural Terminology (CPT) codes you use for clients will likely be the same whether you choose to join a panel or not. The main reason most mental health providers choose to serve on panels as an *in-network* provider is because it allows them to see clients who cannot afford to pay out of pocket. On the downside, it means filing a lot of paperwork and being paid by the insurance carrier when and what they want to pay you. Providers who choose not to be a part of any panels take payment directly from clients at whatever rate the provider chooses. This, of course, limits you to work with only those clients who are willing and able to pay out of pocket. Nonetheless, you can still be considered an *out-of-network* provider when you do this. In this case, you provide your clients with a receipt they can submit to their insurance carrier. The carrier then reimburses the client directly for whatever amount they have set for out-of-network services.

For coaching, we use the same codes as we do for psychotherapy (because coaching is an empirically validated intervention for clients with ADHD); however, it may be wise to indicate to insurance companies that you are not engaged in traditional treatment with clients. That way, if any insurers have issue with reimbursing sessions, you have been up front about your services. Figure 7.1 is an example of what you might want to include on your receipt for coaching sessions.

As you build and refine your practice, there will always be new decisions to make and crises to resolve. Whether you have a solo practice or a staff of 50, owning a business is a commitment different from working for someone else and getting to leave your work at the office. Your practice is a part of you, and ultimately the success or failure of that business lies on your shoulders. It is a tough road and not one to be taken lightly. However, if you take the appropriate steps and position yourself well, it will be one of the most rewarding decisions of your career. Despite the challenges, owning your own practice also means answering only to yourself, taking vacation at times that work for you, and being more available to your family—and, of course, there is the pride and joy you will feel every time clients realize one of their goals as a result of your services.

FIGURE 7.1

Barry Helpful, PhD
Licensed Clinical Psychologist
555 Coaching Lane
Healthy, FL 55555

Employer Identification Number: XXXXXX
License Number: XXXXX

Client Name: _____ DOB: _____

Date of Service: _____ Payment Received: _____
                                                             Cash _____ Check _____ Credit _____

Services Rendered:

_____ 90791 Diagnostic evaluation
_____ 90832 Psychotherapy 30 minutes (therapy with client or family member)
_____ 90834 Psychotherapy 45 minutes (therapy with client or family member)
_____ 90837 Psychotherapy 60 minutes (therapy with client or family member)
_____ 90847 Family therapy with client present
_____ 90846 Family therapy without client present

DSM–IV and *ICD–10* Code and Diagnosis:
_____

Next Appointment: _____

Signature: _____

*Barry Helpful, PhD, specializes in a cognitive–behavioral therapeutic coaching intervention. The client above is a recipient of these services to help reduce the symptoms associated with his or her mental health disorder.

Example of a coaching session receipt.

Summary

1. ADHD coaching and psychotherapy are two different processes. It is important to determine how your practice will integrate these two approaches.
2. HIPAA requires appropriate safeguards to protect the privacy of personal health information and sets limits and conditions on

the use and disclosure that may be made of such information without client authorization.
3. Boundaries recognize the inherent power inequity of the therapeutic relationship and set limits for the therapist's expression of power. Boundaries also set a structure for the relationship, providing a consistent, reliable, predictable, and knowable frame for a process that remains somewhat mysterious.
4. The General Principles and 10 Standards of APA's (2010) "Ethical Principles of Psychologists and Code of Conduct" are all relevant in varying degrees to coaching practice.
5. The APA Ethics Code Standard on Informed Consent states that psychologists obtain appropriate informed consent to therapy or related procedures, using language that is reasonably understandable to participants.
6. In terms of Boundaries of Competence, the APA Ethics Code maintains that psychologists only provide services with populations and within areas that are within the boundaries of their competence, based on their education, training, supervised experience, consultation, study, or professional experience.
7. A business plan is an official document you create for your business that helps you to think through some of the tough questions and think long term.
8. You might choose a sole proprietorship, an LLC, a corporation, or a partnership. Alternately, you might choose a nonprofit organization.
9. As a small business owner, you may hire people as independent contractors or as employees. IRS.gov offers seven tips for business owners making this decision.
10. Successful marketing generally involves a good website and the use of social media.
11. Additional marketing tools include professional referral networks; online video sharing; webinars, interviews, and podcasts; and professional directories.
12. You will need to make clearly thought-out financial decisions about fees, billing, and insurance.

Resources

BUSINESS PLANNING

- Small Business Administration: http://www.sba.gov
- SCORE (free small business advice, how-to resources, tools, and templates): http://www.score.org

- IRS Publication 15-A, Employer's Supplemental Tax Guide, Publication 1779, Independent Contractor or Employee, and Publication 1976, Do You Qualify for Relief under Section 530? These publications and Form SS-8 are available on the IRS website or by calling the IRS at 800-829-3676 (800-TAX-FORM).
- Department of the Treasury's Employer's Supplemental Tax Guide: http://www.irs.gov/pub/irs-pdf/p15a.pdf

MARKETING

- Facebook
- Twitter
- YouTube
- CHADD.org (Children and Adults With Attention-Deficit/Hyperactivity Disorder)
- Psychologytoday.com
- Goodtherapy.org

ACCOUNTING SOFTWARE

- QuickBooks
- Quicken

ELECTRONIC HEALTH RECORDS

- Practice Fusion: http://www.practicefusion.com
- Therapy Notes: https://www.therapynotes.com
- Office Ally: http://www.officeally.com

ADHD COACHING CASE STUDIES | II

Case Study
ADHD Coaching With a Middle-Aged Adult

8

This chapter illustrates how to work with an adult client with attention-deficit/hyperactivity disorder (ADHD) who is well beyond the world of academia but struggling with all of life's "other" problems, from maintaining his relationships at home and work to keeping his health on track. Although many people still think of ADHD as a school-based issue, more and more adults are getting diagnosed well into their 30s, 40s, 50s, and even 60s, after noticing distressing patterns repeated throughout their lives. In this chapter, we outline how to approach these complicated cases in terms of beginning, middle, and final sessions.

The client is a 48-year-old man, Chris, who was recently remarried after his first marriage ended in divorce. He was diagnosed with ADHD (combined presentation) by a neuropsychologist 3 months ago, after his wife saw a news segment about adult ADHD and suggested he get tested. Chris barely finished college with a business degree and has had a

---

http://dx.doi.org/10.1037/14671-009
ADHD Coaching: A Guide for Mental Health Professionals, by F. Prevatt and A. Levrini
Copyright © 2015 by the American Psychological Association. All rights reserved.

variety of "careers" over the past 20 years, including dog walker, truck driver, restaurant manager, and most recently a failed moving company business enterprise. At times, Chris has been quite comfortable financially; at other times, he has been on the brink of financial ruin. When he is under a lot of stress, he tends to lash out at those around him. Because of his up-and-down pattern of behavior and emotional outbursts, he was misdiagnosed and on medication for bipolar disorder for several years. Through it all Chris has remained optimistic and is always excited by his next adventure. However, his new wife is 10 years younger, wants a child as soon as possible, and, according to Chris, is "scared to death" by his unstable track record. Chris doesn't want a second marriage to end in divorce, and he hopes that coaching can help him "settle down" and create a safe and secure environment for his future family.

Case in Action: Beginning, Middle, and End

INITIAL ASSESSMENT

Chris had previously undergone rigorous neuropsychological testing to diagnose his ADHD and identify other areas of mental health concern. Because he had already been assessed, the only instrument the coach used with Chris was the Coaching Topics Survey (CTS). The coach then reviewed all of the measures and developed the following working hypotheses and questions.

1. Chris exhibited a mild amount of anxiety and depression (previous testing). The coach would need to determine whether the affective issues would be a detriment to coaching and whether Chris would need to be in mental health counseling before or simultaneously with coaching.
2. Chris's primary areas of executive functioning deficit were self-management to time, decision making, and maintaining goal-directed behavior. He also seemed to have difficulties regulating his emotions.
3. As determined by the CTS, Chris's areas of concern centered on establishing routines and good habits, planning and prioritizing, making decisions and solving problems, and figuring out the next step in his career.

With these tentative working hypotheses in mind, the coach conducted the initial intake interview.

BEGINNING SESSIONS

Chris gave his coach a powerful handshake before emptying the contents of his back pocket onto the table, then settled down on the couch. He wore a hooded sweatshirt, jeans, and work boots, with a baseball hat turned backward on his head. He complimented the coach on her office decor, flashing a mouth full of gleaming white teeth. Then he stretched, sighed, and put his feet up on the ottoman.

Initial sessions with adults tend to be more straightforward than when working with children. Most adults generally know why they are there and what they would like to accomplish. They may or may not arrive with a working knowledge of what ADHD coaching is, so part of the intake may mean educating them about the coaching structure. Adults will also vary on their level of understanding ADHD as a disorder and how it affects their life. Some will have been diagnosed as children and have a good understanding of their symptoms. Others, like Chris, may be new to ADHD and only understand it based on what they have heard or have seen in the media. If an adult client has any other mental health diagnosis related to ADHD, you will want to briefly explore this and consider your options (see Chapter 11 on working with comorbid disorders). Adult clients often have a plethora of problems they could address, so beginning sessions can often be about establishing those goals that should be considered high priority and addressed first.

With the CTS responses in hand, the coach begins a dialogue with Chris on what he hopes to achieve from coaching.

Chris: So basically I just want to be able to stay on top of things better, and the medication is only helping so much.

Coach: Can you describe the things you have in mind that you'd like to stay on top of?

Chris: Oh, sure. Well, like, my work. I need to get a stable, full-time job. My wife won't have a kid until that happens. I think that would solve a lot of my problems.

Coach: Anything else?

Chris: Well, a lot of it is related to not working, I think, but I get stressed out and snap at my wife when I don't have a job with money coming in. And when I'm stressed I eat and drink too much.

Coach: So you've covered four general areas there. Sounds like you want to make improvements to your career path, your financial management, your nutritional choices, and perhaps, most important, your relationship.

Chris: Yes, that sounds about right.

Coach: Now I see you didn't very highly endorse "eating healthfully" or "exercising" on the Coaching Topics Survey. As you think more about those items, are those things you feel you need to work on?

Chris: Yeah, I guess those aren't things that brought me in or things my wife complains about necessarily, but as we are talking I can see how important they are to decreasing my stress overall.

Many adult clients like Chris need help thinking linearly and staying on track. Sometimes this means eliciting further thought on a response; and other times it means breaking down or rephrasing what your client has said in a more organized way. Imagine a tennis match with you as the instructor, coaching your clients on where to hit the ball; if they hit the ball too far or wide, it will land out of bounds, if they hit it short, it won't make it over the net. As an ADHD coach, you are playing a similar game, guiding your client toward realization and behavioral change. Early on, while establishing rapport, this should be done gently as the coach demonstrated in the dialogue you just read, first by encouraging further response and then by summarizing what Chris said into four distinct areas. As the relationship progresses, a coach may find that he or she needs to be more forceful or confrontational with a client who is struggling with accountability.

Coach: I also want to touch on something else you said about "drinking too much." Did you mean alcohol?

Chris: Yes, that's what I meant.

Coach: Can you tell me about how much and how often you are drinking? And are you using any other substance to de-stress?

Chris: Yeah, I should probably clarify. I really dislike drinking in theory, so my idea of "too much" is probably a lot less than most people's. Most days I drink nothing—oh, and I don't use any drugs either. Promise. But anyway, when I'm stressed I might have 3 or 4 beers that night, and that's maybe twice a month.

Substance use and abuse is common in both teens and adults with ADHD, so it is important to address any concerns that might arise in sessions. As a mental health professional, you most likely have access to inventories that assess substance use behavior and referral resources should you discover a client is in need of further help. Make sure to take the same precautions in coaching as you would in your traditional therapy sessions. In Chris's case, after discussing the issue further, the coach assessed that he was not abusing alcohol and that by establishing healthy habits to reduce his stress he would likely decrease his desire to turn to alcohol. The coach then made a note to check back in with Chris's alcohol use throughout the coaching process.

Because adults in their 30s, 40s, 50s, and beyond have been struggling with most issues for a long time, they may have also tried many ways to take charge of their symptoms, either on their own or with the help of another professional. To better understand the specifics of each general area that Chris is struggling with and what, if anything, he has previously tried to better his outcomes, the coach engages Chris in a conversation about his money problems.

Coach: Tell me a little bit about your financial history as you see it relating to your ADHD.

Chris: Money burns a hole in my pocket, as you might guess. I guess that's the impulsivity, huh? My wife is always complaining that I buy stupid stuff that we don't need.

Coach: How are you getting your money now, and what kind of savings do you have?

Chris: Well, my wife is working and I've got some odd jobs. I just came from helping a buddy build his deck and he's paying me. We're getting by but barely. Any savings we have is because my wife has hid it from me and socked it away before I could get to it [*laughs uncomfortably*].

Coach: Well, I'm glad you are getting by. If I do my job right, I hope I can end up saving you money rather than just spending it on my services. Have you worked with a financial planner before?

Chris: No, but I'd love to get some help there. I don't even know what things cost or how to budget, to be honest. I think that would help my relationship too, because my wife would see that I care and I'm making an effort. You'll just have to help me with the impulsive spending part, too.

Coach: Those are some great ideas that we'll be sure to address. Now, I'd like to ask you some questions about your work history.

Adults like Chris who come to coaching for the first time, especially those who have tried traditional insight-oriented therapy to treat their ADHD, are often excited and energized after the first couple of sessions when they see that coaching is a results-oriented, practical, tool-building experience. This energy can often propel them to successfully complete many of their first, second, and even third week's objectives without a hitch. As the newness of coaching wears off, however, it is important to notice signs of complacency and continuously adjust your methods so that clients remain engaged in the process.

Assessing Mental Health Functioning and Motivation

On the basis of Chris's mental health history, the coach wanted to determine the level of his anxiety and depression. With adult clients with ADHD, some coexisting anxiety or depression (or both) is present more often than not. It appeared that Chris was under a great deal of current stress, and the coach needed to determine whether his resulting levels of anxiety and depression needed further treatment.

Coach: Talk to me a little more about the effect that stress has on you, and your behavior as a result.

Chris: Well, you know, I just get really tense and angry, and my patience gets really short. I end up doing things I regret like yelling at my wife.

Coach: We all get stressed, and feeling tense as a result is completely normal and okay. I'd even go as far as to say it's almost impossible to control feeling that way. But what we can control is how we behave as a result of what we are feeling, don't you think?

Chris: Yes, I guess you're right. Although, it's really hard for me. It's like a switch goes off. I'm just . . .

Coach: Impulsive?

Chris: Yeah . . . oh—yeah! That keeps coming up, huh? So maybe if I can learn to be less impulsive I won't feel as bad because I won't do as many things that I'll regret later.

Coach: I think that's a great starting point. We can work together to come up with some healthy ways to relieve your stress and also some systems to help you keep from getting stressed out in the first place.

The coach was able to establish that Chris's anxiety and depression were mild to moderate and not likely to interfere with the process of coaching. In fact, his affective symptoms appeared to be primarily related to his ADHD-related difficulties and would likely dissipate when he was able to gain momentum on his goals. The coach was able to provide education about the nature of anxiety and depression as it relates to ADHD while simultaneously evaluating Chris's level of distress. The coach also made some comments that give Chris immediate hopefulness that his symptoms are normal and manageable.

Brainstorming Rewards and Consequences

Adults may initially have a hard time coming up with ideas for rewards and consequences for several reasons. Some feel they already reward themselves or indulge far too much. Others think behavioral modification techniques are only for children. However, when applied in a creative and personal manner, incentives can be the most influential part of coaching in terms of reinforcing accountability.

The following questions can be helpful in pinpointing rewards and consequences that adults find helpful:

- What gets you out of bed in the morning?
- What goes through your mind when you are trying to fall asleep?
- Can you name three things you would you rather do than work?
- Can you think of three tasks that would happily surprise your wife/husband/significant other if you completed them?

As adults begin to think of ideas for rewards and consequences, they should use the first week of coaching to see what they are doing or gravitating toward instead of what they should be doing or are avoiding. Some common examples include watching TV, using the computer, using a cell phone, listening to music, or visiting with friends. These ideas can be helpful, but if you help your client dig a little deeper, you can usually come up with some far more creative and personal suggestions. After getting to know Chris a bit, his coach discovered he was an avid fisherman. Together they decided one of his weekly consequences could be an automatic withdrawal from his bank account in the amount of $15 to an antifishing or animal rights organization if he did not meet his financial objective that week. However, if he did meet his objective, that money could be redirected into a "fishing trip fund" account. The incentives related to the overall financial goal and forced him to follow through. Following is the complete list of Chris's list of rewards and consequences he and his coach brainstormed in the beginning stages of coaching:

Rewards
1. Buy and grill a good steak.
2. Add money to a fishing trip fund.
3. I get the remote for a night.
4. Hire a neighborhood kid to mow the lawn for that week (rather that do it myself).
5. Skip making the bed.
6. Get my car detailed.

Consequences
1. My wife picks an extra chore for me.
2. Watch a Lifetime movie with my wife.
3. Send money to animal rights organization.
4. Wash my car and my wife's.
5. Mow my neighbor's lawn.
6. Additional 20 minutes of exercise.

Using the CTS

Adults can run the gamut in terms of which items are highly endorsed on the CTS. As mentioned earlier, often the challenge can be figuring out which items rank the highest in terms of priority. Adult clients can sometimes become overwhelmed if they find themselves circling 1s and 2s on nearly every item, so you may need to ease their mind by explaining that the items are there for that very reason; these issues are common to many individuals with ADHD and it's okay if they fall into many of the categories.

One strategy we recommend when reviewing the CTS with adults who have endorsed many items is taking four or five different-colored highlighters, then highlighting each individual item by "topic." For example, *improving time management*, *managing long terms assignments*, and *establishing good routines* all relate to time management and could be highlighted in yellow. Likewise, *doing laundry, exercising, eating healthfully*, and *getting to bed* can all relate to healthy lifestyle and could be highlighted in green. Once your client sees that all of these items can be broken down into just a few overarching themes they will likely relax and begin to see how to structure their long-term goals.

Creating Long-Term Goals

When working with married or committed adults like Chris, you will often need to take into account the suggestions of their partner of family members. Sure, the client is your primary concern, but many times clients will be there in part because of a loved one's frustrations and insights. When prioritizing and writing out long-term goals, make sure to discuss this impact and write the goal in a way that your clients feel will satisfy both their own needs and the needs of their loved one. Exhibit 8.1 includes a list of the long-term goals Chris and his coach worked together to create.

As with the anxious client described in Chapter 11, Chris and his coach reviewed the ways his goals could potentially overlap and influence each other. For instance, by taking charge of his job search, finances, and lifestyle choices, he would likely reduce his stress and lash

> **EXHIBIT 8.1**
>
> **Chris's Long-Term Goals**
>
> **GOAL 1:** Create and follow through with a schedule that includes exploring my career path, updating my resume and applying for appropriate positions (two per week minimum after completion of parts 1 and 2).
>
> **GOAL 2:** Complete one exercise to increase communication and improve relationship with wife outside of session each week, then discuss in following session.
>
> **GOAL 3:** Construct a breakdown of my monthly expenses and a somewhat flexible budget for the family. Review in session every other week.
>
> **GOAL 4:** Review my current lifestyle choices with my coach (eating, drinking, exercise) and develop and then implement a stepwise schedule to decrease negative choices and increase healthy ones.

out at his wife less frequently, thereby improving their relationship. Similarly, by taking charge of his job search and finances, and improving his relationship, he would likely feel less of a need to use unhealthy coping strategies like eating unhealthy foods or drinking alcohol. In most cases, improvement in one area will mean improvement in others, so make sure to point out this trickle-down effect to your clients.

MIDDLE SESSIONS

The middle sessions of coaching involve (a) working through the long-term goals via weekly objectives (between-session assignments; see Chapter 5), (b) identifying weekly successes and using those to define strengths and coping mechanisms that can be generalized to other tasks, (c) identifying barriers that can be overcome with the problem-solving approach, (d) using rewards and consequences to keep the client motivated, (e) helping the client develop specific skills and strategies, and (f) helping the client reach the point where he or she can conduct all of these tasks on their own, without the help of a coach.

When working with adults who are attempting to make changes in several areas of life at once, like Chris, it becomes especially important to make sure they remain focused and use each session to its fullest. Many adults with ADHD display hyperactivity in conversation (known as being *hyperverbal*). Couple this with difficulty staying focused and the ability to defer responsibility, and it is not hard to see how an entire session could potentially be spent reviewing one objective and why it did not occur, leaving no time for anything else. As the coach, it is your job to serve as your client's "stop sign," bring them back to attention, and model appropriate time management throughout each session.

Creating Weekly Objectives

In the next chapter, we take you through the process of formulating objectives for Week 1 with your client. Here, we focus on the coaching process once clients have completed the beginning stages and are beginning to fine-tune the path toward long-term goal success. Exhibit 8.2 is an example of Chris's objectives from Week 4.

Make sure to continuously monitor where your adult client's priorities lie. Some weeks, you may choose to focus on all goals, other weeks on just one or two. Occasionally, a goal may change altogether. After several weeks of considering Chris's ideal job match and updating his resume, a wonderful opportunity arose in Week 5 with an associate's landscape company. It had just so happened that after a few interest inventories and discussion, this was one of the areas Chris felt passionate about but knew that creating his own business, requiring management of schedules and finances, would not be a wise choice. With the new position working for someone else, Chris would be managing people on jobs (something he was very skilled at), but he would not be required to do paperwork in the office. Together, Chris, his wife, and his coach decided he should jump on the offer. He did and quickly shifted his career-related long-term goal to reflect maintaining responsibilities at his new job.

Reviewing Weekly Objectives

As stated earlier, ADHD is often seen as a disorder that primarily affects adults at work; however, as we've noted elsewhere, it interferes with the routine tasks of daily living and can cause great frustration in relationships. This means you will have to be able to address just about every area of life with adult clients and help them to create appropriate objec-

EXHIBIT 8.2

Chris's Objectives From Week 4

Objective A (Goal 1)	Objective B (Goal 2)	Objective C (Goal 3)
Make suggested changes to my resume and e-mail to coach.	Spend 30 minutes in conversation with wife then rate myself in terms of positive listening.[a]	Using the budget that my coach and I created, review bank account and expenses on Tuesday and Friday.

Objective A (Goal 4)	Objective B (Goal 4)
Continue to log food choices in journal.	Walk/jog with the dog for 30 minutes on Saturday.

Note. [a]See Levrini and Prevatt (2012), pp. 103–104.

tives on a weekly basis. The best ADHD coaches are not just knowledgeable about ADHD; they are also skilled in financial planning, couples and parenting issues, exercise, nutrition, and home organization, to name only a few areas. In Chapter 6 on specific strategies, we took you through some tools you may want to keep handy. The following are some suggestions for weekly objectives tied to common goals for adults.

Finances
- Limit "extra" weekly spending (e.g., coffee, Amazon) to $50.
- Use the credit card no more than five times.

Exercise and Nutrition
- Add one fruit or vegetable to every meal.
- Take the stairs to third-floor office every time.

Medication Management
- Put reminder alarm on phone for medication.
- Schedule doctor appointment for refill.

Improving Relationships and Social Skills
- Call one good friend whom I haven't talked with in awhile.
- Attend one activity outside of my social comfort zone.

Getting Stuck and Cognitive Reframing
- Use the "Unstuck" App when I encounter a stuck moment (see Chapter 6 on Specific Strategies).
- Write my positive mantra (see Chapter 6) on my bathroom mirror (with dry erase marker) and repeat three times every time I go in the bathroom.

Here, the coach and Chris discuss his struggles with exercise:

Chris: So I tried walking and jogging with the dog and I'm doing it, but I just don't think it's something I can keep up. I really hate it.

Coach: Can you tell me what specifically you hate about it?

Chris: Good question. I didn't mind it as much in the first few weeks, but I think one thing is that it's starting to get cold and stay dark later in the morning. It's really hard to get out the door.

Coach: Great insight. That can be a pretty big roadblock if the payoff isn't worth it. We could explore one of two options: Upping the ante in terms of consequence and reward, or (my preference), exploring another exercise opportunity you can more easily sustain, even in bad weather.

Chris: Yeah, let's shoot for the second option.

Chris and his coach talk a bit about the things he seems to enjoy that are relatively active. During the discussion, Chris brings up that he used to play basketball, first on the high school team and then in a pickup league throughout college. After a little surfing on the Internet, Chris found that the gym three blocks from his house had a co-rec adult league on Saturdays. He committed to the team, and his wife decided to join him, helping even more to keep Chris accountable. Not only was he able to get his exercise and enjoy it in the process, he and his wife bonded through the experience.

Once Chris had gained control of his employment, lifestyle choices, and finances, he became distressed in session when discussing things at home with his wife. He felt that he had made a lot of improvements, and although things did seem to be better in a lot of ways, he still found himself getting defensive and angry at times. Here, Chris's coach guides him toward uncovering what may be a "hot-button" issue with his wife that they may have overlooked.

Coach: So you feel you are communicating better after doing the positive listening exercise?

Chris: Yeah, I thought so. We're having a lot of fun playing basketball and everything seems to be okay when we are out, but when we get home, she's on my back.

Coach: What do you mean by that? What does she say?

Chris: Ummm . . . she's just, "This place stresses me out, blah, blah."

Coach: So your home is stressful to her? Why could that be?

Chris: Oh, well, she can't find anything. It's a mess.

Coach: Ah. And why is that?

Chris: Okay, I see where you are going. It's me [*laughs*]. I didn't really think it was that big of a deal. It's not like there are empty pizza boxes all over, but I guess it is pretty disorganized. She does all the cleaning, and I guess you could say I do all the messing up.

Coach: Well, you are doing really well with your other goals. Do you think it would be valuable to spend some time learning strategies to keep you better organized? With a baby in the future, you are only going to find yourselves with more stuff and more mess to deal with. Maybe we can be proactive here and create a space into which you can both feel good about bringing a child.

Chris: That's a good point. A kid is going to be stressful enough without her yelling at me that she can't find the baby's diapers or whatever. Plus, it would probably save me a lot of time if I didn't have to go running around the house looking for things all the time.

Over the next several weeks, Chris and his coach determined the areas of his home that he needed to organize, in order of priority. Some ideas coaches may want to use with adult clients with organizational goals include the following:

- Divide large spaces into smaller, less overwhelming ones.
- Have clients take "before" and "after" photographs to help with accountability and reminders of what a space should look like.
- Pick specific, strategic spots for everyday items.
- Use transparent containers and open shelving for ease of finding and accessibility.
- Try the "keep, throw, or donate" rule when rummaging through items in storage.

Final Sessions

As it becomes clear that your adult clients are well on their way toward maintaining their goals, it is important to use time in the final sessions to review what did and did not work well for them. If your client created and filed away ideas in his Inspiration Toolbox (see Chapter 6), now is the time to bring it out and review his inspirations together. Talk about how each idea or tool might be used going forward in different contexts. This can also be done simply by flipping through the pages of their weekly objectives and remembering their successes and struggles, then discussing what caused things to turn out one way or another in each situation. Or, as illustrated in the next chapter, you may want to do a more formal assessment of change as a result of coaching.

As Chris nears completion of his long-term goals, he and his coach discuss the things that helped him succeed when it came to managing his finances, as well as the pitfalls he encountered in relation to the same goal.

Chris: So I think one big thing that helped was setting up automated payments for everything I could. Oh, and using the mobile app for banking.

Coach: So what about those two things were helpful?

Chris: Well, for the first part, knowing that I struggle to pay bills on time and pay attention to money in and out like I should, it just took things out of my hands. It was like delegating the responsibility to someone else in a way. For the second, just the ease and accessibility of it.

Coach: Can you think of other situations in which those two strategies could be helpful in the future?

Chris: Oh, for sure. I mean, I think I was smart in taking a job that in a way delegates my weaknesses to others and allows me to focus on my strengths. I can try to do that at home with my wife too. Maybe I'm not the best at cleaning, but I enjoy cooking and I could offer to do that more. As for the ease of the app, well, there are apps for everything, right?!

Coach: [*laughs*] Definitely. Those are some great ideas. What do you think some pitfalls were in terms of finances?

Chris: I think my pitfalls are basically the opposites of my strengths. For example, if it's too easy, I'll buy it. Like Amazon. I should probably trash my Amazon app and cancel my Prime membership. And what I can't delegate I really need to develop a system for, to make sure it gets done. I can do that in other areas of my life too.

Coach: First, delegate. Then, regulate. That's a great mantra.

Chris: Oh, my gosh. That's really great. So easy to remember. I'm using that! [Chris immediately records his voice saying the mantra on his phone, then sets it as his morning wake-up alarm.]

Chris and his coach continued the process for each of his long-term goals so that he left with a complete set of tools to tackle his ADHD symptoms going forward. Regardless of the method you use to review your clients' progress in the final sessions, make sure they leave coaching with their helpful hints documented in some way, whether it's a box full of ideas, the Barkley Deficits in Executive Functioning Scales (see Chapter 5), or an excel spreadsheet. Ultimately (as stated many times throughout this book), the goal of coaching your adult clients is to not only help them reach their goals throughout the coaching experience itself but also to be able to take and apply what they have learned in various situations throughout their lives.

Summary

1. Help clients figure out which goals take top priority if they seem to want to address many areas of their life.
2. Identify the strategies clients have already attempted in or out of treatment and analyze what has and has not been helpful.
3. Create long-term goals that address the needs of loved ones and family members and that may positively affect multiple areas of clients' life.
4. Pay attention to changes in priorities and adjust when necessary.
5. Help clients stay focused and on track.
6. Reexamine the tools used throughout coaching (such as the Inspiration Toolbox), and reinforce support techniques.
7. Review and reflect on what worked and why, and discuss possible future scenarios in which helpful tools may be used in different ways.

Case Study

ADHD Coaching With a Young Professional Adult

9

This chapter gives a second example of working with an adult client who is struggling with a variety of issues related to work and healthy lifestyle. Building on the concepts identified in the previous chapter, the case of Lanicia further illustrates how working with an adult client is different from adolescents or college students. Although the key symptoms of attention-deficit/hyperactivity disorder (ADHD) are similar in all age groups, as individuals mature and age, the behavioral manifestations of their symptoms change. Insight and motivation tend to be at a higher level; however, challenges remain as these individuals struggle to find a way of coping with work and demands of being a self-sufficient, independent adult.

Lanicia is a 32-year-old woman with a master's degree in biology, employed as a research assistant working on genetics research and writing grants. Her pediatrician informally diagnosed her with ADHD in elementary school. Her parents resisted putting her on medication and were not aware of

---

http://dx.doi.org/10.1037/14671-010
ADHD Coaching: A Guide for Mental Health Professionals, by F. Prevatt and A. Levrini
Copyright © 2015 by the American Psychological Association. All rights reserved.

any other forms of treatment. However, they had been quite supportive of her, and she had done well in school. As an adult, she presented as bright, articulate, well dressed, attractive, and outgoing. She had a good job that she liked, sang in her church choir, and was passionate about tennis. However, Lanicia was near tears during the first session. She was afraid that she was going to lose her job, she felt that her supervisor was upset with her performance, and she reported having to work much longer than the other researchers in the lab to complete her work. She had not disclosed her ADHD diagnosis to her supervisor and was worried that if he found out, he would "stereotype" her and be further critical of her performance. Lanicia had never taken medication but was currently considering that option.

Lanicia hadn't been dating for several years because she'd had no time to do so. She had recently purchased a small condominium but was feeling overwhelmed with the prospect of paying the mortgage and keeping up with repairs on her own. She reported that her finances should be in good shape, but she had student loan debt to pay off, credit card debt, and just couldn't come up with a system for being efficient with her finances. Finally, she reported being exhausted much of the time because of sleep difficulties.

Case in Action: Beginning, Middle, and End

INITIAL ASSESSMENT

Lanicia had never been formerly assessed for ADHD or other mental health disorders. Therefore, before the first session, the coach had her complete an Application for Services, the Barkley Deficits in Executive Functioning Scale (BDEFS), the Client Symptom Checklist (CSC), the Coaching Topics Survey (CTS), the Outcome Questionnaire—45 (OQ–45), and the Rosenberg Self-Esteem Scale (refer to Chapters 4 and 5 for more information on these instruments). The coach reviewed these measures and developed the following working hypotheses and questions.

1. Lanicia exhibited a moderate amount of anxiety and depression, with low self-esteem (CSC, OQ–45, Rosenberg). The coach would need to determine whether the affective issues would be a detriment to coaching and whether Lanicia would need to be in mental health counseling before or simultaneously with coaching.

2. Lanicia's overall level of distress was high, especially with regard to work issues. It appeared that she was highly motivated to make some changes (OQ–45).
3. Lanicia's primary executive functioning deficit areas were self-management to time and self-organization/problem solving. She also seemed to have difficulties regulating her emotions. Self-restraint and self-motivation did not appear to be problematic (BDEFS).
4. Lanicia's areas of concern centered on time management, organization, and healthy lifestyle, such as sleep habits, diet, and exercise (CTS).

With these tentative working hypotheses in mind, the coach conducted the initial intake interview.

BEGINNING SESSIONS

Lanicia presented as remarkably articulate and self-aware. She had prepared some notes before the session and, possibly because of her scientific background, laid out her story in a logical and structured manner. She also brought a long list of issues in her life, and it was clear that one of the first tasks would be to help her prioritize them. As mentioned earlier, beginning sessions with adults tend to be more straightforward than when working with children. Most adults generally know why they are there and what they would like to accomplish. However, many adults with ADHD also struggle with being realistic about what they can expect to accomplish. Explaining this and helping clients refine their expectations can be an important part of the psychoeducational phase of coaching.

One useful area to explore with high-functioning adults is how they have managed to do well despite their symptoms of ADHD. What coping mechanisms have worked in the past? What strategies do they already possess that can be used as areas of strength to build on? In Lanicia's case, her parents had provided a great deal of structure, collaborated with her teachers, and used a back-and-forth notebook system to ensure that assignments and homework were accomplished. Lanicia's father was an attorney, so she had a role model for high achievement. Her mother worked as a homemaker and was available on a daily basis to provide support and structure. From this foundation, Lanicia had learned how to work hard, had good reading and verbal skills, had high aspirations for success, and was good at analyzing issues and engaging in problem solving. Once her strengths were established, it was time to consider what areas of concern were high priorities and help her to select some concrete goals.

Lanicia: I like my job. Right now I'm doing grant writing. And I think I'm a really good writer. But it takes me forever. I get on the Internet, I start doing literature reviews and find one source, then I go to another, and before I know it, 5 hours have gone by and I've accumulated so much information that I can't possibly organize it.

Coach: So you think you have good writing skills, it's the organizing part that is difficult for you?

Lanicia: Yes, that's right. I need a way to stop myself sooner from gathering so much information and just get it down on paper.

Coach: Okay, that's a good start. Are there other areas? I see on the Coaching Topics Survey that you gave a score of 1 with two big exclamation marks for "Getting to bed on time."

Lanicia: OMG, yes. One reason I'm having so much trouble in my job is that I'm just exhausted. I sometimes don't get to bed until 2 a.m.

Coach: Why is that? What keeps you up?

Lanicia: Well, this is sort of embarrassing, but I have shows that I record and then the only time I can watch them is at night, and I promise myself that I'll only watch one, but then that morphs into four or five shows.

Coach: Do you want to still be able to watch the shows, while getting to bed earlier? Or do you want to figure out a way to limit your TV watching?

Lanicia: Well, maybe a little of both. They help me relax, but if I watch so much, I'm not getting to do anything else I need to, like pay bills or practice singing.

The coach relies on the CTS to elicit possible areas for long-term goals; however, it is usually important to also ask about areas of concern in an open-ended manner. In this way, all possible topics for consideration are generally uncovered. It is usually the case that clients' verbal assessment of issues is congruent with what they reported on the CTS; however, this cannot be taken for granted. After inquiring about areas of concern, the coach will clarify these issues, without assuming what direction the client wants to take. For both of these issues, the coach asks questions to help the client identify the exact nature of the concern. This will be helpful when determining specific objectives later on.

Assessing Mental Health Functioning and Motivation

Based on the precoaching assessment, the coach was concerned about Lanicia's level of anxiety and depression. It appeared that

Lanicia was under a great deal of current stress, which might bode well for her motivation to engage in coaching. However, the coach needed to determine whether this stress was so extreme as to be counterproductive.

Coach: I see you marked quite a few symptoms on this checklist (referring to the CSC). Let's see, you checked "yes" for *depression, feeling that you're losing control, feeling hopeless, anxious, worried,* and *difficulty sleeping.* Tell me more about those symptoms.

Lanicia: Well, most of that has to do with my work. I constantly feel behind and get worried every time my supervisor wants to talk to me. I'm just imagining that he is going to fire me.

Coach: Sometimes anxiety is justified and is based on real fears. What evidence do you have that you might be fired?

Lanicia: Well, none really. My evaluations are usually good. And my work is really good. Maybe I just think he can read my mind and knows how crazy I get trying to meet deadlines. [*laughs*] If he knew I was awake half the night worrying about something I'm writing, he'd fire me for incompetence just on general principle!

Coach: Okay, that's good to know. Just because you're not realistically in danger of being fired doesn't mean your anxiety isn't real. So let's figure out what we can do to help you with your work; we may want to set some goals having to do with organization and time management. But tell me a little more about the depression. How does that affect you?

Lanicia: Oh, I don't think that's a huge thing. It's not like some big dark cloud. I think when I was filling out those forms, everything just seemed grim. Most of the time it's not too bad.

Coach: Well, it's pretty common for adults with ADHD to feel depressed at times, but again, we can set some goals so that things don't seem quite so overwhelming.

The coach was able to establish that Lanicia's anxiety and depression were mild to moderate and not likely to interfere with the process of coaching. In fact, her affective symptoms appeared to be primarily related to her ADHD-related difficulties and would likely dissipate when she was able to feel more effective in her job. Her anxiety actually served as a good motivator to work on areas of difficulty. The coach was able to do some education about the nature of anxiety and depression while simultaneously evaluating Lanicia's level of distress. The coach also made some comments that give Lanicia immediate hopefulness that her symptoms are manageable.

Creating Long-Term Goals

Lanicia indicated quite a few areas of concern on the CTS, in the intake application, and during the intake interview. Even after highlighting general areas that needed work, Lanicia still had trouble prioritizing her concerns. The coach spent the remainder of the interview helping Lanicia with this and then assisting her in selecting an appropriate number of long-term goals.

Coach: We've talked about quite a few things that are going on in your life. I think you are really well suited to coaching. You seem motivated to work on these things, you seem to have a good idea of what your issues are, and you've already made some suggestions about specific things you can do. So let's spend the rest of this session picking the top three things you want to work on. You can do a little bit in each area each week, or you can work on them sequentially. Keep in mind that the goal of coaching is not to solve all your problems but to give you a blueprint for coping with ADHD. By working on a few key areas, you'll be able to learn problem-solving skills so that you can work on other areas on your own. Sound okay?

Lanicia: Sure, that makes sense. So where should we start?

Coach: Well, I have an idea that might help us gain better insight into where you are currently putting your efforts versus where you should be putting them. It may allow you to see where your priorities lie more clearly.

Lanicia: That sounds great. Let's try it!

Lanicia and her coach then draw and discuss the Eisenhower Matrix (described in Chapter 6, Specific Strategies for ADHD Coaching). Lanicia's final matrix is shown in Figure 9.1.

FIGURE 9.1

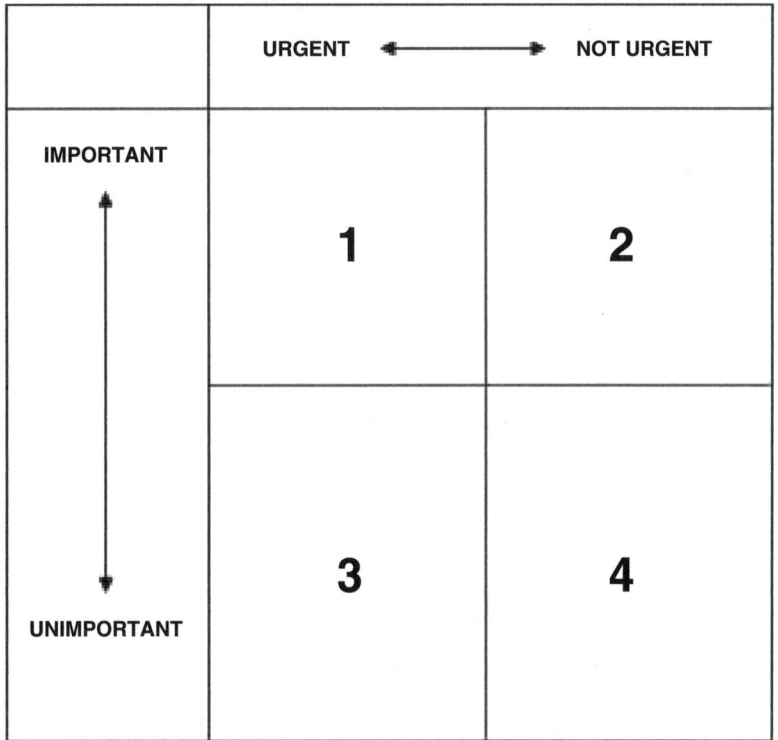

Lanicia's final Eisenhower Matrix. 1 = *getting proposals done for work, paying bills, practicing songs for Sunday church service;* 2 = *exercising, dating, improving time management and organization, decreasing overall stress;* 3 = *watching my shows before I find out what happened through someone else;* and 4 = *not sleeping at night because I'm worrying about things I can't control.*

Coach: So, going in order from 1 to 4 on the matrix (the order in which you should be addressing your tasks), it seems that your work issues are a high-priority item.

Lanicia: That's right, and work causes me the most stress.

Coach: It seems like you're pretty good at grant writing in some areas. What gives you the most trouble?

Lanicia: Definitely the time thing. I could spend months on something, but I always have definite due dates when proposals are due, and if I miss those deadlines, that's it—no second chances. I'm good at gathering lots of details, but can't seem to narrow down and just start writing.

Coach: That's really specific. I think we could work with that as a goal. Can you think of a single sentence or phrase that best describes that process? Later, we'll fill in a lot of details with weekly objectives and specific things you need to do. But right now, let's try to come up with the big picture.

Lanicia: Okay, how about getting proposals in on time?

Coach: Is it primarily the time thing? Or do you want to include something about *how* you write them?

Lanicia: Oh, good point! You're right; I need to work on spending less time on the idea stage. I need to work on closure. I need to be able to move on and decide on the right methods for the proposal. If I could do that, the time issue would solve itself! Okay, let's see. How about organizing proposals and moving through the process without getting stuck on the idea stage?

Coach: That sounds good. It's broad, but not too broad. We can develop some objectives to go with it. And it's specific enough that you will know if you're successful.

This section illustrates the collaborative process of developing a long-term goal. The coach gives small ideas and encouragement and models for the client types of strategies to employ. The coach gives specific examples of what a goal should entail. At the end of this exchange, it is likely that the client will feel ownership of this goal. This is important for motivational purposes. If the coach (or parent or spouse or employer) is in charge of telling the client what needs to be fixed, the client is less likely to work hard to achieve this goal. In Lanicia's case, two other long-term goals were also identified. Exhibit 9.1 is a list of the long-term goals Lanicia and her coach worked together to create.

Although Lanicia develops three long-term goals, in this chapter, we will use just the first one to demonstrate the following aspects of coaching: goal development, creation of objectives, use of rewards and consequences, identifying successes and barriers, problem solving and modification of objectives (using the Client Goals and Objectives form and weekly progress notes), and closure.

> **EXHIBIT 9.1**
>
> **Lanicia's Long-Term Goals**
>
> **GOAL 1:** Practice organizing my proposals and moving through the process without getting stuck in the idea stage by creating and sticking to steps and a strict timeline for the next 2 months.
>
> **GOAL 2:** Develop and implement a plan to improve my work environment (may include disclosing my attention-deficit/hyperactivity disorder to my supervisor). One weekly objective each week must pertain to this goal for next 2 months.
>
> **GOAL 3:** Create and maintain a nightly routine (which includes reducing nightly television) to help me improve my sleep schedule and keep a sleep journal for next 2 months.

MIDDLE SESSIONS

The middle sessions of coaching involve (a) working through the long-term goals via weekly objectives (between-sessions assignments); (b) identifying weekly successes and using those to define strengths and coping mechanisms that can be generalized to other tasks; (c) identifying barriers that can be overcome with the problem solving approach; (d) using rewards and consequences to keep clients motivated; (e) helping clients develop specific skills and strategies; and (f) helping clients reach the point where they can do these tasks on their own, without the help of a coach.

Creating Weekly Objectives to Promote Long-Term Goals

After all long-term goals have been selected, the coach helps the client break these down into manageable tasks. This is a common area of difficulty for those with ADHD. Many clients with ADHD are able to come up with "big picture" ideas and can become quite enthused about making plans. However, they are not as good at the day-to-day, nitty-gritty, detailed steps that go into accomplishing that task. Several items on the BDEFS exemplify this skill. In reviewing that measure, the coach confirmed that Lanicia had indicated difficulty on the following items:

- I have trouble considering various options for doing things
- I am unable to come up with or invent as many solutions to problems as others seem to be able to do.
- I have trouble doing things in their proper order or sequence.

Individuals with ADHD may quickly encounter failure because they are not effective at planning the individual steps that lead to goal completion. A primary objective of coaching is to help them learn how to plan and implement these steps. We use the Client Goals and Objectives form each week as a visual supplement to reinforce the plans that are made in session. This form also helps clients remember their plan because poor memory skills can also be associated with ADHD.

Coach: Now that we've identified your long-term goals, let's pick just one to work on this first week. We call this a between-session assignment, or BSA for short. I want to start slow to make sure you'll be successful. Where would you like to start?

Lanicia: I guess it makes sense to start with number one, my work stuff, since we established that it should be my priority.

Coach: Okay, we've identified organizing proposals and moving through the process without getting stuck on the idea stage as your first long-term goal. Let's write that here on your Goals and Objectives form. Now, let's talk about some of the things that go into that, and then let's pick one thing you can do this first week to work toward changing your typical approach.

Lanicia: Wow, I'm not sure I know where to begin. . .

Coach: Okay, let's pretend your supervisor just gave you a new assignment. Walk me through that.

Lanicia: Oh, okay. Well, we'll have a meeting, the new grant and the deadline will be described, and he'll assign it to one of the grant writers. If it's mine, then I have to do a bunch of research for background. He'll have given me the tentative idea of what the method will be, based on what we've done in the past. Usually my part is the literature review that specifically justifies that method. So I can use a lot of previous stuff. I need to get some new stuff too. I need to figure out a general outline. . .

The coach takes several minutes here to walk Lanicia through the specifics of her general approach.

Coach: Okay, that's really helpful. Now I can see in a sequential fashion exactly what you need to be doing. Do you have a new grant you're working on?

Lanicia: Actually, I just started on a new one last week. My deadline is 2 months from now.

Coach: Perfect. We can start at the beginning of your assignment.

This segment illustrates a key concept in coaching. Lanicia is struggling to go from the "big picture" of her work assignment to the building blocks that go into completing that task. The coach does not provide those for her; rather, the coach suggests a strategy, sequentially imagining a past event and using that to build a timeline of the steps that comprise the task. With this strategy, Lanicia is able to move forward and grasp the concept of breaking down a task into discrete steps. The process is clearly collaborative; with the coach making some suggestions while the client contributes much of the content.

Coach: So you're just starting on a new assignment. What have you done so far?

Lanicia: Not much really. We've been having a few meetings to go over the guidelines for this particular grant, and I've got a good handle on the basic method of what we're proposing. I need to work up all the background information.

Coach: So a good first step would be?

Lanicia: I think a good place to start is to review past grants and see what information I can use.

Coach: How many do you need to review?

Lanicia: Probably eight to 10.

Coach: What's a reasonable time frame to review all those?

Lanicia: Probably 2 weeks.

Coach: So how many could you normally review each week?

Lanicia: Well, four to five makes sense.

This segment further illustrates the use of the collaborative approach. You notice that the coach rarely makes a direct suggestion. Rather, the coach asks numerous questions of Lanicia to help her think through the situation. The coach gently guides her until a point is reached where some closure seems appropriate. It's important that the coach give some direction; clients will get quite frustrated without this. The key is to make the ultimate solution one that works for clients because they have provided the majority of input.

Refining Objectives

Once a tentative objective is selected, the coach and client work together to carefully consider that objective. This is often a new skill for individuals with ADHD. Because of their impulsivity, they tend to make a decision and immediately rush ahead with no thought as to how that might actually work out. This can result in unanticipated difficulties and an inability to continue with that idea. Rather, when minor obstacles are encountered, an easy and immediate solution is to give up.

Coach: So let's tentatively say that your BSA for this week will be to review about four prior grants. Let's talk about how you'll do that and what barriers might get in your way. Let's start with specifics. What exactly does that entail?

Lanicia: Well, I need to download each previous grant and get useful information from each of those.

Coach: How do you know what information to get?

Lanicia: Okay, first I need to plot out the key ideas I'm searching for that will be relevant to this grant.

Coach: It sounds like a first step is to do that before you pull the grants. Should we revise our objective to say that you'll plot out all the key ideas you'll need in the new grant?

Lanicia: Right, good point. That makes more sense.

In this segment, the coach again helps Lanicia with prioritizing and sequencing. It's useful to be specific about what clients need to do to accomplish a task. Otherwise, they may leave with only a general sense of what they need to do but no plan for how to do it.

Coach: Okay, so what might get in the way of plotting out key points for the new grant? What obstacles have you encountered in the past?

Lanicia: Time is one. I'm not sleeping well, so I find it hard to get to work at a reasonable time. I really need to figure out how to get up in the morning.

Coach: Right, you've decided that one of your other long-term goals will be to work on getting a good night's sleep. So now it's becoming clear how that's related to this goal. But let's hold off a minute before we move to that one. Let's see if there are other things that are more directly related to the way in which you're trying to organize your writing. Then we'll move on to sleeping.

This segment is a classic example of working with clients with ADHD. Because of their impulsivity and lack of focus, it is common for them to jump from one topic to another. The coach does not downplay the importance of the second issue but does help Lanicia focus first on the task at hand. It is difficult for many mental health practitioners to keep their clients from diverging and allowing their thoughts to go in whatever direction they seem to go. After all, in counseling 101, we learned the value of "free association" and how a good therapist does not lead his or her clients in any particular direction. However, when it comes to coaching clients with ADHD, it is imperative that you keep them on track. After all, their ever-changing stream of consciousness has likely contributed to their difficulties in reaching their goals and thus to their coming to you for help.

Coach: Let's think some more about your task of plotting out key points for this grant. What, other than not getting to work on time, might get in the way of that?

Lanicia: I don't know—I'm blanking.

Coach: Let's try visualizing the process. Where do you do this task? What time of day? Is anyone else involved? Do you need any specific materials?

Lanicia: Okay, that helps. I do it at my desk on my laptop. No specific time of day, but I work best in the morning. I sometimes get help from Roberto, he's one of the postdocs, and he's really good at meeting with me and helping me to start a plan.

Coach: Good thoughts! Now, what might get in the way of those?

Lanicia: Well, sometimes I really need to talk to Roberto, but he's in the middle of lab work and won't meet with me for days. Actually, that almost always sets me back.

Coach: And a possible solution might be?

Lanicia: Ha! This sounds really simple, but I guess if I actually made an appointment with him early on I'd have a better chance of meeting with him.

This segment illustrates two concepts. First, it's important to guide the client into identifying obstacles and solutions. The coach may have many preconceived notions about what may work in any given situation. What works for the coach or what has worked for other clients are important to keep in the back of one's mind. These ideas can be used as suggestions if necessary. However, it's always a good idea to help clients learn the process of problem solving for themselves. In this case, it would have been easy for the coach to be more direct and come up with solutions. However, the coach chose not to try to tell Lanicia what to do. Soon, Lanicia was able to reflect on her experience and come up with a scenario that was relevant to her experience. Second, and closely related, is the notion that the coach does not have to be an expert in all the content areas that a client presents. A coach may not be familiar with grant writing and have no background in genetics research; however, the coach is an expert on organizational skills, problem solving, and using detailed questions to guide a client. Sometimes novice coaches are worried that they don't have specific skills in all areas that might be difficult for a client. A basic training in key foundational areas is necessary, but the coach will primarily be teaching problem solving by guiding clients to determine solutions that work for them.

Using Rewards and Consequences With Weekly Objectives

The previous chapter demonstrated how to brainstorm a list of possible rewards and consequences with adult clients at the outset of coaching. In the following segments, we give more details about using that process when setting weekly objectives with your client.

Coach: So to get started on your first-week objective, you need to make an appointment with Roberto, and then follow up by plotting out key points you need to write about. Will this be difficult for you? Is this an inherently enjoyable task, is it something you enjoy? Do you need a motivator to help you do this?

Lanicia: I don't mind making the appointment or talking to Roberto, but plotting out the ideas we discuss and getting them down on paper is not my favorite task.

Coach: Is that something that you need a little motivation to do?

Lanicia: Actually, some motivation might be good!

Coach: Some people motivate themselves by giving themselves a reward. For daily or weekly tasks something small is fine. Like a favorite TV show or a glass of wine. Other people use a consequence; we call that a negative reward. Perhaps take away something you would normally get to do, like not watching that favorite television show. Or you can make yourself do something unpleasant, like clean the bathroom.

Lanicia: Okay, I'm definitely a stay-away-from-bad-things kind of person. I think if I do that last one, threaten myself with something negative, that would really work for me.

Coach: Let's be specific with how this will work. Do you want to do this daily or weekly?

Lanicia: I think every day is best. Let's say that every day I need to do one page of an outline. And if I don't do it, hmmmm... If I don't do it I have to iron one thing from my stack of wrinkled clothes. I really despise ironing!

Coach: Sounds good! Do you think you'll stick to this? Do you need any reminders from me?

Lanicia: That would be great. Can you text me every evening and just say, "Do you need to iron?" That will hold me accountable. [*laughs*]

In this segment, the coach identified the type of motivators but is again careful to let the client decide what will work for her. Avoiding ironing a blouse may not be an incentive for everyone, but this is Lanicia's choice. The coach is also careful to go into detail about how consequences will work. Fully thinking through all aspects of weekly plans is crucial. Finally, the coach inquires about some additional motivation in the form of reminders or checking in during the week. This is entirely up to the coach and his or her personal preference. Some coaches use texts and e-mails routinely with clients. If you choose to use phone calls, keep in mind it can be hard to reach clients, and the time burden on the coach can be excessive. However, a text or e-mail can be a quick an efficient way of helping clients to stick to their goals. We explain to clients that we will do this more often in the beginning phases of coaching and less so near the end as clients learn to take more responsibility for their actions.

The Client Goals and Objectives form (see Figure 9.2) shows how the coach has helped Lanicia to fill in the first long-term goal and write out specific objectives. Lanicia also gives three ratings regarding her motivation to work on this task, how well this objective matches her goal, and how much she enjoys this type of activity. If the ratings are low on the match question, a decision might be made to revise the objective. If there is low motivation to attempt the objective, the coach will be sure to discuss the use of incentives in the form of rewards or consequences. Similarly, if the activity is not one the client finds inherently enjoyable, the coach will spend some time discussing barriers to completion. A copy of this chart is made for the client to take home as a visual reminder of what he or she is to accomplish.

After several sessions, Lanicia and her coach reflect on her progress thus far and discuss where to go next.

Coach: How did your week go? Tell me about your weekly objectives. Here, let's look at the Goals and Objectives form as we talk through this.

FIGURE 9.2

CLIENT GOALS AND OBJECTIVES
NAME *Lanicia* **WEEK** *1* **DATE** *Sept 3* **NEXT SESSION** *Sept 10*
GOAL 1: *Organizing proposals and moving through the process. Avoid getting stuck at idea stage.*
GOAL 2:
GOAL 3:
GOAL 4:

Objective A (Goal   )
Call Roberto to make appointment. Discuss key ideas for grant. Write one page per day M through F.

What is your level of motivation to do this objective?
0 — not at all motivated   1 — somewhat motivated   2 — moderately motivated   3 — very motivated   ● 4 — completely motivated

How well does this objective match with a goal?
0 — not at all a match   1 — somewhat a match   ● 2 — moderately a match   3 — very much a match   4 — completely a match

In general, I enjoy this activity.
0 — strongly disagree   ● 1 — disagree   2 — neutral   3 — agree   4 — strongly agree

Objective B (Goal   )

What is your level of motivation to do this objective?
0 — not at all motivated   1 — somewhat motivated   2 — moderately motivated   3 — very motivated   4 — completely motivated

How well does this objective match with a goal?
0 — not at all a match   1 — somewhat a match   2 — moderately a match   3 — very much a match   4 — completely a match

In general, I enjoy this activity.
0 — strongly disagree   1 — disagree   2 — neutral   3 — agree   4 — strongly agree

Objective C (Goal   )

What is your level of motivation to do this objective?
0 — not at all motivated   1 — somewhat motivated   2 — moderately motivated   3 — very motivated   4 — completely motivated

How well does this objective match with a goal?
0 — not at all a match   1 — somewhat a match   2 — moderately a match   3 — very much a match   4 — completely a match

In general, I enjoy this activity.
0 — strongly disagree   1 — disagree   2 — neutral   3 — agree   4 — strongly agree

Lanicia's goals and objectives form.

Lanicia: It was pretty good! I made an appointment with Roberto for Wednesday. He was really helpful. So I didn't waste a lot of time trying over and over to see him.

Coach: So that was a success! Let's talk a bit about what you learned from that. Was that different from your normal way of doing things?

Lanicia: Well, I think the key was that I didn't spin my wheels waiting on something to happen and waste all my time with a roadblock.

Coach: And would that be useful in the future?

Lanicia: Hmm . . . I think it taught me that if I thought things through a little better and made a specific plan, I would save a lot of time. Oh, plus talking to Roberto made me realize that asking for help is good, and I don't have to do everything myself.

Coach: Okay. Those sound like good strategies. Making a plan and asking someone for help. We'll keep those in mind if you have roadblocks on other BSAs.

This segment illustrates that accomplishing an objective is important primarily as a way of learning lessons for the future, when the coach is no longer there. As coaches, we hope there will be many instances of specific successes for your clients: being on time for a meeting, getting an *A* on a paper, organizing a closet, or paying a bill on time. Although these are important and can build self-confidence, the key to these specific successes is to teach the clients how they accomplished these objectives and what processes they can use to accomplish other tasks in the future. In the previous segment, the coach guides Lanicia in the process of identifying what worked. There will be plenty of barriers in working on weekly objectives, and the lessons learned from successes are important building blocks.

Coach: Your other BSA for the week was to write a page a day about key ideas for your grant. How did that go?

Lanicia: Not so good. I did write one, not two pages. But that was pretty much a flop.

Coach: Tell me about it. What got in the way?

Lanicia: [*Laughs*] What didn't get in the way?! Let's see. One day my mom called and really needed me to help her with a problem with my cousin, and that got me all stressed out. One day I got a lot of things online but then started reading all this other stuff. Hmmmm. . . One day I think a lot of people just kept showing up in my office, and I didn't get anything done. I think mostly I just did my normal routine of way too much time online and getting lots of stuff, but not being able to organize it.

Coach: OK, that's a good job of figuring out what the barriers are. It sounds like organization is the key one, do you agree?

Lanicia: Definitely.

Coach: So let's do some problem solving. Do you remember the steps we talked about earlier in figuring out what to do next?

Lanicia: Um, no, I think I forgot.

Coach: OK. Let's write the steps down this week. I'll put them in your weekly Progress Notes. But to summarize, we'll do five things. One, let's come up with different ideas for how you can organize your writing. Two, we'll talk though them and decide on a good possibility. Three, we'll talk about what might get in the way of doing it that way. You should be able to use your experience this week to troubleshoot for next week. Four, we'll narrow down and be very specific about how to do it. Then we'll use that for a BSA for next week. We'll also add consequences or rewards if needed to motivate you.

This segment illustrates the way in which lack of completion of a weekly objective is turned into a learning experience. We try to avoid the terms *failure* or *problems*. Rather, we try to reframe the client's experiences as barriers that can be overcome. In our early work with coaching, clients were sometimes reluctant to admit they had not achieved their objectives. They seemed to anticipate disapproval based on their failure. By reframing their weekly actions as problem-solving opportunities, we were more likely to engage them in productive brainstorming. Although we do not emphasize the notion of failure, we do deconstruct the activity to determine what happened. To help Lanicia gain further insight, the coach has her complete the ratings on the Client Goals and Objectives form and then discuss the process (see Figure 9.3).

These ratings help the client to better understand their behaviors. The first rating (How easy was it to complete this objective?) is important in discussing motivation. For objectives that were quite difficult to complete, it is useful to understand the type of motivators that helped the client persevere. The second and third ratings (quantity and quality of completion) can be used to create weekly graphs to chart progress. These are especially helpful for younger clients, although clients of all

FIGURE 9.3

FOLLOW-UP
How easy was it to complete this objective?
Ⓞ   1   2   3   4   Not at all   Somewhat   Moderately   Very   Completely   easy   easy   easy   easy   easy
How much of this objective did you complete?
0   ①   2   3   4   None   25%   about half   75%   totally completed
Regardless of how <u>much</u> of the objective you completed, what was the <u>quality</u> of the work that you did do?
0   1   2   ③   4   Not good at all   OK   really good work
Barriers to not completing objective (check all that apply):   ___forgot, ___lack of ability or didn't know how, ✓confused about how to do it, ___fear or avoidance of task, ___just not motivated, other → _____

Lanicia's goals and objectives rating sheet.

ages can enjoy looking at a chart that plots an upward trajectory. The final rating (barriers) helps to identify exactly what got in the way of completing a BSA. As should be evident, these possible reasons would lead to quite different interventions or approaches to the next week's task. Text reminders, specific skill builders, written directions, self-confidence builders, or different rewards or consequences might be justified based on the answer to this rating.

Lanicia rated the BSA of writing a page of key grant ideas each day as *not at all easy*, with 25% completion, with a quality rating of 3 (between *OK* and *really good work*). She listed her barrier as *confused about how to do it*. The coach engaged Lanicia in a discussion of each of these areas, focusing on what Lanicia learned from the process.

> *Coach:* To summarize, you felt you did good work with what you accomplished, but you didn't do as much

Lanicia: as you had planned on and weren't sure about how to fix that.

Lanicia: Yes, that pretty much sums it up. I definitely need a new way of doing this writing.

Coach: Was your consequence of ironing helpful?

Lanicia: Ha! It motivated me to *want* to write, but I just wasn't good at getting it done. I did iron one night though, so that was helpful on its own!

Coach: So it sounds like the motivator is not the issue so much. But you might need to figure out a better strategy for doing the writing.

Lanicia: Definitely.

In this segment, we identify possible reasons for not accomplishing goals. Helping the client to analyze the process is key in determining where to go next. A coach might be tempted to ask a client what went wrong and what the client thinks he or she should do differently. This approach is often too vague. Many clients will struggle to identify specific ideas. By teaching clients to dissect their past performance, new strategies are more likely to emerge.

The coach engaged Lanicia in a brief strategizing session, being careful to allow her to make the resulting idea her own. Again, the coach may have some ideas about effective writing and organizing, and it's fine to make suggestions. However, the ultimate plan needs to be something that works for the client, regardless of whether the coach thinks it will be effective. If the plan does not work out, that will emerge in succeeding weeks, and the coach can continue to work with the client on modifications. The more involvement the client has in creating the plan, the greater the likelihood of success.

For specific strategies to help clients write more effectively, you might select some of your favorite online writing tools.

Coach: Okay, I think we ought to write down the steps you've come up with.

Lanicia: Good, I want to get a whiteboard and put this over my desk at work.

Exhibit 9.2 is the outcome of Lanicia's discussion with her coach on creating a writing plan. Lanicia was able to come up with a plan, based on her barriers of the previous week. She was able to create specific steps, which the coach detailed in a weekly progress note (see Figure 9.4). These notes can be helpful in dealing with memory issues that many clients encounter. You can use these notes or keep a binder with copies of the client's long-term goals, rewards and consequences

EXHIBIT 9.2

Lanicia's Plan for Efficient Writing

- Pick one key point from list generated with Roberto.
- Select one prior grant. Briefly skim grant looking just for key points.
- Record areas that need literature review. Flag no more than five areas.
- Identify no more than 10 key terms.
- Go online using 10 search terms.
- Make a chart. Cross off terms as you find them.
- Decide within 2 minutes if an article is relevant by skimming abstract.
- If an article is relevant, put key terms onto separate chart.
- Stop after 1 hour to take 10-minute snack or exercise break.

FIGURE 9.4

Progress Note

Session 2   09/10/2013   Coach: Frances Prevatt

Lanicia is a 32-year-old African American woman, with a master's degree in biology, employed as a research assistant working on genetics research and writing grants. She reported difficulties with her work, especially in the area of writing, timeliness, and organization. Additionally, she reported sleep difficulties and issues with financial management. Lanicia has a diagnosis of ADHD but has never been on medication. She has not disclosed her ADHD diagnosis to her supervisor.

<u>Long-Term Goals</u>

- Organize proposals and move through the process; avoid getting stuck at idea stage.
- Work on healthy sleep habits
- Self-disclose ADHD to supervisor

<u>Prior Week Progress</u>

Progress Toward Last Week's Objectives:

- Objective A: Lanicia completed the objective of scheduling an appointment and meeting with Roberto.
- Objective B: Lanicia wrote two pages out of her goal of five pages.

Weekly Successes and What Contributed to Successes:

- Lanicia found that having a plan helped her to avoid wasting time.
- Lanicia found that asking for help was very beneficial.

Obstacles:

- Lanicia encountered numerous obstacles with regard to writing.
- Lanicia decided that her lack of a system for writing was her greatest obstacle.

Progress note for Lanicia.

list, and ongoing weekly objective pages for the client to bring home each week. Another option is to use a cloud-based document-sharing program for clients who might lose papers or prefer to see everything on screen (just be sure the program is compliant with Health Insurance Portability and Accountability Act regulations).

In subsequent sessions, a similar process is used: check on progress from the previous week, build on successes, identify barriers, and use problem solving to modify the plan. When a goal has been accomplished, the client can start to work on a new goal. Often, clients will be working on more than one goal simultaneously. This depends on the complexity of each goal, the difficulty in accomplishing weekly objectives, and whether the goals are highly related. For example, Lanicia's goal of improving her sleep routines was highly related to her goal of being more effective during the day with her writing, so we chose to work on those simultaneously. In addition, she was not comfortable working on her goal of self-disclosing her ADHD status to her supervisor until she had completed her objectives involving her work performance.

Figure 9.4 shows a weekly progress note for Lanicia. The background section remains the same in each note. Normally, the long-term goals also remain stable; however, some clients complete all long-term goals before the end of the 8 weeks and select new goals to work on. Alternatively, some clients decide to change their long-term goals after gaining insight into their areas of difficulty. The progress notes detail the successes and barriers encountered in meeting the previous week's objectives and then document the plan for the upcoming week.

FINAL SESSIONS

Although not a necessary component of coaching, you may want to consider using some inventories as a postmeasure of success for coaching clients. This could depend on time, the client's willingness to do so, whether a client really "completes" coaching or impulsively quits, and a number of other factors.

Before her final session, the coach had Lanicia once again complete the BDEFS, CSC, CTS, OQ–45, and Rosenberg Self-Esteem Scale. Her ratings had improved on the BDEFS for self-management to time, self-organization and problem solving, and self-motivation. Her scores had not changed significantly on self-restraint or self-regulation of emotions; however, these had not been problematic initially. She showed less anxiety and depression on the CSC, and her CTS showed substantial improvement on the areas she had concentrated on in coaching (time management, organization, long-term assignments, planning and decision making, solving problems, waking up, staying up, getting to bed, and understanding and explaining ADHD to others). Her OQ–45 showed improvement in overall distress, and her Rosenberg Scale showed improvement in her self-esteem. The coach summarized these results and reviewed the progress notes and charts created from the Client Goals and Objectives form. These documents provided a basis for discussing Lanicia's progress in coaching. The coach then asked Lanicia for her opinion of coaching.

Coach: Tell me how you think you have changed as a result of coaching.

Lanicia: I think I mainly learned that I can do a lot of this stuff on my own. The weekly accountability was great.

Coach: Do you think you will continue on your own without the accountability?

Lanicia: I think so, yes. Those charts were sometimes a bit of a pain, but looking back, I think they really taught me how to think about my problems in a different way. I'm not nearly as likely to get stressed out or give up and say, "Oh, I just can't do that." I really like the rewards and consequences too. It took me a while to get the hang of that. And it takes a lot of willpower! I think it helped me more to reward myself with breaks rather than to force myself to do something I didn't want to do, and no one was making me do.

Coach: What did you learn about yourself?

Lanicia: I think I have more respect for myself. I'm really pretty good at a lot of things, and maybe I won't get down on myself so much now. I'm glad I made the decision not to take medication. I know you are kind of fond of that, and I understand why. But with my job it just makes me nervous, and I'm pretty sure I can manage without it.

Coach: What do you think will be your biggest barrier in the future?

Lanicia: Well, I've gotten better at it but probably still a tendency to get down on myself, not believe in myself.

Coach: And what do you think you can do now about that?

> *Lanicia:* Just stick it out. Maybe make up a list of my good points! I can't believe I'm becoming such a list maker!

These are just some of the questions that can be used in the final session to elicit further summarization and forward thinking from your client. Like many coaching clients, Lanicia was motivated, intelligent, articulate, hardworking, and insightful—she just needed her coach's help to bring these qualities to the surface. She did not have serious comorbid disorders, which invariably slow down potential progress in coaching. Although she identified a number of areas of difficulty, it appears she developed some core organizational, time management, and problem-solving skills that will allow her to cope more effectively on her own.

Summary

1. In the initial assessment, the client may need to complete standardized self-report forms.
2. The coach uses the assessment information to develop working hypotheses, as well as questions for the intake interview.
3. During the intake, the coach evaluates the client for potential mental health issues, as well as motivation to participate in coaching.
4. The CTS is combined with detailed interviewing to develop three or four long-term goals.
5. Collaboration involves a careful balance of giving suggestions while allowing clients to "own" their goals.
6. The BDEFS can be helpful in identifying areas to pursue as weekly objectives.
7. One strategy for breaking an objective into steps is to visualize a natural timeline. This helps develop skills in prioritizing and sequencing.
8. The coach will help the client focus by blocking them from impulsively jumping from one topic to another.
9. What might be a good solution for the coach may not necessarily be effective for the client.
10. The coach does not need to be an expert in all content areas.
11. Rewards, consequences, or the absence of consequences can serve as motivators.
12. Between-session texts or e-mails can be used, at the discretion of the coach, as reminders and motivators.

13. Although task completion is important, learning the processes involved in successful task completion is critical to future coping.
14. The coach avoids discussion of failures; rather, the coach focuses on how barriers can be overcome and problem solving can lead to success.
15. The ratings on the Client Goals and Objectives form can be used to evaluate client progress and to modify objectives.
16. Progress Notes can be used to help clients remember specific steps in a weekly task, and to motivate task completion.
17. At the conclusion of coaching, posttest measures can be used to evaluate client progress.
18. Standard questions at the conclusion of coaching help the client to gain additional insight into the lessons they have learned.

Case Study 10
ADHD Coaching With a College Student With Executive Functioning Deficits

This chapter illustrates how to work with college students who are adjusting to the demands of independent academic life. College students in general tend to have difficulties with time management and organization, and this can be exacerbated for students with attention-deficit/hyperactivity disorder (ADHD) who also have executive functioning (EF) deficits. In addition, many younger students with ADHD have relied heavily on their parents to keep them structured and on task, and they may struggle further without this help.

Trey was a second-semester freshman with an undeclared major. His academic dean referred him for an evaluation for possible ADHD after Trey was put on academic probation at the end of his first semester. Trey's GPA had fallen below a 2.0 out of 4.0, which automatically resulted in probation; he had one semester to bring up his grades. After being put on probation, Trey underwent a psychoeducational evaluation and subsequently received a diagnosis of ADHD, combined type. He then entered a coaching program for 8 weeks. He was not

---

http://dx.doi.org/10.1037/14671-011
ADHD Coaching: A Guide for Mental Health Professionals, by F. Prevatt and A. Levrini
Copyright © 2015 by the American Psychological Association. All rights reserved.

on medication at the time of coaching and was unsure as to whether he wanted to pursue that option. Trey was hoping to raise his GPA enough to pursue a major in political science and international affairs.

Trey reported that he had done moderately well in high school but was unprepared for the rigors of college. During his first semester, he admitted to "going a little wild" with his newfound freedom. His parents had been quite strict during high school; they had made driving, going out with friends, and receiving an allowance contingent on keeping up his grades. Without that structure and supervision, his first semester at college, Trey had spent a great deal of time with friends, missed many classes, waited too late to study, and failed to do as well as he thought he was capable of doing. He did not keep a planner, procrastinated when papers were due, and received poor grades on final exams. Trey reported being shocked and overwhelmed by how quickly the semester had gone by. By the time he realized how much trouble he was in, he had no idea how to recover. His parents were understanding yet firm; if he did not improve his grades, they would discontinue supporting him financially, and he would need to find a job and live on his own until he could raise enough money to resume college.

Case in Action: Beginning, Middle, and End

INITIAL ASSESSMENT

Trey had been formerly assessed and diagnosed with ADHD a month before beginning coaching. To gain some additional information, his coach had Trey complete the Application for Services, Academic Success Inventory for College Students (ASICS), Barkley Deficits in Executive Functioning Scale (BDEFS), Client Symptom Checklist (CSC), Coaching Topics Survey (CTS), Outcome Questionnaire—45 (OQ–45), and the Rosenberg Self-Esteem Scale (refer to Chapters 4 and 5 for a summary of these measures). The coach reviewed all of these measures and developed the following working hypotheses and questions.

1. Based on his ASICS profile (see Table 10.1), Trey had some gaps in his basic academic skills. He had a difficult time concentrating both in class and on homework and did not see a connection between his current coursework and his future goals. His grades had suffered because of insufficient studying, primarily because he had spent a great deal of time socializing with friends.
2. Trey exhibited only a mild amount of anxiety and depression, and his self-esteem was in the normal range (CSC, OQ–45, Rosenberg

TABLE 10.1

Trey's Responses on the Academic Success Inventory for College Students

Domain	Trey's score	25th percentile cutoff	X indicates score is < cutoff
Academic skills	33	45	X
Internal motivation/confidence	77	45	
Instructor efficacy	77	46	
Concentration	21	29	X
External motivation future	33	36	X
Socializing	48	57	X
Career decidedness	100	57	
Anxiety	48	29	
Personal adjustment	53	43	
External motivation current	90	52	

Scale). Although he had experienced recent setbacks, he had a healthy view of his abilities and believed he could improve his academic record.

3. Trey's overall level of distress was moderate, especially with regard to schoolwork. It appeared that he was highly motivated to make some changes (OQ–45).
4. Trey's primary executive functioning deficit areas were self-management to time and self-organization/problem solving. He also seemed to have difficulties with self-motivation. Self-restraint and regulating his emotions did not appear to be problematic (BDEFS).
5. Trey's areas of concern centered on time management, organization, and study skills (CTS).

With these tentative working hypotheses in mind, the coach conducted the initial intake interview.

BEGINNING SESSIONS

Although Trey had struggled in high school, he had much support from his parents and teachers, and his symptoms had not been significantly impairing until college. Therefore, his first coaching session began somewhat differently from how it would for someone who had been aware of an ADHD diagnosis for many years. Trey appeared tired and looked as though he had just gotten out of bed. He appeared a little standoffish as he shook his coach's hand and settled quietly into his chair.

Coach: I see from your records that you had a pretty good GPA in high school. How do you think you were *able to do that? What difficulties did you have to overcome?*

Trey: I really worked hard, partly because I didn't have a choice. I'm an only child. My mom doesn't work, and my dad is pretty strict, so they were on me a lot to make sure I got things done. I played soccer all through high school, and I think that really helped to get rid of some of my energy. Plus, between that and my parents, I just didn't have time to get into trouble.

Coach: So you had a good support system, and athletics is a great way to learn discipline, engage your mind, and burn off energy. What about your actual study skills? Were there things you did that were particularly helpful?

Trey: Well, compared with college, most of my high school classes had lots of homework and projects. Everything didn't depend on a final exam. So I had lots of time to get things done. My mom pretty much made me do things on time.

Coach: Did you have a planner?

Trey: Yes, my mom! She knew everything that was going on and talked to my teachers all the time.

Trey is a classic example of the type of student we often see in the college setting. Strong support from parents or teachers serves as a built-in executive function system for a student with ADHD. Do you forget your books? Do you have a tendency to procrastinate on that assignment? Are you unable to get out of bed in the morning or make it to school on time? It's often not seen as a "problem" if mom or dad takes care of it. This is a double-edged sword for students with ADHD. The positive side is that these students do relatively well in school, do enough work to really benefit from their classes, make good enough grades to get into college, and develop some good study habits. The drawback is that they sometimes have not learned how to motivate themselves or structure their lives when on their own. In particular, the executive function area of time management is often lacking. To evaluate this, the coach began the session with Trey by getting a good picture of how he had been used to functioning academically, what had worked for him, and how that changed when he began college.

Coach: Let's take a look at your BDEFS ratings. I see that you marked *very often* for *procrastinates, wastes time, not prepared for tasks,* and *not meeting deadlines.* Were those things a problem for you last semester?

Trey: Oh, definitely. Like I said, most of my classes had a final paper or final exam, and everything just came at once and I wasn't at all ready. I did terrible on finals. One paper in my English class I started about 2 a.m. the morning before it was due. It was horrible.

Coach: We know that poor time management is one of the primary areas of difficulty for someone with ADHD. And it's especially hard if you're in school or at a job where you have deadlines. And it's even harder if you're suddenly in a situation where you don't have much structure and you're not used to having to set and monitor your own time. Imagine if you were in the military at boot camp. You'd have no choice about when to get up or when to do a task. But this year you've had to get used to doing that on your own.

Trey: Great! [*Laughing*] So are you going to become my new drill instructor?

Coach: Well, actually, no. But I am planning to help you figure out how to get that drill instructor to operate inside your own head.

Trey: Okay, fair enough.

In this section, the coach provided some education about ADHD and EF. Because Trey has only recently been diagnosed, he was not familiar with some of the ramifications of having ADHD. Recall from Chapter 6 that we like to use metaphors in coaching when possible, and Trey seems to understand the concept of a drill instructor in his brain. The coach goes on to discuss some of the other findings from the BDEFS and asks Trey for specific examples that elaborate on his self-report responses.

In the following section, we will see how the coach emphasizes areas in which Trey appears to have adequate or good EF, such as emotional regulation.

Coach: Here are some things our drill instructor won't have to work on. I see you marked *never or rarely* for things such as *getting angry, remaining upset,* or *unable to calm yourself down.*

Trey: Yeah, I think that's not a problem. Maybe playing soccer helped with that. I was constantly getting kicked or knocked down. Lots of times I knew it was guys trying to psych me out. If they could really get to me and make me mad, I'd probably get called for

>
> a foul or do some stupid play. My dad helped with that too. He was pretty much a "take your medicine and deal with it" kind of guy.
>
> Coach: Great, so we can check that off our list right away.

It's important to identify both strengths and weaknesses to help clients see a bigger picture and to build on things they already do well. Trey had relatively good self-esteem. However, some clients with ADHD have had many years of negative experiences and fully believe they are "stupid, lazy, or crazy" (Kelly & Ramundo, 2006). It can be useful in the early sessions to identify coping techniques, find out what clients have done well, and give them some positive feedback. This helps with initial motivation and the belief that they can make changes.

The coach may use specific examples from some or all of the pre-coaching paperwork. Some coaches prefer to generate hypotheses from this paperwork but not refer to it in sessions, instead using the interview to elicit information directly from clients. Other coaches go over the BDEFS and other paperwork in detail to specify EF deficits. In the case of college students, the ASICS can be especially important. The ASICS was developed to simultaneously evaluate social, cognitive, and interpersonal variables that are correlated with academic success. The 10 subscales are highly predictive of student's GPA (Prevatt, Li, et al., 2011). Trey's ASICS is shown in Table 10.1. The norms for the ASICS are based on college students and show areas in which the ratings are below 75% of the normative group. The areas marked by an X in Table 10.1 show that Trey had low functioning in four areas.

> Coach: Your answers on the ASICS really confirm some things you've already talked about. One is that you spent a little too much time partying and going out with friends. The other is that you had difficulty concentrating, which is, of course, one of the primary symptoms of ADHD. So no surprises there. But let's look at this scale called Academic Skills. You marked *almost never* for setting homework goals, being organized, studying the correct material for tests, and using organizers such as planners or calendars. I think that gives us a little more detail about what specifically tripped you up in school.
>
> Trey: Whoa. That sounds bad. But it's true... all those things.
>
> Coach: One of the most important things about coaching is to have the strength to face up to some things that sound unpleasant, own them, and then figure out a

	plan for overcoming them. Do you know what the word *denial* means?
Trey:	Yeah. I think so. It's kind of like just pretending something's not true when it really is.
Coach:	Exactly. And people use it all the time. It makes them feel much better! But can you figure out what's not so good about denial?
Trey:	Well, like you said, you feel better, but then you don't do anything to change.
Coach:	Sure. So by identifying and admitting to some of your issues with school, you have the opportunity to change them. All we need to add are some specific strategies and some motivation.
Trey:	Piece of cake. [*A bit sarcastically, but laughing*]

The ASICS can be useful in relating EF deficits specifically to an academic environment. Trey was a remarkably insightful client, and he made it easy to identify specific areas for improvement; sometimes clients are not so forthcoming. However, by using a combination of self-reports, parent reports, interview, and history, the coach is able to develop a good picture of the client's specific strengths and weaknesses. Some coaching programs (particularly group programs) are more structured, with specific activities or content areas discussed each week. These can be useful because the areas covered are quite representative of areas that are important for individuals with ADHD. However, individual coaching is most successful when a general framework is used but tailored to the specific needs of the client.

When using the ASICS, the final step is to compare these findings with the areas marked on the CTS. In Trey's case, this is quite consistent: He has marked that he needs to work on the following areas:

- improving time management,
- establishing routines and good habits,
- organizing school or work,
- organizing personal space,
- getting to class on time,
- studying,
- keeping track of things, and
- paying attention.

These areas were pulled together by the end of the first session to create some long-term goals for Trey. First, however, because Trey was so new to his diagnosis, the coach offered psychoeducation regarding ADHD and EF. See the first section of Chapter 6 for a comprehensive list of ideas for helping clients better understand their disorder.

Psychoeducation

Coach: Before we decide the major areas you want to work on, let's spend a couple of minutes understanding why you might be having difficulties and why I think we'll be able to make some changes. I'm going to give you a short description of something we call executive functioning. Have you ever heard of that before?

Trey: No, I don't think so.

Coach: Later in our work together, we might be using some exercises from a workbook (Tuckman, 2012) about executive functioning. I'll tell you how it's described in the workbook, and you can see if that might make sense for you. Dr. Tuckman, the author of the workbook, believes that there are some important things most adults have to do every day. These include holding memories in your head while you figure out what to do, thinking about the time that is going to pass and making plans to get things done on time, reminding yourself to do things, making yourself get started on tasks, and using your past to plan and change how you do things in the future. Are you with me so far?

Trey: Yes, kind of like an internal drill instructor?

Coach: Right! Executive functions are those things that happen in our brains that let us do all those things on a day-to-day basis without really thinking about them. Are you aware, most days, of actually thinking about those things? For example, when you came here today, did you have a plan that you thought out for how long it was going to take and remind yourself when you needed to start getting ready? And did you relate that information to the first time you came to ALEC and parking was a problem?

Trey: Uh, no, not really. I don't really think I thought about all that.

Coach: Well, that's normal. Most of those things go on automatically, because you've learned over time to think that way. That's the executive functioning part of your brain. Dr. Tuckman goes on to say that adults without ADHD are better at acting automatically because their brain takes tiny pauses all the time. During these tiny pauses, the brain is saying to itself, "Wait, think, focus." Or maybe the brain is saying, "Ignore those two people talking, just keep reading."

>
> Or the brain is saying, "We've got 10 minutes to walk to the office, we'd better not stop and get a cup of coffee now." The brain is constantly pausing to make these little adjustments. But adults with ADHD tend to have brains that don't always pause. Does that make sense? Any questions?
>
> Trey: No, I'm still with you. So maybe when my brain should be pausing it's just going straight to the finish and not listening to anything? [*The coach goes on to give some additional information about EF.*]
>
> Coach: Okay, so to pull it all together, you and I are going to come up with some goals. Given what we've already discussed, I think some of your goals are going to be related to executive functioning. So we're going to come up with some strategies to help you remind yourself to pause or to create situations where it doesn't matter if you don't pause.

To help Trey better understand and identify the specific EF tasks he needed to address and how much of an impact they were making, the coach decided to have him depict his EF struggles by creating an ADHD Life Wheel (see Chapter 6). Trey rated and marked how satisfied he felt in each area of EF on a scale from 0 to 10 and then drew lines connecting each area. Figure 10.1 depicts Trey's completed wheel.

> Trey: Wow, I really see now how much room for improvement I have. That's one tiny pizza worth of executive function.
>
> Coach: [*Laughs*] It is. But I like how you said that—it just means there is a lot of room for improvement.

The coach may engage in many areas in psychoeducation with the client. This will vary somewhat depending on how long it has been since the client's diagnosis (although it is never safe to assume that a client with a long-standing diagnosis is well versed in factual information). Common areas that require some psychoeducation involve the biology and etiology of ADHD, common areas of difficulty, medication, and self-advocacy. Although a lot of this conversation can happen in the beginning stages of coaching, it is also important to give your client small segments throughout coaching to highlight different concepts. As can be seen in the previous section, the coach was careful not to make this sound like a lecture. She paused frequently to make sure Trey was following and used creative techniques to make it more interesting and engaging. The continued use of the drill instructor metaphor was helpful in that Trey could continually relate to this in a way that became more personal to him—make sure you pay attention to images or ideas that

FIGURE 10.1

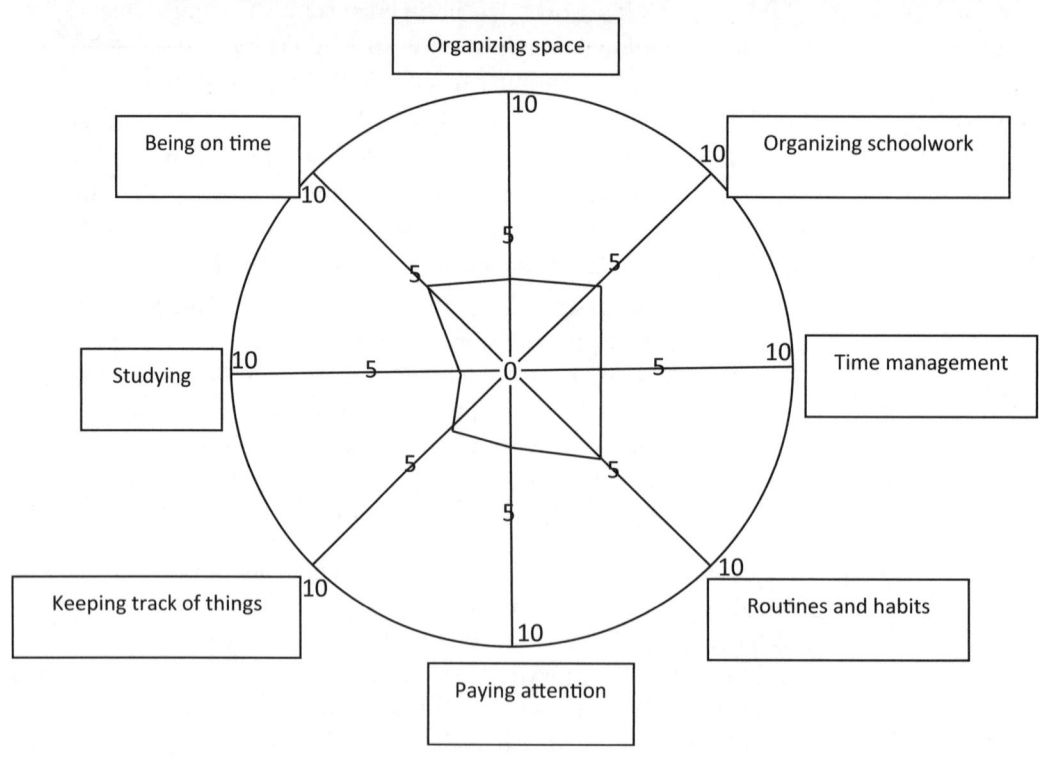

Trey's completed ADHD Life Wheel.

seem to resonate with your clients. See Chapter 6 on specific strategies for ADHD coaching as well as the list of resources on psychoeducation and executive function that concludes that chapter.

Creating Long-Term Goals

Because the coach had spent a great deal of time during intake going over the BDEFS, ASICS, and CTS, when it was time to create long-term goals, the areas in which Trey was having the most difficulty were already fairly apparent. Specific details on how to create long-term goals are given in other case study chapters. For example, recall that in Chapter 9 (Lanicia's case study), we discussed giving encouragement to clients before they begin to plan their goals, as well as giving specific examples of what a goal should entail. It is important that clients feel ownership of their goals. After going through the problem-solving process with Trey, he decided on three long-term goals (see Exhibit 10.1).

> **EXHIBIT 10.1**
>
> **Trey's Long-Term Goals**
>
> **GOAL 1:** Become a more punctual person and arrive on time for 90% of scheduled classes, appointments, and activities this semester.
>
> **GOAL 2:** Complete all course assignments at least 5 days in advance this semester.
>
> **GOAL 3:** Utilize homework and study time more efficiently this semester by creating weekly schedules and deadlines.

Trey's long-term goals were all highly interconnected, which was helpful. His successes on one goal would directly affect the other two. All were also directly related to his referral issue of having been put on academic probation. As such, he was highly motivated to achieve these goals to earn As and Bs in his classes. From an EF perspective, his goals were likely going to be most affected by difficulties in time management, organization, and motivation. Let's move now to the middle sessions where the coach works on weekly objectives and try to tie those objectives to specific EF skills.

MIDDLE SESSIONS

As a reminder, the middle sessions of coaching involve (a) working through the long-term goals with weekly objectives (between-session assignments); (b) identifying weekly successes and using those to define strengths and coping mechanisms that can be generalized to other tasks; (c) identifying barriers that can be overcome with the problem-solving approach; (d) using rewards and consequences to keep clients motivated; (e) helping clients develop specific skills and strategies; and (f) helping clients reach the point where they can do these tasks on their own, without the help of a coach. Also, recall that the coach uses the weekly Client Goals and Objectives form throughout the process, emphasizing a collaborative approach with the client to determine a weekly objective and then discusses potential barriers and solutions. Together, the coach and client create consequences or rewards, and the client analyzes his or her motivation to complete the objective. Clients use the ratings on the weekly Goals and Objectives form to help them understand their behaviors, both before and after attempting the weekly objective. Weekly written progress notes can help the coach and client remember their plan. After attempting the week's objectives, the coach and client evaluate the attempt using a problem-solving approach. The client is able to learn from both successes and failures as he or she determines the next week's objectives.

On the basis of his three long-term objectives (punctuality, completing assignments, more efficient studying and work completion), Trey developed 17 weekly objectives over the course of the 8-week coaching program. Rather than just pick out one or two, as was done in some of the other case study chapters, the following is a look at an entire coaching program's worth of Trey's Weekly Objectives. Table 10.2 summarizes his weekly objectives, as well as his corresponding reward or consequence.

An examination of Trey's objectives reveals that many of them were directly related to his EF goals. Many dealt with time management (create a study schedule, make a weekly plan, track time in journal, leave home earlier). Others involved problem solving (decide on a planner, make a decision about spring break), and still others involved organizational skills (organize the room, use a planner and whiteboard, use list). Many of Trey's objectives actually improved his abilities (writing class, learning how to do literature searches, join a study group, consider medication). Some changed his strategies (timers, lists, whiteboards, online planner). Finally, Trey altered the situation when he decided to join a soccer team because this allowed him to use his excess energy to his advantage.

Using Rewards and Consequences With Weekly Objectives

Initially, Trey chose not to use an incentive for his weekly objectives because he thought he would not need one. You should encourage clients to try incentives, but if they can manage without them, that is a successful solution. It is best to leave this decision up to them and handle it during the weekly discussion of barriers and subsequent problem solving. If clients are not able to accomplish their objectives without incentives, they generally come to their own conclusion that more motivation is needed. Trey was quite motivated in the beginning and did not use incentives for the first 2 weeks. However, after some initial successes, his weekly objectives became more tedious, and he began implementing incentives going into the fourth week.

Some clients prefer to set an incentive for every objective, and some prefer only one incentive, regardless of the number of objectives. Again, leave these decisions up to the client. Keep in mind that one of the general rules of coaching is that the solutions have to work for the client, not for the coach. Trey preferred a single reward or consequence because he thought tracking too many things was more confusing than helpful. He tended to use rewards rather than consequences but acknowledged that consequences (cleaning the bathroom) could be motivating because even if he failed to meet his objective, he achieved something positive with his self-imposed "punishment."

TABLE 10.2

Trey's Weekly Objectives

Week	Objective	Reward or consequence
2	Decide whether to use a paper planner or an online planner. After making a decision, either buy the planner or figure out how to use the online planner. Write assignments and tests for the spring semester into the planner.	None. Trey thought that this activity was so motivating, he would not need any incentives.
3	Create a study schedule for classes and do this on a weekly basis. Update this every week in coaching session. Clean room so it is organized and he can find things.	Trey was happy with his progress the previous week and again thought he would not need any incentives.
4	Every Friday afternoon at 2:00, make a study plan for the week to determine in advance how much time will be left over for social activities on the weekend. Put a reminder on phone for 2:00 p.m. Friday. Track in a journal the time Trey leaves the house, how long it takes him, and whether he is late.	Watch a movie on his computer.
5	Based on journal, leave house 10 minutes earlier for each event. Join the soccer club to use up energy and help with being able to study later. Join a study group for political science class.	Clean the bathroom if he does not complete his objectives.
6	Set appointment with library assistant to learn how to search for research articles. Put a whiteboard in bedroom to supplement online planner. Write test dates and assignments on board. Attend the writing session at the university tutoring center.	Go out with friends on Friday night.
7	Try again to set appointment with library assistant to learn how to search for research articles. Use an "I HAVE TO DO THIS" list. Use a timer to study for 30 minutes, then take a 10-minute break.	Play video games on his phone for a few minutes after each 30 minutes of studying.
8	Stay in town over spring break rather than go away. Make plan for some studying, some writing, and some fun things. Make an appointment at the student health center to talk about getting on medication.	Plan several fun activities as a reward for not going away over spring break. Also, earn parent's pride in this decision is a motivator and a reward in itself.

The most difficult aspect of rewards and consequences is that they take willpower and motivation. It is certainly easy for clients to simply ignore them. Trey admitted that at times he did things (e.g., playing video games on his phone) without completing the objective (studying). Sometimes methods to automate incentives or use outside support for accountability are necessary. Some clients report that just having to report back to the coach is an ongoing incentive. Others use the inherent satisfaction of getting better grades, being more efficient at work, or pleasing parents or friends. Although there is a general belief that internal motivation is preferable to external motivation, this has not been empirically documented in the research regarding adults with ADHD. Again, we try to let the client guide this process and use the weekly problem-solving and planning time to discuss motivation and incentives. We find the process of discussing this, and letting clients discover what will work for them, to be an important product of coaching.

Overcoming Obstacles

Each week involves a discussion of barriers to meeting objectives and problem solving to determine how to overcome those barriers. Recall that the weekly Client Goals and Objectives form helps the client categorize the obstacles into the following: forgot, lack of ability, didn't know how, fear or avoidance, or not motivated. Trey encountered numerous obstacles during coaching; most of his obstacles involved lack of ability or lack of motivation. However, he was quite effective at analyzing his obstacles and using them to achieve eventual success. Many of his later objectives helped him with skill deficits (writing, studying). Other times he learned to engage in simple persistence. For example, if one week Trey failed to complete an objective (e.g., meet with the librarian), rather than give up, he would determine what went wrong and attempt it again the next week.

Going into his final week of coaching, Trey decided that although he was making good progress, he was still having difficulties with concentration. During his seventh session, Trey and the coach discussed the possibility of using medication. Many college student clients have been on medication and quit because of side effects, are currently on medication, or have recently been diagnosed and are considering medication. ADHD coaches need to have a working understanding of the issues surrounding medication.

Discussing Medication

Many clients will want to discuss the pros and cons of medication. Some believe that ADHD medication is a wonder drug and will magically cause their symptoms to disappear—that it will alleviate all their difficulties. Alternatively, others worry about possible side effects or are afraid of depending on anything other than their own "free will." Many facts associated with medication should be discussed. For example, clients can be encouraged to know that 70% of adults respond positively to a stimulant, and response rates increase to greater than 90% when nonresponders are switched to another stimulant (Wigal, 2009). However, an estimated 10% to 30% of patients have an inadequate response, cannot tolerate side effects, or have conditions for which stimulants are contraindicated (e.g., prior substance abuse, mood disturbance, comorbid tic disorders; Mohammadi & Akhondzadeh, 2007). Trey had never been on medication, and after some difficulties in meeting his weekly objective regarding studying, the subject was raised.

Trey: I'm still having a really hard time paying attention in class. I really can't go more than about 10 minutes before I get distracted or my mind starts to wander. I know I said before I didn't want to take drugs, but maybe I might want to try that.

Coach: Okay, sure. Let's talk about the pros and cons. First, it might be good to make sure you understand how medication works. Have you done any reading or talked with anyone about that?

Trey: Not really. I think you use something called Ritalin and it's a stimulant. Like caffeine or something. But I know it also calms you down so you're not so hyper.

At this point, the coach used another analogy to describe how medication works and brought up concepts such as neurotransmitters and the effect of drugs on attention, memory, concentration, and regulation of emotions. The coach might use a figure (many can be found on the Internet) to describe the function of dopamine, norepinephrine, and serotonin, as well as some basic biological terms such as *synapses*, *receptors*, and *reuptake*. The level of complexity will depend on the particular client; however, we have found that many clients are quite interested in knowing the science behind the medications they might be taking. Other aspects of psychoeducation, such as nutrition, can also be useful.

Coach: Nutrition can also play an important role in all of this. Some experts believe that you can make your own dopamine by eating foods high in protein, such as fish, meat, dairy, soybeans, or nuts (e.g., Monastra, 2014). If you do this first thing it the morning, then your system can be making its own dopamine, which can help you get through the day. What do you usually eat for breakfast?

Trey: Well, usually I don't. I'm usually running late and might just wait and have something at lunch.

Coach: That's likely to cause you to crash in the early afternoon and have an even harder time concentrating.

There are many ways to discuss medication with a client. As with any complicated information that you give to clients with ADHD, it is helpful to keep it short, use a handout or drawing, make it less like a lecture and more like a story, allow time for questions, make sure they are following you, and have it written down as a backup so they can refer to it later. A common belief among clients is that medication will work well and will work immediately. Always caution them that not everyone responds the same way to the same drug.

FINAL SESSIONS

Before his final session, the coach had Trey once again complete the BDEFS, ASICS, CSC, CTS, OQ–45, and the Rosenberg Self-Esteem Scale. His ratings had improved on the BDEFS for self-management to time, self-organization/problem solving, and self-motivation. He did not show significant change in self-restraint or self-regulation of emotions; however, these had not been problematic at the start of coaching. Trey did not show significant change in anxiety and depression on the CSC, but again, these had not been problematic for him. Trey's CTS showed substantial improvement in the areas he had concentrated on in coaching (time management, getting to class on time, organization of school and personal space, and study). He did not show improvement in keeping track of things; however, this had not been a focus of his weekly objectives.

Trey's OQ–45 showed slight improvement in overall distress, and his Rosenberg Scale score showed slight but nonsignificant improvement in his self-esteem. The coach summarized these results and reviewed the progress notes and charts created from the weekly client Goals and Objectives form. These documents provided a basis for discussing Trey's progress in coaching. Trey also drew another ADHD Life Wheel to illustrate how much the "size of his slice of pizza" had grown—or, in other words, how much his executive skill set had improved. The coach then asked Trey for his opinion of the coaching.

Coach: Tell me how you think you changed as a result of coaching.

Trey: I think the best thing was just realizing that I could do some things on my own. I really didn't like doing those forms every week, but at the end it really changed how I thought about things.

Coach: In what way did your thinking change?

Trey: It's hard to put into words, but I think I sort of get now that my mom and dad were pretty much responsible for getting me through high school. But now I think I can do what they did. I can do it myself. But I'm still sort of worried that without coming in here every week and writing out my schedule with you, I won't be so good at this.

Coach: That's a reasonable fear. So, let me list some things about you that I think have changed. One, I think you are good at looking at what goes wrong and turning that into a plan for how to make it go right. Two, I think you figured out that you don't have to do it all yourself, and you know you can get help from tutors, friends, doctors, or librarians. And three, I think you have good motivation, which is actually kind of rare, and that will really help you to keep at this. And you know, you can always come back in again for some booster sessions if that drill instructor in your head slacks off. Anything you want to add to that list?

Trey: Okay, you're right. That's all good. Can you put that in my note [*i.e., progress note*] this week? I'm definitely going to read that one!

Summary

1. Behaviors that are problematic in individuals with EF deficits include self-management of time, self-organization and problem solving, self-restraint, self-motivation, and self-regulation of emotions.
2. The BDEFS is a self-report checklist that measures a large number of specific behaviors. A subset of those behaviors has been shown empirically to be especially characteristic of college students.
3. EF skills are particularly necessary to deal with the academic demands of college.
4. The initial assessment information can be used to develop hypotheses that use an EF framework.
5. Having supportive parents can be a double-edged sword for a student.

6. A single metaphor can be used throughout coaching to tie the session together and help the client understand and remember difficult concepts.
7. It can be useful in the early sessions to identify coping techniques, find out what clients have done well, and give them some positive feedback. This helps with initial motivation and the belief that they can make changes.
8. The ASICS subscales are highly predictive of student's GPA and can be used to identify areas of both strength and weakness.
9. Psychoeducation can be needed in a variety of areas; EF and medication are two of those areas that may need to be discussed with college students.
10. Psychoeducation is more effective if done in small segments at a time, if it does not sound like a lecture, and if handouts or written reminders are used.
11. EF deficits can be changed by improving one's abilities, using different strategies, or altering one's situation.
12. Weekly objectives can be paired with an incentive, which can be a reward or a consequence.
13. Weekly problem solving is used to discuss obstacles and make plans to overcome the obstacles and turn them into successes.
14. Many college students will benefit from a discussion of the pros and cons of medication.

Case Study 11
ADHD Coaching With a Young Adult With Comorbid Mood Disorders

This chapter illustrates how to work with clients with mood conditions, such as anxiety and depression, that commonly co-occur with attention-deficit/hyperactivity disorder (ADHD). More individuals with ADHD have a comorbidity than do not, and striking a balance in treating all issues simultaneously can sometimes be tricky (Larson, Russ, Kahn, & Halfon, 2011). In the following pages, we outline how to approach these dual-diagnosis cases.

The client is a female master's-level student who is experiencing academic failures and school avoidance as a result of her ADHD and performance anxiety. Audrey demonstrates how an ADHD dual diagnosis can be a complex, "chicken and egg" situation requiring the practitioner to sort out which disorder is causing what behavior, whether the ADHD symptoms have caused the mood disorder, or whether the two are interdependent. Audrey, now 25 years old, was diagnosed with ADHD (inattentive presentation) as an undergraduate at age 20. After pulling

---

http://dx.doi.org/10.1037/14671-012
ADHD Coaching: A Guide for Mental Health Professionals, by F. Prevatt and A. Levrini
Copyright © 2015 by the American Psychological Association. All rights reserved.

countless all-nighters just to graduate with a 3.0 GPA, she struggled with depression off and on, and took a few years off from academia before applying to graduate programs. Audrey felt ready, but the fast pace and demanding assignments of graduate school caused her confidence to waiver, and she eventually fell behind in her coursework. In the mornings, she gets ready for class, then some days suffers from panic attacks and refuses to leave her home. Unable to attend several of her classes, Audrey has fallen even further behind. She doesn't want to lose this opportunity and knows she will enjoy her career, once she can get through school.

In some cases, a client may come to you with an ADHD diagnosis from a previous doctor or clinician. When there is a clear indication of a mood disorder as well, it is important that you take the previous diagnosis into account but also keep in mind how the professional arrived at his or her conclusion and whether further investigation is needed. Sometimes what appears to be ADHD because of a client's difficulty concentrating, lack of motivation, impaired working memory, or other common ADHD symptom is actually a result of depressed or anxious mood. If you have any questions as to the true nature of your client's dysfunction (whether it is truly an executive functioning deficit resulting from ADHD or rather a mood disorder that is clouding his or her ability to think clearly), refer the client to someone who specializes in this type of psychological testing. As practice experts, we can sometimes be limited in terms of uncovering the true nature of a diagnosis, so do not hesitate to enlist a colleague if you are unsure whether your client's ADHD symptoms could not be better explained by another mental health disorder.

Audrey had undergone rigorous testing, and after reviewing her report, her coach felt confident that the previous practitioner had been thorough and that both ADHD and coexisting mood conditions were present. As a result of his diagnostic interview and assessments, the previous clinician had surmised that Audrey's anxiety and depression were largely a result of her struggles with ADHD. During the time she took off from school, Audrey saw a psychologist for talk therapy twice a week for over 2 years. Through this experience, she felt she had gained a better understanding of the ways in which her failures had affected her mental health and learned some methods to fight her negative thoughts. However, after some time, she felt that until she learned some new behaviors to overcome areas of weakness, she would continue to struggle with her confidence and self-esteem.

As a trained therapist who is already experienced in more traditional theoretical approaches (e.g., cognitive behavior therapy [CBT], psychodynamic, client centered), it is important to know that ADHD coaching methods can often be intertwined with other approaches to provide additional relief for issues such as anxiety and depression in addition to ADHD. This is because, in terms of the model presented here, ADHD coaching is simply an offshoot of CBT. Think of it as a CBT intervention, or a model-based in cognitive behavioral principles, rather than a separate entity altogether. Many of the strategies you, as a therapist, already use in your practice can be integrated into the coaching format, and similarly, coaching interventions can be integrated into a more traditional therapeutic model. There are instances in which comorbidities may be inappropriate for a coaching setting; this includes depression or anxiety, if severe enough, even if you are a licensed therapist who is able to treat these disorders. It is up to you as a professional to know your ethical and professional limitations when it comes to treating clients with coexisting conditions and to realize when an intervention is not helping a client. Begin by assessing your client at the outset of treatment using the Client Symptom Checklist (CSC) or another depression and anxiety inventory. Also, take into consideration whether the client has had previous therapy. Finally, revisit the section on Suitability of the Client for Coaching and the section on Motivation in Chapter 3. On the basis of this information, you can decide whether the client seems ready for coaching.

Sometimes, even if clients pass the first phase of the "readiness" assessment, it becomes clear at some point that they are not on track with the ADHD coaching model because their mood disorder is overwhelming their ability to address the ADHD symptoms. If you begin to feel your client needs a different or additional approach to treatment, you have three choices:

1. Refer the client to a more appropriate practitioner and discontinue coaching.
2. Treat the client for the mood disorder yourself, but make it clear that he or she needs to take a step back from coaching or take a different approach in dealing with some issues in coaching.
3. Continue to coach the client for particular goals while he or she receives therapy from a colleague to work on concerns related to the mood disorder.

To help make this decision, keep in mind Standard 2.01 of the APA "Ethical Principles of Psychologists and Code of Conduct," which addresses Boundaries of Competence: "Psychologists provide services, teach and conduct research with populations and in areas only within the boundaries of their competence, based on their education, training, supervised experience, consultation, study or professional experience" (APA, 2010).

Case in Action: Beginning, Middle, and End

INITIAL ASSESSMENT

Audrey had previously undergone rigorous psychological testing to identify her specific mental health concerns. She was given the following *International Classification of Diseases, 10th Revision*, diagnoses:

- F90.0 ADHD, predominately inattentive presentation
- F41.1 Generalized anxiety disorder, with expected panic attacks (in school setting)
- F34.1 Persistent depressive disorder, mild severity, with early onset, with pure dysthymic syndrome

Because she had already been assessed, the coach decided to only give Audrey the CSC to measure her current level of symptoms and the Coaching Topics Survey (CTS). Figure 11.1 lists Audrey's responses on the CSC.

USING THE CTS WHEN MOOD DISORDERS ARE PRESENT

The main difference you should see on a CTS when a mood disorder is present is a rating of 1 or 2 on two items: "Decreasing negative self-talk" and "Managing stress/anxiety." If these are the only items that receive a 1 or 2, this may be an indication that the client is not experiencing executive functioning deficits at a level that makes coaching appropriate but rather that a traditional counseling setting may be more effective. Also, remember that even if the client does highly rate executive functioning–related items, this may be a result of anxiety, depression, or his or her ADHD. It is your job as the professional to explore this further if you are not sure and to refer the client to another practitioner if necessary. Figure 11.2 shows Audrey's responses on the CTS.

On the basis of her coach's initial assessment, and after reviewing her CSC and CTS, the coach felt even more confident that the previous provider's assessment was correct; Audrey's anxiety and depression symptoms seemed to be highly related to her difficulties in school (as a result of her ADHD symptoms). The coach then developed the following working hypothesis and questions:

1. Audrey was experiencing a moderate to high amount of anxiety and depression (previous testing, CSC) as a result of her deficits in executive functioning. The coach would need to monitor her mood disorder symptoms throughout coaching to assess whether coaching was helpful or if Audrey needed additional mental health counseling.

FIGURE 11.1

Symptom Checklist

Please indicate which of the following is currently or has been a problem:

Symptom	In general Yes	In general No	When studying, taking tests, or thinking about academics Yes	When studying, taking tests, or thinking about academics No
Nausea or stomachaches	___	_X_	_X!_	___
Difficulty following instructions	_X_	___	_X_	___
Depressed mood	___	_X_	_X_	___
Easily distracted	_X_	___	_X_	___
Restless	___	_X_	_X_	___
Careless	___	_X_	___	_X_
Feeling of losing control	_X_	___	_X_	___
Poor concentration	_X_	___	_X_	___
Anxious or worried	___	_X_	_X!_	___
Cannot sit still, fidgets	___	_X_	___	_X_
Feeling hopeless	___	_X_	_X!_	___
Poor organizational skills	_X_	___	_X_	___
Palpitations, increased heart rate	___	_X_	_X!_	___
Act as if "driven by a motor"/have nonstop energy	___	_X_	___	_X_
Irritable	___	_X_	___	_X_
Trembling or shaking	___	_X_	_X!_	___
Forgetful	_X_	___	_X_	___
Difficulty sleeping	_X_	___	_X_	___
Act without thinking, impulsive	___	_X_	___	_X_
Fail to finish tasks	_X_	___	_X_	___
Talk excessively	___	_X_	___	_X_
Shortness of breath, dizziness	___	_X_	_X!_	___
Feel sluggish, low energy, or fatigued	_X_	___	_X_	___
Difficulty sustaining attention	_X_	___	_X_	___

Audrey's symptom checklist.

2. Audrey's overall level of distress was high, especially with regard to school issues. It appeared that she was highly motivated to make some changes.
3. Audrey's primary executive functioning deficit areas were self-management to time and self-organization. She also had severe difficulties regulating her emotions.
4. Audrey's areas of concern centered on time management, organization, and reducing negative self-talk/managing anxiety (CTS).

With these tentative working hypotheses in mind, the coach conducted the initial intake interview.

FIGURE 11.2

Coaching Topics Survey

For each of the following items, circle the number from 1 to 5 that indicates the degree to which you need to work on that area.

	Do Need to work on				***Don't*** need to work on
Improving time management	(1)	2	3	4	5
Establishing routines and good habits	(1)	2	3	4	5
Organizing (School)work	1	(2)	3	4	5
Organizing Personal Space	1	(2)	3	4	5
Getting to class/work on time	1	2	(3)	4	5
Studying	1	(2)	3	4	5
Scheduling classes/meetings	1	2	3	(4)	5
Paying attention in class/at work and taking good notes	1	2	3	(4)	5
Managing long-term assignments/projects	(1)	2	3	4	5
Planning and prioritizing	(1)	2	3	4	5
Making decisions and solving problems	(1)	2	3	4	5
Keeping track of things	1	2	(3)	4	5
Doing laundry	1	2	3	(4)	5
Exercising	1	2	3	(4)	5

Audrey's coaching topics survey.

FIGURE 11.2

Eating healthfully	1	2	3	④	5
Waking up and staying up	1	2	3	4	⑤
Getting to bed	1	2	3	④	5
Taking medication	1	2	3	4	⑤
Making friends	1	②	3	④	5
Keeping friends	1	②	3	④	5
Getting along with others	1	2	3	④	5
Getting along in group situations	1	2	3	④	5
Decreasing negative self-talk	①	2	3	4	5
Managing stress/anxiety	①	2	3	4	5
Establishing realistic goals	1	②	3	4	5
Understand more about my disorder(s)	1	2	③	4	5
Figuring out the next step in my career/job	1	2	③	4	5
Other:					

Audrey's coaching topics survey.

BEGINNING SESSIONS

Audrey was upbeat and polite to the coach at their first meeting. She wore her long black hair in a ponytail and dressed in jeans with a pretty blue top. Her brown eyes sparkled, but her nails were bitten down to the cuticle. Upon closer inspection, her coach could tell she had heavy foundation covering dark circles under her sparkly eyes, and as she sat down in the office, she began to wring her hands.

At the outset of treatment, when working with a client who has a long-standing history of ADHD but also suffers from anxiety or depression, it is important to pinpoint as best as possible how the two are intertwined. Although the coach had a good indication that Audrey's mood issues were related to ADHD, she needed to better understand the impacts of the ADHD symptoms on her resulting cognitions, behaviors, and emotions over the years (think Ellis and Beck cognitive behavioral principles and the thought–emotion–behavior interplay; Beck, 1967; Ellis, 1957). As mentioned at the beginning of this chapter, sometimes this conversation is a bit like the "chicken or egg" dilemma, even with a strong working hypothesis. First, many clients have trouble remembering back that far. Moreover, by the time most clients come to coaching, their ADHD and mood symptoms have snowballed into such an entangled mess, they can be difficult to sort out. Problems related to ADHD when a person is young lead to issues with friends, family, and school, which lead to depression or anxiety (or both), which lead to issues with friends, family, and school, which lead to increased problems with executive functioning, which lead to more problems with friends, family, and school, and eventually work, marriage, and money. . . and so on.

By separating emotions, thoughts, and behaviors for clients, you begin to help them see that they do not have to be a victim to their neurobiology; they can take control in any or all areas and have a direct impact on the others. Having ADHD may not be something over which they have any control, but they can control the way their ADHD symptoms affect their thoughts, actions, and emotions. Coaching clients can learn new ways to cope and view their world that will directly and indirectly affect positive change in their mood and outlook as they simultaneously improve their executive skill set.

Audrey: I just don't know if I can do it anymore. School is literally making me sick. I'm just so tired of this.

Coach: That sounds awful. I'm really sorry to hear that. What about it makes you feel so sick?

Audrey: Everything. I thought I could do this, but it's like I just can't keep up. I'm always playing catch-up, and even my all-nighters sometimes don't cut it.

Coach: It sounds like you don't think you can perform like you need to. Have you always felt this way in school? Was there a time you felt you were keeping up and that you could be successful?

To help establish rapport with any client, client-centered skills such as positive regard and empathy are always helpful. However, unlike most therapy, because coaching is generally more action oriented, the coach quickly shifted to lead Audrey toward insight and movement around her anxiety rather than allowing her to dive too deeply into her emotions. Clients with ADHD that initially present with a more generalized anxiety can often pinpoint more precise reasons, relating back to problems with executive functioning that affected them in specific ways. In Audrey's case, "school" was not the actual catalyst for her anxiety. School has many facets. No one is allergic to cake; people are allergic to a particular ingredient or ingredients in the cake. Similarly, no one gets anxious because of "school"; they get anxious because of a particular aspect or aspects of it. It is important to understand the ingredients in school that Audrey was avoiding—social rejection, evaluation, underperformance, for example. The coach also attempted to uncover when the anxiety began for Audrey, while offering a chance for her to recall some positive and hopeful memories.

Audrey: I didn't always hate school, but I was never very good at it. I've always struggled with time management, organization, and staying focused as a result of my ADHD, but I loved the social aspect. Even now, I've made some really good friends in my classes. And I actually enjoy the courses—that's what's so funny! Staying focused isn't as much of an issue since I enjoy it so much. I just can't keep up with the workload.

Coach: It sounds like you know what you are fighting for here: a satisfying career and some important connections. That will be useful information when it comes to motivation each week.

As mental health professionals know, in addition to an external system of rewards and consequences, helping clients identify positive aspects or internal motivators can be a crucial component in their success when it comes to mood disorders. If they are attending coaching simply because a loved one is "making" them come, or if clients have unrealistic expectations about what coaching can and cannot do for them, their chances of success are significantly lower. Another reason it is important to identify internal motivators when clients are highly anxious or depressed is that the use of external motivators can sometimes increase stress and should not be used in this case.

Brainstorming Rewards and Consequences

At the outset of treatment, help your clients identify the internal motivators, or metaphorical "light through the darkness," that they are hoping to find or regain. The following questions can be helpful in pinpointing your anxious or depressed client's incentives:

- Can you tell me what life was like before you began to feel this way?
- Are there aspects of your current situation that you enjoy and wish you could feel more of?
- What would you be doing if you weren't weighed down so much by anxiety or depression?

It may be helpful to document these ideas—the things the client is fighting to get back. You can make a simple written list of rewards and consequences, or you and your client may want to come up with another system. The idea here is to create a reminder for you and your client as you progress from week to week, so that you always keep these things in mind. Clients can do this with a big note on their wall or a message on their phone—whatever makes sense to them. It should simply be something that will help fight negative thoughts when they creep in and threaten to undercut the plans. Audrey and her coach decided making an Inspiration Toolbox (see Chapter 6) would be a good method to help Audrey keep track of her positive thoughts. For clients who use electronic devices such as tablets and smartphones, there are many options to make sure the message is seen on a daily basis:

1. Set a computer or tablet password to something like, "DoIt ForYourFriendsAndJob".
2. Take a photo of a handwritten note and have clients set it as their wallpaper. Artistic clients can add an illustration. In this case example, Audrey chose to draw a picture of herself as the career woman she hoped to become and wrote the message "Do it for your friends and job!" by it.
3. Have clients manipulate a photo of themselves when they were feeling good using an application that allows them to put a message on the photo, then use that as wallpaper.
4. Clients can enter positive messages or daily affirmations into a smartphone or an app that automatically displays them with a pop-up at random times throughout the day.

With clients such as Audrey who have symptoms of depression or anxiety, begin by adding only reward ideas on your list of rewards and consequences. Try not to include things that add too much time or would be stressful to complete, even though they might be enjoyable (e.g., "Going to a movie would be fun, but I'd just be thinking about all the other things I have to do!" "If I eat ice cream, I'll get fat and I'll feel bad about myself"). Instead, think of things that are healthy, relaxing, and simple to complete. Here is Audrey's list of rewards that she and her coach brainstormed in the beginning stages of coaching:

1. Transfer $20 to my "fun money" account.
2. Boyfriend lets me control the remote all night.
3. Wear my favorite outfit to class.
4. Grab a (healthy) smoothie after class.
5. Study at my favorite park.
6. Take a bubble bath instead of a shower.

Creating Long-Term Goals

When creating long-term goals with clients who have comorbid depression or anxiety, you will want to factor in the effect each behavioral goal will (both directly and indirectly) have on the client's self-talk (cognitions) and mood symptoms (emotions). Exhibit 11.1 lists the long-term goals Audrey and her coach worked together to create.

As you can see, Goals 1 and 2 specifically relate to Audrey's executive functioning deficits as a result of her ADHD, whereas Goal 3 relates to her cognitive distortions and anxious thought patterns; however, all three goals will help to effect positive change in her overall mood. Many coaching goals can do double duty as these do, even for clients who are not clinically depressed or anxious. In fact, most clients with ADHD who have struggled with symptoms severe enough to warrant

EXHIBIT 11.1

Audrey's Long-Term Goals

GOAL 1: Construct and follow through with a schedule that helps me get my school work done in a timely manner *(thus indirectly addressing and reducing my anxiety).

GOAL 2: Maintain organization of my school documents from week to week *(thus indirectly addressing and reducing my anxiety).

GOAL 3: Complete one cognitive reframing exercise per week in session and one exercise per week out of session *(thus directly addressing and reducing my anxiety).

coaching have probably suffered at least some hit to their mood or self-esteem and can benefit in the same regard.

MIDDLE SESSIONS

The middle sessions of coaching involve (a) working through the long-term goals via weekly objectives (BSAs), (b) identifying weekly successes and using those to define strengths and coping mechanisms that can be generalized to other tasks, (c) identifying barriers that can be overcome with the problem-solving approach, (d) utilizing rewards and consequences to keep the client motivated, (e) helping the client develop specific skills and strategies, and (f) helping clients reach the point where they can do a–e on their own, without the help of a coach.

Creating Weekly Objectives:

When working with an individual like Audrey, it becomes especially important to pay attention to your client's emotional and visceral reaction to ideas about weekly objectives or strategies to try and to constantly (informally or formally) assess your client's mood. If an idea or suggestion seems to be "too much" for them, you can quite often see it in their body language, facial expression, or verbal display (e.g., shoulders tense, teeth grit, uncomfortable mutters, "Uhhh. . ."). Even more than in your sessions with clients who do not have comorbid disorders, make sure to start small so that clients can celebrate successes and build momentum as they start to tackle their weekly objectives. Exhibit 11.2 is an example of Audrey's Weekly Objectives.

It may be helpful to use a mood-tracking app, program, or chart with these clients so that they can constantly check in with their emotional status in relation to their objectives and outcomes. Clients can use paper and pen to create their own simple rating scale or use a more sophisticated method such as mood-tracking apps or computer

EXHIBIT 11.2

Audrey's Weekly Objectives for Week 3

Objective A (Goal 1)	Objective B (Goal 1)	Objective C (Goal 2)
Review notes for class by Tuesday	Attend class on Wednesday	File away old papers and clean out backpack
Objective D (Goal 3)	**Objective**	**Objective**
Create five coping cards		

programs. Ideally, as you work through the long-term goals you and your clients have set, you should start to see a shift in mood due to both the indirect (i.e., Audrey's Goals 1 and 2) and direct (i.e., Audrey's Goal 3) goals you have set.

Refining Objectives

In addition to being mindful of your clients' emotional vulnerability when co-creating appropriate weekly objectives, it will be equally, if not more, important to consistently help clients reflect on their emotional status in relation to the goals set that only indirectly correlate with their mood. Here, the coach and Audrey talk about her anxiety in relation to her first goal of improving time management.

Coach: So this is the third week you have followed through with the homework and study schedule we created. How are you feeling about your progress there in relation to your anxiety?

Audrey: I'm feeling. . . calmer. My head seems less noisy, and I've noticed my nails are longer—less biting!

Coach: What specifically about managing your time better has contributed to you feeling calmer, do you think?

Audrey: I'm realizing that the discomfort of putting things off is much more intense and painful than the discomfort of actually doing those assignments that I used to dread. So in a way it's calming to do my work. Because I know the sooner I get to it, the sooner the uncomfortable feeling will be behind me.

The coach and Audrey made sure to rate her mood on her mood tracking app as it related to her progress in the area of time management. They also decided to add the statement "The sooner I get to it, the sooner the uncomfortable feeling will be behind me" to an index card for her Inspiration Toolbox. A similar approach should be taken with Goal 2 in this scenario.

When dealing with anxiety head on (Goal 3), there are a number of helpful strategies you can use from week to week. If you are experienced with CBT exercises or exposure therapy, you have a huge head start. If not, the following are some suggestions on how to directly tackle anxiety and depression with your coaching clients.

- Have clients write a list of the imagined negative outcomes they have created. Existence of thoughts is not support of them. Have clients write down some of these negative thought patterns, and

teach them to overrule the urge the thought creates. For example, if someone announces a fire alarm is about to be tested, you can more easily resist the urge to flee when it rings. Likewise, clients can learn to "self-talk" themselves down in situations where anxiety or depression may have previously rendered them helpless.
- Engage clients in mindfulness meditation strategies to aid in relaxation.
- Have clients use their Inspiration Toolbox to store "Coping Cards" with messages they can refer to on days where they are struggling. For clients with coexisting mood conditions, these may include statements such as:
  - I am stronger than my fear/anxiety/depression.
  - Just because I'm scared/sad doesn't mean I can't do it.
  - Scary/Sad thoughts can never hurt me.
  - It's OK to be scared/anxious/sad.
  - I know I can do this because. . .
- For anxiety, especially when you have identified specific triggers, use exposure-therapy tactics. Anxiety is usually temporary and harmless. Let your client experience anxiety and learn this firsthand. To overcome anxiety, you must "dive into it," just as you dive into a large wave rather than run away from it (recall that metaphor from Chapter 6). (Audrey created a poster with a picture of the beach, together with this statement, so she could look at it before school each day.)

A basic and effective way to combine exposure strategies with coaching fundamentals is for you and your client to create steps and reward each behavior. To address Audrey's school avoidance, she and her coach created these steps for her to follow each morning:

- Get up at the right time, when my alarm goes off—reward (Skittle).
- Get dressed as if I am going to school—reward (Skittle).
- Next, get in the car as if I am going—reward (seeing the note on my steering wheel saying, "Audrey Rocks!").
- Drive to school—reward (my friends waiting by my parking space).

For added reinforcement, Audrey used a goal-tacking app on her phone to chart these behaviors and when they were completed each day. She enjoyed opening the app to reflect on her successes throughout her day.

Another aspect to consider is whether your clients are getting reinforcement for their anxiety-driven behavior. If so, make it a less attractive option—"water the seeds, not the weeds." Often loved ones unknowingly give more attention to the maladaptive behavior than the healthy one. Here Audrey's coach gently guides her toward insight related to reinforcement.

Coach: Where is your boyfriend on the days you end up skipping class due to your anxiety?

Audrey: He works at home. He's really sweet and always makes me a nice breakfast when I come back upset.

Coach: So he helps to make it appealing to come back home, huh?

Audrey: Yeah, I guess he does. He probably shouldn't, right? He really wants to help me, so I guess I need to tell him he shouldn't make me breakfast. I'll have to settle for cereal.

Not only did Audrey's boyfriend stop making her breakfast, but he hid the TV remote control and only allowed Audrey to open her homework for necessary school assignments. Once she had completed her work and only if she had attended class that week, Audrey's boyfriend would often draw her a bubble bath (one of her weekly reward ideas).

FINAL SESSIONS

When you are treating clients with anxiety or depression and approaching the end of coaching, some may experience what professionals refer to as an *extinction burst*—an increase in the frequency or intensity of the targeted behavior or feeling when extinction has been used in the treatment. (An example of extinction in Audrey's case is when her boyfriend stopped making her breakfast or hid the remote control to stop providing positive reinforcement when she didn't go to school or do her homework.) Extinction bursts can also occur in clients without a mood disorder (e.g., a coaching client with an exercise goal). The important thing to remember is that if the behavior seems to be getting better, then suddenly worse, this can nonetheless mean that things are working. However, when it comes to anxiety, it is extremely important to not create a crisis situation for your clients; help them realize that the recurrence of a behavior during treatment is not unusual.

After meeting for several weeks, consistently staying on track with her time management and organizational goals, and attending class regularly without incident, Audrey experienced a panic attack before class one day. She called her coach, asking to be seen earlier than their scheduled appointment and came in looking like a deer in the headlights. Audrey and her coach discussed the recent situation.

Audrey: I just freaked. I just... I don't know. I just freaked! What's wrong with me? All this work for nothing. I'll never get better!

Coach: So you're still human? That's good to know. You're three quarters of the way up the mountain, and you stumbled off the path. What next? Do you start back at the bottom, or regain your footing and continue?

Audrey: So I'm not at square one?

Coach: Let's look at the evidence.

Audrey and her coach pulled out the weekly objectives worksheets they had compiled and her mood- and goal-tracking apps. They reminisced about her successes and talked about what helped to make her successful week after week.

Audrey's brain was making a last-ditch effort, so to speak, to engage in homeostasis and revert back to its catastrophic, black-and-white thinking. Her coach used humor to downplay Audrey's intensity and model calm behavior. Audrey and her coach then slowly eased her back on track, and several weeks later, she stated that "the panic is gone. That last little bit that was making my toes tingle, it's like it just slipped away. It's almost hard to believe that was me."

Once clients are well on the road to recovery from anxiety or depression and have taken charge of their ADHD-related struggles, it is important to use the final sessions to reflect on what strategies they can use going forward in different situations. Of course, this is a fundamental goal of every coaching relationship to ensure future success, but it can be even more important for high-risk clients such as Audrey. Remind them that the road will not always be easy, and their symptoms may creep in again, but now they are armed with an arsenal of tools to combat these negative feelings.

Summary

1. Many adults with ADHD have one or more mental health disorders in addition to ADHD, most commonly depression or anxiety (Cumyn, French, & Hechtman, 2009; Murphy & Barkley, 1996; Sobanski, 2006), so it is imperative that as a coach you have some understanding of this impact.
2. Help clients separate their ADHD from other diagnoses as much as possible, and pinpoint causal relationships.

3. Identify the positive rewards the client is fighting for and leave out the consequences.
4. Create long-term goals that address anxiety indirectly, directly, or both.
5. Pay attention to emotional reactions to weekly objectives and adjust accordingly.
6. Combine CBT approaches with coaching strategies.
7. Beware of the potential for an extinction burst and use evidence from written objectives to reframe and anticipate backslides with the client.
8. Review and reflect on what worked and why, and discuss possible future scenarios where helpful tools may be used in different ways.

Case Study 12
ADHD Coaching With an Adolescent

This chapter illustrates how to work with adolescent clients with attention-deficit/hyperactivity disorder (ADHD) or executive functioning impairments while juggling interactions with their parents or caregivers. Working with a younger population also means working with their families. ADHD has a high degree of heritability (Schachar, 2014), and this often means the "apple doesn't fall far from the tree," adding additional treatment challenges. Coaching teens also means understanding the additional learning challenges these clients often come with.

You may have noticed that we did not include a chapter on coaching children. The reason for this, as we noted in the Introduction, is that we do not recommend individual coaching for clients under the age of about 12. For children with ADHD, the treatment should focus on teaching parents or guardians strategies so that they can best help their children at home. It is important for the child to be involved, but ultimately the parents need to understand how to support and guide their children at younger ages.

---

http://dx.doi.org/10.1037/14671-013
ADHD Coaching: A Guide for Mental Health Professionals, by F. Prevatt and A. Levrini
Copyright © 2015 by the American Psychological Association. All rights reserved.

When working with an adolescent client, it is important to keep in mind that you are guided by the same ethical and legal principles as you would be in any other counseling and therapy situation in terms of informed consent and assent, confidentiality, and other concerns with clients under age 18 years. As a coach, you will need to decide how much to involve parents in sessions, and this will most likely differ for each client. Some adolescents have strong relationships with their parents, whereas others, like Apple, whom we feature in this case study, harbor a lot of anger and resentment. Some are fiercely independent; others are still struggling to stand on their own two feet and still look to their parents for much-needed support. You may want to consider these factors even before the intake session to determine how much you will involve the client's parents in that first conversation, which can be critical in determining the relationship you will have with your client going forward. After the intake, you and your client can decide together how and when to use parental support throughout coaching.

In the following pages, we outline how to approach ADHD coaching with adolescents and their families in terms of beginning, middle, and final sessions.

The client is a 15-year-old female high school sophomore named Apple, who was diagnosed with ADHD—inattentive presentation (previously inattentive subtype) in first grade. Every few years, she has undergone complete psychoeducational testing by a psychologist, which has consistently confirmed that she has no other learning or social-emotional diagnosis outside of ADHD but that has relative weaknesses in several areas, including reading and writing. Apple is by all accounts a thriving teenager. She has many friends, plays on the JV soccer team, and loves her photography class. Her teachers report that she seems upbeat and happy when interacting with her peers but often can't find or forgets her homework, is late to class, has trouble listening in the classroom, and struggles with test taking, even when allowed extra time. Apple's parents state that at home they see a different kid—one who is angry and argumentative and prefers to lock herself in her room with her phone and computer rather than talk to them. Like most teens, Apple didn't want to come to coaching but begrudgingly agreed after her parents offered her a shopping trip as an incentive.

The single most important factor when beginning to work a younger client (in any setting, not just coaching) is trust. If you miss this critical step, you are setting yourself and your client up for a long road of resistance. Coaches who are also therapists actually have a disadvantage here when working with kids and teens. This is because most kids simply do not want to go to a therapist. Children see the world in black and white, good and bad, with little in between. Seeing a therapist to them means they are bad, broken, messed up, or stupid. Similarly, ADHD to them means they are bad, broken, messed up, or stupid. Therefore, although your client's parents might see it as a good thing that you have this extra credentialing, we can assure you that your client does not. In the beginning sessions and throughout, try to set aside your "therapist" hat (but don't set it too far away) and put on your "coach" hat.

Case in Action: Beginning, Middle, and End

INITIAL ASSESSMENT

Apple had undergone psychoeducational testing on multiple occasions and was formally diagnosed with (*International Classification of Diseases, 10th Revision;* World Health Organization, 2010) F90.0 ADHD, predominately inattentive presentation. Because she had already been assessed, the coach decided to give Apple only the Client Symptom Checklist (CSC; to make sure no depressive symptoms were present) and the Coaching Topics Survey—Child Version (CTS–Child). Apple's CSC confirmed that she was not exhibiting symptoms of depression or anxiety.

USING THE CTS WITH CHILDREN AND ADOLESCENTS

In earlier chapters, we outlined the differences between our adult and child versions of the CTS. In addition to having your teenage client fill out the inventory, it may be appropriate and helpful for a parent or caregiver to complete the CTS as well. We do not suggest parents complete the form in place of a teen—after all, as a coach, you are trying to empower your client. But most individuals (even adults) with ADHD are not very accurate in terms of self-assessment, and most teens can be self-absorbed; therefore, your younger clients may be blinded by a positive illusory bias when it comes to rating themselves on areas of relative weakness. Parents, in contrast, often arrive at the coach's office at their wit's end and may paint their child in an overly negative light. Because of these two tendencies, your best bet is to assume the true answer lies somewhere in the middle. Of course, have a conversation about each item with your client and the parent to clarify any discrepancies.

In terms of specific items, most adolescents who come to coaching will rate highly executive function–and school-related topics such as "improving time management" or "paying attention in class." Parents may also tend to give high ratings to things such as "waking up and staying up" or "doing laundry." In fact, we find a lot of parents get excited when they see those items, saying things like, "You can help with *that?*" Younger clients may downplay the more social–emotional items, so make sure you do not take their rating of these topics at face value. Never force these issues with younger clients, but stay open to signs and check in with them from time to time. You will likely find that as your relationship with your clients develops and their comfort with you grows, teenagers will begin to open up about problems when it comes to friends and negative self-talk. Figure 12.1 shows Apple's responses on the CTS, and Figure 12.2 shows Apple's parents' responses.

The coach reviewed Apple's previous testing in addition to both her and her parents' CTS scores and developed the following working hypotheses and questions.

1. Apple did not exhibit symptoms of anxiety or depression (previous testing/CSC) but was struggling with her relationship with her parents, causing her to become angry and withdrawn at times. The coach would need to determine whether the affective issues would be a detriment to coaching and how much to involve Apple's parents in the process or refer out for additional family counseling.
2. Apple's primary executive functioning deficit areas were self-management to time, self-organization, studying, and paying attention.
3. Apple's priority areas of concern centered on scheduling class work and study time, developing study skills and strategies, organizing schoolwork, making decisions, and learning strategies to increase focus in the classroom (CTS).

With these tentative working hypotheses in mind, the coach conducted the initial intake interview.

Beginning Sessions

Apple's coach decided to bring both parents back at the same time as Apple for their initial session. Although it was apparent she was not pleased with her parents lately, she also appeared nervous about the session, anxiously tapping her foot and cowering down in her waiting-room chair. Apple shyly smiled as her coach shook her hand, and then followed her parents back to the office, where she looked around for clues as to where she actually was. She wore a hooded sweatshirt with the name of her high school on it, and her blonde hair in a messy ponytail. As she plopped onto the wingback chair, she dropped her large, heavy backpack to the ground with a thud. Then she pulled out her

FIGURE 12.1

	Does need to work on				Doesn't need to work on
Improving time management	1	**_2_**	3	4	5
Establishing routines and good habits	1	2	**_3_**	4	5
Organizing schoolwork	**_1_**	2	3	4	5
Organizing personal space	1	2	**_3_**	4	5
Getting to class on time	1	**_2_**	3	4	5
Studying	1	**_2_**	3	4	5
Scheduling classes	1	2	3	**_4_**	5
Paying attention in class and taking good notes	**_1_**	2	3	4	5
Managing long-term assignments/projects	1	**_2_**	3	4	5
Planning and prioritizing	1	2	3	**_4_**	5
Making decisions and solving problems	1	2	3	**_4_**	5
Keeping track of things	1	2	**_3_**	4	5
Doing laundry	1	2	3	**_4_**	5
Exercising	1	2	3	4	**_5_**
Eating healthfully	1	2	3	4	**_5_**
Waking up and staying up	1	2	3	**_4_**	5
Getting to bed	1	2	3	**_4_**	5
Taking medication	1	2	3	**_4_**	5
Making friends	1	2	3	4	**_5_**
Keeping friends	1	2	3	4	**_5_**

Apple's coaching topics survey responses. Apple's responses are shown in bold underline.

(continues)

FIGURE 12.1 (Continued)

	Does need to work on				Doesn't need to work on
Getting along with classmates or siblings	1	2	3	4	**<u>5</u>**
Getting along in group situations	1	2	3	4	**<u>5</u>**
Decreasing negative self-talk	1	2	3	4	**<u>5</u>**
Managing stress/anxiety	1	2	3	**<u>4</u>**	5
Establishing realistic goals	1	2	3	4	**<u>5</u>**
Understanding more about his/her disorder(s)	1	2	3	**<u>4</u>**	**<u>5</u>**
Using accommodations	1	2	3	**<u>4</u>**	5

Apple's coaching topics survey responses. Apple's responses are shown in bold underline.

FIGURE 12.2

	Does need to work on				Doesn't need to work on
Improving time management	**<u>1</u>**	2	3	4	5
Establishing routines and good habits	**<u>1</u>**	2	3	4	5
Organizing schoolwork	**<u>1</u>**	2	3	4	5
Organizing personal space	**<u>1</u>**	2	3	4	5
Getting to class on time	**<u>1</u>**	2	3	4	5
Studying	**<u>1</u>**	2	3	4	5
Scheduling classes	**<u>1</u>**	2	3	4	5
Paying attention in class and taking good notes	**<u>1</u>**	2	3	4	5

Apple's parents' coaching topics survey. Apple's parents' responses are shown in bold underline.

FIGURE 12.2

	Does need to work on				Doesn't need to work on
Managing long-term assignments/projects	1	**2**	3	4	5
Planning and prioritizing	1	**2**	3	4	5
Making decisions and solving problems	1	**2**	3	4	5
Keeping track of things	**1**	2	3	4	5
Doing laundry	1	**2**	3	4	5
Exercising	1	2	3	**4**	5
Eating healthfully	1	2	**3**	4	5
Waking up and staying up	1	**2**	3	4	5
Getting to bed	1	**2**	3	4	5
Taking medication	1	2	3	**4**	5
Making friends	1	2	3	4	**5**
Keeping friends	1	2	3	4	**5**
Getting along with classmates or siblings	1	2	3	4	**5**
Getting along in group situations	1	2	3	4	**5**
Decreasing negative self-talk	1	2	**3**	4	5
Managing stress/anxiety	1	2	**3**	4	5
Establishing realistic goals	1	**2**	3	4	5
Understanding more about his/her disorder(s)	**1**	2	3	4	5
Using accommodations	**1**	2	3	4	5

Apple's parents' coaching topics survey. Apple's parents' responses are shown in bold underline.

phone and began to check for messages as her parents addressed the coach. The coach smiled at her parents, then addressed Apple directly.

Coach: Apple, can you tell me why you're here today?

Apple: Not really. Because I'm not doing well in school and I have ADHD?

Coach: That sounds about right. I'm guessing this wasn't your idea, huh?

Apple: [*Laughs*] Yeah, no.

Coach: Your mom told me you play soccer?

Apple: Yeah.

Coach: That's great. Soccer takes a lot of talent and hard work. And since you play soccer and have a coach, you must know a little about coaching. Why don't you tell me what your coach does for you?

Apple: Well, she teaches us new plays and helps us to get better at the game.

Coach: Good answer. And that makes it a lot easier for me to explain my role. I call myself a coach, too—an ADHD coach. So it's my job to help teach you new plays and help you get better at things that might be affected by your ADHD. In a lot of cases for teenagers like you, that means school. You might have trouble organizing your assignments, taking tests, or writing papers. And I can help you learn new ways to approach your schoolwork so that you can get better at it. Make sense?

Apple: Oh, okay. Yeah. I guess that could help.

In the first meeting with your client and the parent or caregiver, address the client first. Often the parents will start speaking. If this happens, don't cut them off; allow them to say what is needed. But the first response out of your mouth as the coach should be directed to your client. This begins the long road of establishing trust and rapport so that your client knows that you work for him or her. Also important is the way in which you explain coaching to your new client. By high school, most kids have had at least some experience with an athletic coach, musical director, scout leader, or some other instructor whose job was to help them develop and grow their skills in a particular area. Teachers do this too, of course. But do your best not to compare yourself to teachers. Your clients are there because they have had negative experiences with school, and most likely (and unfortunately) have negative associations with teachers. You are much better off joining your clients in their feelings and supporting them by saying that although teachers try their best, they may not have been trained sufficiently about how different students with ADHD think and approach things, and most mainstream schools just aren't set up for an ADHD learning style.

Coach: What do you know about ADHD?

Apple: I know it means I have trouble focusing on my work. Like I can't pay attention.

Coach: That's right, but that's not all of it. Let's keep your parents in here for a while longer while we talk a little bit about ADHD and how it's affected you throughout the years, and then we will kick them out for the last few minutes. Sound good?

Apple: Sure, I guess.

Coach: I don't want to bore you with another lecture—I'm sure you hear plenty of those—so instead I'm going to paint a couple of mental pictures for you to help explain what ADHD is about and how coaching can help. Are you learning to drive yet, Apple?

Apple: Yeah, I've got my learner's permit.

Coach: Great. Then let me try to explain it this way: Imagine you are in your car trying to get from your house, on one side of town, to a party at your friend's house, on the other side of town. Only, when you try to get onto the highway, you don't have enough money for the tollbooth, so you end up taking all these back and side roads, get lost a few times, and finally make it to your friend's house an hour late and frustrated.

Having ADHD is kind of like watching everyone else take the highway and get where they want to go as fast as they want, while you struggle and feel lost, then end up being late and missing out on the party.

Apple: Wow. Yeah. I do feel that way, I guess.

Coach: Well, I know it may feel like you're the only one, but trust me, you aren't alone. Kids who have ADHD sometimes struggle because they are trying over and over to access the highways with everyone else, but never have enough money. It's tiring and frustrating to see everyone else get there faster, and it makes you want to give up. But in coaching, we can start to build some new roads and express lanes. We can help you get to the party just as fast as everyone else but in a different way.

Apple: Oh, that makes sense. Not sure how you're going to do that, but it sounds good, I guess. That doesn't sound like I thought this was going to be, like analyzing my thoughts or dreams or something.

Coach: [*Laughs*] No, nothing like that. And don't worry about how we're going to do it just yet either. You are obviously a talented person, which will make that part a lot easier. You have a lot of friends, which means you have a lot of what we call social intelligence. You also are good at soccer, which means you have great physical intelligence. And you are good at photography, which means you learn well kinesthetically. That means learning by doing in a hands-on sort of way.

Apple: I didn't realize you could be smart in so many different ways. I pretty much just thought there was only one way.

By using metaphors and ideas that Apple could relate to and focusing the attention on the young client, the coach was able to begin developing rapport with her. (To learn more about why metaphors are helpful and which ones to use, see Chapter 6.) After discussing the benefits of coaching and hearing what Apple's parents had to say about their ideas for coaching goals, the coach asked them to please have a seat in the waiting room so Apple and the coach could speak privately.

Assessing Motivation

As previously mentioned, most teens like Apple do not ask their parents for an ADHD coach. Therefore, motivation for change can be one of your biggest hurdles when coaching this population. Motivational interviewing techniques can help adolescents see the benefits of coaching, as can well-thought-out rewards and consequences (demonstrated in the next subsection). During the initial sessions and when they were alone, Apple's coach assessed her motivation to change.

Coach: So I'll be frank. This isn't going to be a helpful process if it's something only your parents want for you—not something you want to do. So I'd like to know, after hearing what I had to say about how I can help you, is this something you'd like to try?

Apple: Okay, I'll be frank too . . . that means honest, right? I really didn't want to. My parents had to bribe me to come here. But it was because I was scared you were just going to say I was messed up and broken and try to figure out how to fix my screwy brain. But the way you said it, I just think differently, not wrong, and maybe I've just been expecting things to work for me that work for everyone else? So, to answer your question, yes, I'll try it out. We'll see how it goes.

Coach: That's great, and I'm glad you heard me when I said that ADHD is about differences and not right or wrong, good or bad, broken or fixed. Keep in mind, I *chose* to work with kids with ADHD. And I did so because I think kids like you are really fun, creative, and interesting people to work with.

Apple: Okay, okay. Enough of the sales pitch [*laughs*]. You've got my attention. . . for now!

Brainstorming Rewards and Consequences

For minors whose parents are legally and financially responsible for them, almost all rewards and consequences will need to get mom and dad's stamp of approval, especially those that involve time with friends, money, or recreational activities. However, all ideas and suggestions for rewards and consequences should come from the minor client. When parents tell you they have tried using an incentive system before without success, the first question to ask is, "Who came up with the incentives?" Nine times out of 10, it was the parents. Often, putting the power and ownership back into the child's hands is enough to make the incentive effective.

Try to encourage adolescents to steer clear of reward and consequence ideas that their mom or dad, or other caregiver, has used before (e.g., no cell phone) or those that may be harmful to their already fragile and budding social image (e.g., skip the school dance). The following questions can be helpful in pinpointing rewards and consequences that young people may find useful:

- If you weren't forced to do homework every day, what would you be doing?
- If a friend was upset about something, what would you do to help make him or her feel better?
- What are three things no teenager should live without?

Remind parents that by recognizing the desired behavior, they are not bribing their kids or rewarding them for what they should already be doing. Older kids and teens with ADHD have not yet developed an internal sense of self-regulation, and by setting up a system that immediately reinforces accountability, incentives become an extremely valuable coaching tool. The coach asked Apple the questions just suggested, and based on her answers, they developed the following list of ideas together:

Weekly Reward Ideas
1. New lip gloss
2. Don't have to walk the dog for 3 days
3. Movie with friends
4. A latte with mom
5. Skip making bed for one week
6. Picnic dinner in front of TV
7. Download an MP3

Weekly Consequence Ideas
1. No makeup to school
2. Make dinner
3. Do a load of laundry
4. Make brother's bed for a week
5. Buy my mom a latte (but none for me)
6. No TV for 3 nights
7. Give dog a bath

Creating Long-Term Goals

Make sure that parents and caregivers understand that although you have the ability to work on many facets of ADHD with their child, you will need to focus on the areas that are of highest priority first, so as not to overwhelm the adolescent by trying to do too much, too soon. Also, building rapport usually takes slightly longer with younger clients, so parents and caregivers often need reminders to be patient about bringing up grades or other signs of improvement. Such achievements may be the ultimate goal, but nothing good comes out of a child's refusing to return to coaching because the coach forced lots of extra-hard work on him or her. Considering both Apple's needs and the needs expressed by her parents, she and her coach worked together to create a list of long-term goals (see Exhibit 12.1).

EXHIBIT 12.1

Apple's Long-Term Goals

GOAL 1: Create and follow through with an after-school schedule that incorporates homework, study time, and projects and that does not interfere with my extracurriculars or time with friends.

GOAL 2: Utilize my planner to keep track of due dates and corresponding class times and update weekly.

GOAL 3: Organize my subject papers in a way that gets my parents off my back, makes sense to me, and makes maintaining organization easier for me than binders.

After writing her long-term goals, Apple shared them with her parents, who gave their approval. Although her mom and dad had hoped to see something about more respect in the home or getting chores done, they accepted that school was the priority. They understood that as Apple and her coach worked together on these ideas, and as the parents backed away, their relationship with their daughter would likely improve as a direct result. If the coaching sessions were successful, the need for a specific goal about family interactions could be eliminated.

MIDDLE SESSIONS

The middle sessions of coaching involve (a) working through the long-term goals with weekly objectives (between-session assignments), (b) identifying weekly successes and using those to define strengths and coping mechanisms that can be generalized to other tasks, (c) identifying barriers that can be overcome with the problem-solving approach, (d) using rewards and consequences to keep clients motivated, (e) helping clients develop specific skills and strategies, and (f) helping clients reach the point where they can do these tasks on their own, without the help of a coach.

When working with a younger client like Apple, it becomes especially important to make sessions as fun and "non–school-like" as possible. Put up a small basketball hoop, and let them take shots between objectives, play Uno as an icebreaker, or let artistic clients create their own collage on their Inspiration Toolbox (Chapter 5). The following are some suggestions for other coaching strategies to use with children or adolescents:

- keep LEGOs, Play-Doh, or other items handy to keep kids' hands busy in session;
- exercise working memory with a game of Distraction, Simon, or Don't Break the Chain;
- brainstorm fun acronyms or sayings to help kids remember steps they must take ("Car Shops Have Tools" for "[Hang] Coat, Snack, Homework, [Set] Table"); or
- make objectives into art—create collages or posters for kids to hang for motivation and encouragement.

Creating Weekly Objectives With Adolescents

Exhibit 12.2 is an example of Apple's Weekly Objectives from Week 2.

Although parents should begin to relinquish control as their child gets older, they are still legally and financially responsible for them until the age of 18 (and financially sometimes longer). Taking this into account, you and your younger client should come up with a way to make mom

> ### EXHIBIT 12.2
>
> **Apple's Weekly Objectives From Week 2**
>
> | Objective A (Goals 1 and 2) | Objective B (Goal 3) | Objective C (Goal 4) |
> | --- | --- | --- |
> | Follow schedule for studying geometry as coach and I outlined in my planner. | Using the colored folders that I bought for my subjects, write subject name on each and file papers accordingly. | Make a photo collage of cool celebrities with attention-deficit/hyperactivity disorder. |

and dad aware of the objectives set up each week. As stated earlier, this may differ depending on your client's developmental stage and needs, and there are a number of ways parent involvement with weekly objectives can be handled. For some clients, the coach may choose to bring the parents into the session for the final 10 minutes each week and review the weekly objectives as a group. Other clients may prefer to talk to their parents after the session on the car ride home or at dinner that night. Just make sure that your client is staying accountable to this when you check in at the beginning of the following session or midweek as needed. Still other clients may prefer electronic methods such as e-mailing the objectives or putting them on a cloud-based drive so that parents (and the coach) can access them at any time. No matter which method is chosen, make sure your client approves and owns it first. Coaching adolescents empowers them to make smart decisions and wise choices, and the more ideas that come from these young clients, the more successful and hopeful they will feel.

Reviewing Weekly Objectives

When it comes to scheduling with younger clients, paper planners tend to work best. Not only are most electronic devices not allowed in schools (except in emergencies), the temptation to click on the Facebook or Twitter icon is often too much for kids who are trying to keep a calendar on their phone. However, there is a place for these devices: many teachers now allow students to take photos of assignments written on boards for easy transfer. Also, most schools use electronic systems to post assignments on a regular basis. Although these are all helpful tools, they will only help with knowing what the assignments are, not outlining when your client is to complete them. Therefore, you and your client may want to pull up photos or assignments during your sessions together, but using a paper planner to create a schedule is equally if not more important than simply being aware of assignments.

After reviewing assignments for the coming week and creating a homework and study schedule that worked around Apple's soccer practice (Goals 1 and 2), she and her coach discuss approaches to organization (Goal 3).

Apple: My teachers have all these requirements on how to keep my stuff, but I'm lucky if I can find it buried at the bottom of my bag.

Coach: But you have an accommodation that allows you to organize things in a way that makes sense to you. So let's talk about what *does* work.

Apple: It needs to be fast. I won't take the time to flip through tabs. And bright. If it catches my eye, I might use it.

Coach: How about folders with pockets? Would you open those?

Apple: Yeah, that sounds simple enough. And lighter weight so I could just keep them all in there and not worry about having to transfer things in and out. That's when they get lost.

Coach: I know they make them in lots of different colors. . .

Apple: Oh, I just had an idea! What if I did like green for earth science, and red for math because red is an angry color and I hate math?

Coach: [*Laughs*] I think that's really creative. . . as long as seeing the folder doesn't make you even madder!

Apple: [*Laughs too*] No, I don't think it would. But I'll see it and know quickly which folder to pull out. I'll probably find it funny and laugh, so maybe it'll make math seem less annoying.

Organization is not one-size-fits-all, despite how schools attempt to create strict guidelines on how to keep track of papers for each class down the binder size and specific tabs that should be used.

Academic Accommodations

Most students with an official ADHD diagnosis have or should have some sort of academic accommodations that can help bypass typical requirements such as organizing notebooks, and understanding things such as Section 504 and an individualized education plan (IEP) is an important part of being a coach.

Section 504 is a U.S. federal law designed to protect the rights of individuals with disabilities in programs and activities that receive federal financial assistance from the U.S. Department of Education; this includes students in any public elementary, middle, or high school. Under Section 504 of the Rehabilitation Act, any child who has a legitimate disability has the right to seek appropriate accommodations for a wide range of physical and psychiatric disabilities, including ADHD, to obtain an appropriate and adequate education, equal to their nondisabled peers. The document associated with this act is often referred to as a *504 Plan*, which lists the student's accommodations. Accommodations may be defined as assistive devices or adaptations that serve to ease the impact of the disability on a particular activity. Several tools and devices can help adolescent clients with communicating, writing, staying organized, remembering important information and dates, or keeping track of time. Accommodations may also mean making slight adjustments to their school environment to work efficiently and effectively, such as having additional time for tests, presenting information orally rather than creating a written report, or taking tests alone in a quiet space (Levrini & Prevatt, 2012).

An IEP is a plan or program developed to ensure that a child who has a disability identified under the law and who is attending a public educational institution receives specialized instruction and related services. Not all students who have disabilities like ADHD require specialized instruction, so not all will be granted an IEP. However, every student who has an IEP also has a team that works together to ensure his or her success. Therefore, you will want to understand these processes and outcomes not only to help your client during the coaching process, but also to be prepared if you are requested to be part of a client's team. For more information on 504 and IEP, visit the Department of Education website (http://www2.ed.gov).

Make sure to ask parents for a copy of any 504 Plan or IEP that your younger client has, and be prepared to educate parents who do not know about their child's rights. Keep in mind that many adolescent clients may not even be aware of their accommodations and will need your help to understand their rights as well.

Psychoeducation

Younger clients also tend to have less understanding about the realities of and myths about ADHD, so a decent amount of psychoeducation is often necessary (even if they don't think it is). Again, make this as fun as possible. Apple decided to create a photo collage of celebrities with ADHD, such as Justin Timberlake, Michael Phelps, and Adam Levine (front man for the band Maroon 5), to help her feel more "normal." Apple and her coach also complete the Juggling Activity (see Chapter 6) to help her better understand ADHD.

Coach: Here, Apple, I want you to try and juggle this ball. Just throw it up and down and catch it.
[*Apple begins to toss the ball up in the air and then catch it.*]

Apple: Uh, okay. That's pretty easy.

Coach: Great. Here, now take this one and try to juggle them together.
[*Apple easily juggles two balls between her hands.*]

Apple: [*Getting ahead of herself*] Oh, give me three! I can actually do three. My uncle taught me!

Coach: [*Laughs*] Okay, here you go. Let's see it!
[*Just as she stated, Apple successfully juggles the three balls.*]

Coach: So . . . how about just one more?

Apple: Oh my God. Um. Okay, I'll try.
[*Apple throws the four balls into the air, and they come bouncing down to the ground.*]

Apple: Yeah, not so much. [*Laughs*]

Coach: So, I bet you're guessing where the lesson is in this. I want you to think of each one of those balls as something you have to keep track of in your mind: your soccer games, your tests, who's dating who, what your mom asked you to do before Friday . . . as you can see, the more things you have to "keep in the air," the harder it is to keep track of them, right? Get too many things, and they all come crashing down, don't they?

Apple: Oh, wow! That is so cool! And makes total sense. But y'know, coach, when I write them down and use other things to help me it's a little bit like adding another hand to keep the balls in the air.

Coach: Don't ever accuse a kid with ADHD of not being smart!

FINAL SESSIONS

When coaching adolescents, you will need to keep track of how the child is progressing with his or her own goals (through both child and parent assessment), and also check in with how your client believes that his or her parents are reacting to the process. It is best if this conversation can be broached organically—when you feel the child is ready to open up rather than shut down if you bring up the topic. Some teens may even bring it up themselves, which is even better.

After several weeks of coaching, Apple was progressing well with her academics. Not only had her grades improved, but she was also actually enjoying some of her coursework that she previously would dread. Her confidence also skyrocketed as she began to understand what ADHD was and was not, and that it didn't mean she was stupid, lazy, or "bound for failure," as she once thought. Now comfortable with her coach, Apple brings up her relationship with her parents.

Apple: I know they are proud of me for doing better, but it's really annoying that they seem to think it's all me.

Coach: Can you give me an example of why you feel that way?

Apple: Well, my mom *so* has ADHD. It's so obvious. She gets mad at me for not keeping my room clean and then will forget to pick me up from soccer practice or we'll have nothing to eat when I get home. Then my dad gets all stressed when she forgets to pay a bill or something, and I get yelled at. It's like I'm doing better, but I'm still getting crap all the time. I want to do better for me, but sometimes they make me want to say screw it and not try anymore, since it doesn't seem to make a difference.

As stated in the beginning of this chapter, and as overtly suggested with our client's name, often the "apple doesn't fall far from the tree" in families with ADHD. Some parents can be quick to put blame on the child or the child's disorder, when in actuality a chaotic environment has exacerbated ADHD symptoms in their child. In a final individual coaching session with Apple and her parents, her coach showed them all the progress she had made from week to week, and Apple respectfully told her parents how she felt about their home life. Fortunately, Apple's mom and dad agreed to begin their own parent coaching sessions, so that they could learn their own helpful strategies and create a more ADHD-friendly environment in the home.

Summary

1. Developing trust with your young client is a critical first step.
2. Make sure your client understands your role as a coach and how ADHD affects her or his life.
3. Let your young client take the lead when creating rewards and consequences and long-term goals, but make sure to get parents' or caregivers' final approval.
4. Understand the basic principles of 504 Plans and IEPs and be prepared to answer questions or integrate accommodations into coaching.

5. Use games, metaphors, art projects, and other unique ways to make coaching fun and "non–school-like."
6. Pay attention to how your young client learns best, and structure assignments accordingly.
7. As your young client becomes more comfortable with you, he or she may begin to reveal more emotionally driven thoughts and look to you for help. Be prepared for how you will receive this and what you will do next.
8. Review and reflect on what worked and why, and discuss possible future scenarios in which helpful tools may be used in different ways.

Additional Resources

A recent (April 2014) search on the Internet using the word "ADHD" resulted in 32 million hits. There are unlimited resources out there to help you in your own coaching practice. To narrow your search, we list below some of the top books, websites, conferences, organizations, journals, tests, videos, and training clinics that we have found helpful in our own journey as ADHD coaches. These are primarily general in nature. But there are many specific strategies/tools for individual topics such as organization, financial planning, timers, calendars, healthy lifestyle, mediation, or any of the 32 million topics on the Internet associated with ADHD. These resources change rapidly, so we hope you will explore them more on your own. Along with our book, we believe that the list in this appendix will give you a solid foundation in the basics of ADHD coaching. Be sure to refer back to the specific strategies in Chapter 6, as well as Chapter 7 on starting a Coaching business.

Books

COGNITIVE BEHAVIOR THERAPY SKILLS

The first three books listed below are not about ADHD coaching per se, but explain the cognitive behavioral approach to treating ADHD in adults, and are excellent primers for utilizing this therapeutic approach in your Coaching.

Ramsay, J. R., & Rostain, A. L. (2008). *Cognitive-behavioral therapy for adult ADHD: An integrative psychosocial and medical approach.* New York, NY: Routledge.
This book is empirically based on a great deal of published research. It is an excellent source for basic CBT-oriented treatment of adult ADHD. It provides an overview of symptoms, assessment and diagnosis issues for adult ADHD. Using research, case examples, and a combined biological and psychosocial treatment approach, the authors discuss the many complicated factors that go into treatment, relapse prevention, and long-term management of adult ADHD, including a particular focus on comorbidity and medication issues. The authors direct the University of Pennsylvania ADHD Treatment and Research Program.

Safren, S. A., Perlman, C. A., Sprich, S., & Otto, M. W. (2005). *Mastering your adult ADHD: A cognitive-behavioral treatment program.* New York, NY: Oxford University Press.
This empirically based book is an excellent source for basic CBT-oriented treatment of adult ADHD. The structured program is detailed in step-by-step, session-by-session descriptions for therapists who deliver the treatment to clients with ADHD. Each module highlights a different area of impairment. Worksheets and homework assignments are included, as are a companion website and a corresponding client workbook.

Solanto, M. V. (2011). *Cognitive-behavioral therapy for adult ADHD: Targeting executive dysfunction.* New York, NY: Guilford Press.
This book provides evidence-based strategies for helping adults with ADHD build essential skills for time management, organization, planning, and coping. Each of the 12 group sessions—which can also be adapted for individual therapy—is reviewed in step-by-step detail. Features include quick-reference Leader Notes for therapists, in-session exercises, and reproducible take-home notes and homework assignments. Dr. Solanto is director of the ADHD Center at Mount Sinai School of Medicine.

CLASSICS

If you are working in the field of ADHD, you have probably already read these books, but we are listing them here because they are classics in the field. Most of them are a decade or more old; but this is where we got our start as ADHD coaches.

Hallowell, E. M., & Ratey, J. J. (1995). *Driven to distraction: Recognizing and coping with Attention Deficit Disorder through adulthood.* New York, NY: Touchstone Books.

Hallowell, E. M., & Ratey, J. J. (2006). *Delivered from distraction: Getting the most out of life with Attention Deficit Disorder.* New York, NY: Ballantine Books.

(There is a newer book, *Answers to Distraction*, but the originals are classics.)

Kelly, K., & Ramundo, P. (2006). *You mean I'm not stupid, lazy, or crazy?* New York, NY: Scribner.

Nadeau, K. G. (1996). *Adventures in fast forward: Life, love and work for the ADD adult.* New York, NY: Brunner-Routledge.

Nadeau, K. G. (1997). *ADD in the workplace: Choices, changes, and challenges.* Florence, KY: Brunner/Mazel.

Nadeau, K. G., & Quinn, P. O. (2002). *Understanding women with AD/HD.* Silver Spring, MD: Advantage Books.

Quinn, P. O., Ratey, N., Maitland, T. L. (2000). *Coaching college students with AD/HD: Issues and answers.* Silver Spring, MD: Advantage Books.

BOOKS FOR ADULTS WITH ADHD

The books listed below were written as self-help books for adults who have ADHD. You can recommend them to your clients, but we urge you to read them first, as they will give you a wealth of ideas for working with adult clients. They can be useful to use in conjunction with your coaching sessions; for example, you might assign your clients a chapter to read or an exercise to attempt as "homework" during the week.

Barkley, R. A. (2010). *Taking charge of adult ADHD.* New York, NY: Guilford Press.

This self-help book provides step-by-step strategies for managing symptoms of ADHD and reducing their harmful impact. It includes self-assessment tools and skill-building exercises, plus answers to frequently asked questions about medications and other treatments. Specific techniques are presented for overcoming challenges in critical areas where people with the disorder often struggle—work, finances, and relationships.

Levrini, A., & Prevatt, F. (2012). *Succeeding with adult ADHD: Daily strategies to help achieve your goals and manage your life.* Washington, DC: American Psychological Association.

This is the book we rely on most in our coaching work. It is a self-help book that can be used in conjunction with coaching. It is written in a format that will be reader-friendly to those with ADHD. The chapters cover making a plan, using incentives, overcoming procrastination, improving social relationships, organizing your space, learning and study strategies, finding job satisfaction; dealing with stress, anxiety, and depression; and using medication. Each chapter starts with a brief quiz (*Does this sound like you?*), followed by a short, nontechnical explanation of research; a short case example; a list of tips, exercises, or checklists; a description of how to get back on track, and a summary of takeaway ideas.

Ramsay, J. R., & Rostain, A. L. (2015). *The adult ADHD toolkit: Using CBT to facilitate coping inside and out.* New York, NY: Routledge.

(This book was in press at the time of this writing, so we have not actually used this yet. The following is the description by the publisher.) A coping guide for adults living with ADHD that presents useful coping strategies and specific tactics.

Tuckman, A. (2009). *More attention, less deficit: Success strategies for adults with ADHD.* Plantation, FL: Specialty Press.

This guidebook covers many useful topics, including the following: how the ADHD brain processes information, why certain strategies are effective and others aren't, getting diagnosed, treatment options, and practical strategies to overcome common struggles.

Tuckman, A. (2012). *Understand your brain, get more done: The ADHD executive functions workbook.* Plantation, FL: Specialty Press.

This workbook is a follow-up to Tuckman's 2009 book (above) and provides educational and interesting exercises for adult clients.

Zylowska, L. (2012). *The mindfulness prescription for adult ADHD: An 8-step program for strengthening attention, managing emotions, and achieving your goals.* Boston, MA: Trumpeter Press.

This is an area that is beginning to get more research attention, and there are some positive initial studies. In her book, Zylowska describes an eight-step program that includes practices such as sitting meditation, body awareness, thoughtful speaking and listening, development of self-acceptance, mindful self-coaching, and cultivation of a balanced view of thoughts and emotions. She does state that the mindfulness approach can be combined with other treatments, including medications. An audio program of mindfulness exercises accompanies the book.

BOOKS FOR CHILDREN AND ADOLESCENTS WITH ADHD

The books listed below can be quite useful to you as a coach if you plan to work with children or adolescents. You can easily incorporate the strategies and suggestions into your own practice. Alternately, these are good resources to recommend to parents of your child clients.

Barkley, R. A. (2013). *Taking charge of ADHD: The complete authoritative guide for parents* (rev. ed.). New York, NY: Guilford Press.

This book gives empirically based information about ADHD and its treatment. It also presents an eight-step behavior management plan designed for 6- to 18-year-olds with ADHD. This would be useful for parents who need help getting a diagnosis, working with their child's school, learning parenting techniques, using rewards and incentives, understanding medications.

Monastra, V. J. (2014). *Parenting children with ADHD: Ten lessons that medicine cannot teach* (2nd ed.). Washington, DC: American Psychological Association.

This new edition provides practical guidance to parents. Monastra has updated chapters on causes of ADHD; how medications work; and the problems that sleep deficits, poor nutrition, and other medical disorders can cause. The book gives practical tips on improving organization, task completion, problem solving, and emotional control. This edition also has a new chapter on teaching life values such as kindness, generosity, and compassion.

Shapiro, L. E. (2010). *The ADHD workbook for kids: Helping children gain self-confidence, social skills & self-control.* Oakland, CA: Instant Help Books.

For children 6 to 12 years old. This workbook includes more than 40 activities for kids that can help a child with ADHD handle everyday tasks, make friends, and build self-esteem. The activities are designed to be done daily, and take about 10 minutes each. The reviews of this book are positive; however, some reviewers have noted that all the activities are paper-and-pencil tasks, and could be a bit tedious.

Clinics

There are numerous private practice clinics that specialize in ADHD, and you can find those by doing Internet searches of the city in which you are interested. We have listed below some of the clinics that are associated with universities and are conducting research on ADHD. If you are a student in training or are interested in research opportunities, these would be excellent sources.

The Adult Learning Evaluation Center (ALEC). Florida State University, Tallahassee. http://www.coe.fsu.edu/ALEC. ALEC is a not-for-profit psychological assessment clinic specializing in the assessment and treatment of college students and other adults with ADHD and learning disabilities. The center is staffed by doctoral and EdS students earning degrees in school psychology and counseling psychology. The ALEC provides services to the community, training for graduate students, and conducts research on ADHD. Executive Director—Frances Prevatt, PhD; Director—Eve Wettstein, MS.

The Center of Excellence in ADHD and Related Disorders. Mount Sinai School of Medicine, New York, NY. http://icahn.mssm.edu/research/centers/attention-deficit-hyperactivity-disorder-center. For children, adolescents, and adults. The Center of Excellence in ADHD and Related Disorders provides assessment, treatment, consultation, and research. The center's efforts link evidence-based pharmacologic and psychosocial treatments with state of the art research approaches using neuroimaging and genetics, ensuring that advances in the scientific basis of ADHD and its treatment inform clinical care delivery. Medical Director—Jeffrey Newcorn, MD.

The University of Pennsylvania School of Medicine Adult ADHD Treatment and Research Program. Philadelphia, PA. http://www.med.upenn.edu/add/adhd_group.html?2. The ADHD Treatment Program conducts research, and provides evaluation and treatment, including a group ADHD Coaching program. Director—Anthony Rostain, MD; Associate Director—J. Russell Ramsay, PhD.

Journals and Periodicals

ADDitude Magazine: Living Well With Attention Deficit (http://www.additudemag.com/adhd-guide/adult-adhd.html)

This publication is in print and digital editions. It includes links to webinars by experts (e.g., using CBT strategies); suggestions for apps, games, and software; and blogs by experts, parents, and adults with ADHD (e.g., ADHD DAD, ADHD in the City). There are links to discussion groups (e.g., Should I disclose my diagnosis at work?) and book reviews.

The ADHD Report (http://www.guilford.com/journals/The-ADHD-Report/Russell-Barkley/10658025)

This research-focused periodical is edited by Dr. Russell Barkley, and is published eight times per year. Most issues contain several short articles by leading experts in the field, as well as reviews of articles published in other journals.

Attention Magazine (http://www.chadd.org/Membership/Attention-Magazine.aspx)

Published by Children and Adults With Attention-Deficit/Hyperactivity Disorder (CHADD), this periodical is intended primarily for those with ADHD. It contains short applied articles, reviews, and information about support services.

Journal of Attention Disorders (http://jad.sagepub.com)

JAD is a peer-reviewed scientific journal that publishes articles on diagnosis, comorbidity, neuropsychological functioning, psychopharmacology, and psychosocial issues. The journal also addresses practice, policy, and theory, as well as review articles, commentaries, in-depth analyses, empirical research articles, and case presentations or program evaluations. The *Online First* version publishes articles ahead of print, and is an excellent source for the latest research: http://jad.sagepub.com/content/early/recent

Organizations and Conferences

ADHD Coaches Organization (ACO) (http://www.adhdcoaches.org)
The ADHD Coaches Organization is a nonprofit association created to advance the profession of ADHD. Their annual conference is designed for coaches and others working within the ADHD community. In addition to learning and networking, participants can gain hours needed for certification as an ACO coach.

American Professional Society of ADHD and Related Disorders (APSARD) (http://www.apsard.org/)
APSARD is an international membership organization consisting of a broad spectrum of allied mental health experts working to improve the quality of care for patients with ADHD through the exchange of research, best practices and evidence-based insights. APSARD has a strong emphasis on adults. Their annual conference is generally in the fall. This conference will have a higher number of talks by physicians and researchers, as compared with CHADD, which will have a broad range of presenters, including those with ADHD.

Association on Higher Education and Disability (AHEAD) (http://ahead.org/about)
AHEAD is a an international organization for individuals involved in the development of policy and in the provision of services to meet the needs of persons with disabilities involved in all areas of higher education. AHEAD delivers training to higher education personnel through conferences, workshops, publications and consultation. This organization can be especially useful if you have questions regarding ADA issues, accommodations for college students or legal rights for adults with ADHD.

Attention Deficit Disorder Association (ADDA) (http://www.add.org)
This organization provides resources for adults with ADHD. Their mission is stated as "Helping adults with ADHD lead better lives." The website has a Legislative Action Center, webinars, links to find a professional, articles, and FAQ sheets. This association also sponsors a yearly international conference.

Children and Adults With Attention-Deficit/Hyperactivity Disorder (CHADD) (http://www.chadd.org)
This professional organization provides education, advocacy, and support. There is a yearly international conference plus numerous regional conferences attended by parents, educators, researchers, mental health professionals and those with ADHD. CHADD now

also has virtual conferences (online). Their website has experts, blogs, online chats, resources, advocacy groups, local CHADD chapters, continuing education, and an online library. CHADD publishes *Attention Magazine* and supports the National Resource Center on ADHD (see the Websites section in this list of resources).

International Coaches Federation (http://www.coachfederation.org)
Professional coach Thomas Leonard started ICF in 1995 as a nonprofit organization for coaches (including but not limited to the ADHD field) to support each other and grow the profession. ICF created Core Competencies and built a Code of Ethics. An Ethical Conduct Review Process and Independent Review Board (IRB) were established, allowing consumers to file breach-of-ethics complaints. ICF also defined curriculum standards (accreditation), to ensure consistency in coach training, and developed an ICF Credentialing system, requiring renewal every 3 years.

Radio

Attention Talk Radio (http://www.blogtalkradio.com/attentiontalkradio)
This weekly self-help Internet radio show focuses exclusively on ADHD. Topics include managing symptoms of attention-deficit disorder, adults with ADHD, or adults who have children with ADHD. It is hosted by "attention coach" Jeff Copper.

Tests

There are many checklists that can help you to rate the core symptoms of ADHD. The following test is free and can be obtained from the first author. We use it for all of our college students with ADHD, as it allows one to quickly evaluate key areas of academic functioning associated with executive functioning and academic success.

Prevatt, F., Li, H., Welles, T., Festa-Dreher, D., Yelland, S., & Lee., J. (2011). The Academic Success Inventory for College Students: Scale development and practical implications for use with students. *Journal of College Admission, 211,* 26–31.

This 50-item self-report measure gives normed scores in each of the following domains: basic academic skills, internal motivation and self-confidence, current external motivation, future external motivation, career decidedness, anxiety, concentration, excessive socialization, personal difficulties, and beliefs about the efficacy of instructors.

Videos

Levrini, A. [Abigail Levrini]. (2009, October 15). *ADHD coaching tips and strategies part I-Psych Ed Coaches—Abigail Levrini, Ph.D.* [Video file]. Retrieved from http://www.youtube.com/watch?v=Kj0hdNE6MBM

Levrini, A. [Abigail Levrini]. (2009, October 15). *ADHD coaching tips and strategies part II* [Video file]. Retrieved from http://www.youtube.com/watch?v=xaA5NFPLZ2E

This two part video program shows Dr. Levrini doing ADHD coaching with two different clients. These videos were first shown during her 2009 presentation at the CHADD conference.

Levrini, A., & Prevatt, F. (2014). *Adult ADHD* [DVD]. Washington, DC: American Psychological Association. Available from http://www.apa.org/pubs/videos/4310917.aspx

This video shows how Drs. Prevatt and Levrini engage in the coaching process. The video begins with a general explanation of coaching. Then, Dr. Levrini works with a man in his 20s, recently diagnosed with ADHD, who seeks assistance in overcoming distractions and managing his time better. Dr. Levrini incorporates techniques used in the intake, beginning, and middle sessions as she demonstrates core coaching concepts and strategies. Finally, Drs. Levrini and Prevatt answer questions from an academic audience as they expand on the live coaching demonstration.

Websites

There are virtually unlimited resources available on the Internet. We've picked just a few that we tend to access frequently. These are websites that you might refer your clients to if they want basic information regarding ADHD, one ADHD coaching site, as well as one child-oriented site.

Centers for Disease Control and Prevention (http://www.cdc.gov/ncbddd/adhd/facts.html)

This site gives helpful information for you or your client, including prevalence, handouts, fact sheets, posters, research, downloadable booklets, and articles.

Edge Foundation (https://edgefoundation.org)

An executive who has two children with ADHD founded this nonprofit organization is devoted to providing research-based ADHD coaching for students. Their goal is to train and solicit ADHD coaches, and provide those coaches to students, especially those at risk of dropping out of school.

Fin, Fur and Feather Bureau of Investigation (http://www.fffbi.com/info/academy.html)
This website is funded by the U.S. Department of Education. It provides a set of Internet-based games for 8- to 13-year-old kids with ADHD. Each game is designed to teach useful skills and strategies, such as staying organized, managing homework, listening, and staying focused. The games encourage players to complete increasingly difficult tasks. The games use a stop secret spy theme and frequent reinforcements to maintain interest.

National Institute of Mental Health (http://www.nimh.nih.gov/health/topics/attention-deficit-hyperactivity-disorder-adhd/index.shtml#part6)
This site covers a variety of topics related to ADHD, the most helpful of which might be the section on medications, which includes a list of FDA-approved medications, side effects, and warnings.

National Resource Center on ADHD (http://help4adhd.org)
This is a program of CHADD that is funded by the Centers for Disease Control and Prevention, National Center on Birth Defects and Developmental Disabilities (CDC/NCBDDD). The website includes science, general information, resources, support, webinars, FAQs, "Ask the Expert," chat rooms, and a library. Also included are the latest news reports from the CDC, FDA, and the U.S. Surgeon General. The site includes a toll free number to talk with a Health Information Specialist 1-800-233-4050.

WEBMD (http://www.webmd.com/add-adhd/features/adult-adhd-treatment)
This site features articles citing a variety of experts on topics such as organization, employment, marriage and relationships, vitamins and supplements, and sleep disorders. There is a slide show on topics such as foods that help you focus or how to reduce side effects from drugs.

We want to emphasize again that there are numerous resources to help you learn about ADHD. We do not intend this to be an all-inclusive list. We do think that the resources listed here will give you a strong foundation in the science of ADHD and help you in developing ADHD coaching skills. In closing, we want to remind you that perhaps your most valuable resource will be your clients. They will teach you, inspire you, change your beliefs about ADHD, and convince you of the power of individuals to change and grow.

References

Aaron, P. G., Joshi, R. M., Palmer, H., Smith, N., & Kirby, E. (2002). Separating genuine cases of reading disability from reading deficits caused by predominantly inattentive ADHD behavior. *Journal of Learning Disabilities, 35*, 425–435, 447. http://dx.doi.org/10.1177/00222194020350050301

Adler, L. A. (2004). Clinical presentations of adult patients with ADHD. *Journal of Clinical Psychiatry, 65*(Suppl. 3), 8–11.

Advokat, C., Lane, S. M., & Luo, C. (2011). College students with and without ADHD: Comparison of self-report of medication usage, study habits, and academic achievement. *Journal of Attention Disorders, 15*, 656–666. http://dx.doi.org/10.1177/1087054710371168

Alexander, S. J., & Harrison, A. G. (2013). Cognitive responses to stress, depression, and anxiety and their relationship to ADHD symptoms in first year psychology students. *Journal of Attention Disorders, 17*, 29–37. http://dx.doi.org/10.1177/1087054711413071

American Psychiatric Association. (2013). *Diagnostic and statistical manual of mental disorders* (5th ed.). Arlington, VA: Author.

American Psychological Association. (2010). *Ethical principles of psychologists and code of conduct (2002, Amended June 1, 2010)*. Retrieved from http://www.apa.org/ethics/Code/index.aspx

Americans With Disabilities Act of 2008, 42 U.S.C. § 12102 (1)(A) (2008). Retrieved from http://www.access-board.gov/about/laws/ada-amendments.htm

Antshel, K. M., Faraone, S. V., & Gordon, M. (2012). Cognitive behavioral treatment outcomes in adolescent ADHD. *Journal of Attention Disorders, 18*, 483–495. http://dx.doi.org/10.1177/1087054712443155

Anuta, J. (2006). Probing question: Has there been an increase in ADHD? *Penn State News.* Retrieved from http://news.psu.edu/story/141162/2006/02/27/research/probing-question-has-there-been-increase-adhd

August, G. J., & Garfinkel, B. D. (1990). Comorbidity of ADHD and reading disability among clinic-referred children. *Journal of Abnormal Child Psychology, 18*, 29–45. http://dx.doi.org/10.1007/BF00919454

Bagwell, C. L., Molina, B. S., Pelham, W. E., Jr., & Hoza, B. (2001). Attention-deficit hyperactivity disorder and problems in peer relations: Predictions from childhood to adolescence. *Journal of the American Academy of Child & Adolescent Psychiatry, 40*, 1285–1292. http://dx.doi.org/10.1097/00004583-200111000-00008

Barak, A., Hen, L., Boniel-Nissim, M., & Shapira, N. A. (2008). A comprehensive review and a meta-analysis of the effectiveness of Internet-based psychotherapeutic interventions. *Journal of Technology in Human Services, 26*, 109–160. http://dx.doi.org/10.1080/15228830802094429

Barbaresi, W. J., Katusic, S. K., Colligan, R. C., Weaver, A. L., & Jacobsen, S. J. (2007). Long-term school outcomes for children with attention-deficit/hyperactivity disorder: A population-based perspective. *Journal of Developmental and Behavioral Pediatrics, 28*, 265–273. http://dx.doi.org/10.1097/DBP.0b013e31811ff87d

Barkley, R. A. (1997). *ADHD and the nature of self-control.* New York, NY: Guilford Press.

Barkley, R. A. (1998). *Attention-deficit hyperactivity disorder: A handbook for diagnosis and treatment.* New York, NY: Guilford Press.

Barkley, R. A. (2002). Major life activity and health outcomes associated with attention-deficit/hyperactivity disorder. *Journal of Clinical Psychiatry, 63*(Suppl. 12), 10–15.

Barkley, R. A. (2004). Adolescents with attention-deficit/hyperactivity disorder: An overview of empirically based treatments. *Journal of Psychiatric Practice, 10*, 39–56. http://dx.doi.org/10.1097/00131746-200401000-00005

Barkley, R. A. (2005). *Attention-deficit hyperactivity disorder: A handbook for diagnosis and treatment* (Vol. 1). New York, NY: Guilford Press.

Barkley, R. A. (2010). Evaluating executive functioning deficits in everyday life. *The ADHD Report, 18*(6), 9–10. http://dx.doi.org/10.1521/adhd.2010.18.6.9

Barkley, R. A. (2011a). *Barkley Adult ADHD Rating Scale—IV* (BAARS—IV). New York, NY: Guilford Press.

Barkley, R. A. (2011b). *Barkley Deficits in Executive Functioning Scale (BDEFS)*. New York, NY: Guilford Press.

Barkley, R. A. (2013). *Taking charge of ADHD: The complete authoritative guide for parents* (rev. ed.). New York, NY: Guilford Press.

Barkley, R. A., & Fischer, M. (2010). The unique contribution of emotional impulsiveness to impairment in major life activities in hyperactive children as adults. *Journal of the American Academy of Child & Adolescent Psychiatry, 49*, 503–513.

Barkley, R. A., Fischer, M., Smallish, L., & Fletcher, K. (2006). Young adult outcome of hyperactive children: Adaptive functioning in major life activities. *Journal of the American Academy of Child & Adolescent Psychiatry, 45*, 192–202. http://dx.doi.org/10.1097/01.chi.0000189134.97436.e2

Barkley, R. A., & Murphy, K. R. (2011). The nature of executive function (EF) deficits in daily life activities in adults with ADHD and their relationship to performance on EF tests. *Journal of Psychopathology and Behavioral Assessment, 33*, 137–158. http://dx.doi.org/10.1007/s10862-011-9217-x

Barkley, R. A., Murphy, K. R., & Fischer, M. (2008). *ADHD in adults: What the science says*. New York, NY: Guilford Press.

Barry, T. D., Lyman, R., & Klinger, L. G. (2002). Academic underachievement and attention-deficit/hyperactivity disorder: The negative impact of symptom severity on school performance. *Journal of School Psychology, 40*, 259–283. http://dx.doi.org/10.1016/S0022-4405(02)00100-0

Beck, A. T. (1967). *Depression: Causes and treatment*. Philadelphia: University of Pennsylvania Press.

Bekker, E. M., Overtoom, C. C., Kenemans, J. L., Kooij, J. J., De Noord, I., Buitelaar, J. K., & Verbaten, M. N. (2005). Stopping and changing in adults with ADHD. *Psychological Medicine, 35*, 807–816. http://dx.doi.org/10.1017/S0033291704003459

Biederman, J., & Faraone, S. V. (2006). The effects of attention deficit/hyperactivity disorder on employment and household income. *Medscape General Medicine, 8*, 12.

Biederman, J., Faraone, S. V., & Chen, W. J. (1993). Social Adjustment Inventory for Children and Adolescents: Concurrent validity in ADHD children. *Journal of the American Academy of Child & Adolescent Psychiatry, 32*, 1059–1064. http://dx.doi.org/10.1097/00004583-199309000-00027

Bijlenga, D., Van Someren, E. J., Gruber, R., Bron, T. I., Kruithof, I. F., Spanbroek, E. C., & Kooij, J. J. (2013). Body temperature, activity and melatonin profiles in adults with attention-deficit/hyperactivity disorder and delayed sleep: A case–control study. *Journal of Sleep Research, 22,* 607–616. http://dx.doi.org/10.1111/jsr.12075

Birchwood, J., & Daley, D. (2012). Brief report: The impact of attention deficit hyperactivity disorder (ADHD) symptoms on academic performance in an adolescent community sample. *Journal of Adolescence, 35,* 225–231. http://dx.doi.org/10.1016/j.adolescence.2010.08.011

Bledsoe, J. C., Semrud-Clikeman, M., & Pliszka, S. R. (2010). Response inhibition and academic abilities in typically developing children with attention-deficit-hyperactivity disorder-combined subtype. *Archives of Clinical Neuropsychology, 25,* 671–679. http://dx.doi.org/10.1093/arclin/acq048

Bramham, J., Young, S., Bickerdike, A., Spain, D., McCartan, D., & Xenitidis, K. (2009). Evaluation of group cognitive behavioral therapy for adults with ADHD. *Journal of Attention Disorders, 12,* 434–441. http://dx.doi.org/10.1177/1087054708314596

Brown, T. E. (2008). ADD/ADHD and impaired executive function in clinical practice. *Current Psychiatry Reports, 10,* 407–411. http://dx.doi.org/10.1007/s11920-008-0065-7

Brymer, E., Cuddihy, T. F., & Sharma-Brymer, V. (2010). The role of nature-based experiences in the development and maintenance of wellness. *Asia-Pacific Journal of Health, Sport and Physical Education, 1,* 21–27.

Canu, W. H., & Carlson, C. L. (2003). Differences in heterosocial behavior and outcomes of ADHD-symptomatic subtypes in a college sample. *Journal of Attention Disorders, 6,* 123–133. http://dx.doi.org/10.1177/108705470300600304

Carlson, C. L., Booth, J. E., Shin, M., & Canu, W. H. (2002). Parent-, teacher-, and self-rated motivational styles in ADHD subtypes. *Journal of Learning Disabilities, 35,* 104–113. http://dx.doi.org/10.1177/002221940203500202

Centers for Disease Control and Prevention. (2012). *Attention-deficit/hyperactivity disorder: Data & statistics.* Retrieved from http://www.cdc.gov/ncbddd/adhd/data.html

Chandler, M. L. (2013). Psychotherapy for adult attention deficit/hyperactivity disorder: A comparison with cognitive behaviour therapy. *Journal of Psychiatric and Mental Health Nursing, 20,* 814–820.

Charach, A., Yeung, E., Climans, T., & Lillie, E. (2011). Childhood attention-deficit/hyperactivity disorder and future substance use disorders: Comparative meta-analyses. *Journal of the American Academy of Child & Adolescent Psychiatry, 50,* 9–21. http://dx.doi.org/10.1016/j.jaac.2010.09.019

Coffman, T. P. (2014). *The psychometric properties of the Barkley Deficits in Executive Functioning Scale (Bdefs) in a college student population* (Doctoral dissertation). Retrieved from http://diginole.lib.fsu.edu/etd/8961

Connor, D. J. (2012). Helping students with disabilities transition to college. *Teaching Exceptional Children, 44*(5), 16–25.

Cortese, S., Kelly, C., Chabernaud, C., Proal, E., Di Martino, A., Milham, M. P., & Castellanos, F. X. (2012). Toward systems neuroscience of ADHD: A meta-analysis of 55 fMRI studies. *The American Journal of Psychiatry, 169,* 1038–1055. http://dx.doi.org/10.1176/appi.ajp.2012.11101521

Cumyn, L., French, L., & Hechtman, L. (2009). Comorbidity in adults with attention-deficit hyperactivity disorder. *Canadian Journal of Psychiatry, 54,* 673–683.

Davidson, M. A. (2008). ADHD in adults: A review of the literature. *Journal of Attention Disorders, 11,* 628–641. http://dx.doi.org/10.1177/1087054707310878

Dehili, V. M., Prevatt, F., & Coffman, T. P. (2013). An analysis of the Barkley Deficits in Executive Functioning Scale in a college population: Does it predict symptoms of ADHD better than a visual-search task? *Journal of Attention Disorders.* Advance online publication. http://dx.doi.org/10.1177/1087054713498932

Dias, G., Mattos, P., Coutinho, G., Segenreich, D., Saboya, E., & Ayrão, V. (2008). Agreement rates between parent and self-report on past ADHD symptoms in an adult clinical sample. *Journal of Attention Disorders, 12,* 70–75. http://dx.doi.org/10.1177/1087054707311221

Dittner, A. J., Rimes, K. A., Russell, A. J., & Chalder, T. (2014). Protocol for a proof of concept randomized controlled trial of cognitive-behavioural therapy for adult ADHD as a supplement to treatment as usual, compared with treatment as usual alone. *BMC Psychiatry, 14,* 248. http://dx.doi.org/10.1186/s12888-014-0248-1

DuPaul, G. J., Weyandt, L. L., O'Dell, S. M., & Varejao, M. (2009). College students with ADHD: Current status and future directions. *Journal of Attention Disorders, 13,* 234–250. http://dx.doi.org/10.1177/1087054709340650

DuPaul, G. J., Weyandt, L. L., Rossi, J. S., Vilardo, B. A., O'Dell, S. M., Carson, K. M., . . . Swentosky, A. (2012). Double blind, placebo-controlled, crossover study of the efficacy and safety of lisdexamfetamine dimesylate in college students with ADHD. *Journal of Attention Disorders, 16,* 202–220. http://dx.doi.org/10.1177/1087054711427299

Edwards, G., Barkley, R. A., Laneri, M., Fletcher, K., & Metevia, L. (2001). Parent–adolescent conflict in teenagers with ADHD and ODD. *Journal of Abnormal Child Psychology, 29,* 557–572. http://dx.doi.org/10.1023/A:1012285326937

Eisenberg, D., & Schneider, H. (2007). Perceptions of academic skills of children diagnosed with ADHD. *Journal of Attention Disorders, 10,* 390–397. http://dx.doi.org/10.1177/1087054706292105

Ek, U., Westerlund, J., Holmberg, K., & Fernell, E. (2011). Academic performance of adolescents with ADHD and other behavioural and learning problems—a population-based longitudinal study. *Acta Paediatrica, 100*, 402–406. http://dx.doi.org/10.1111/j.1651-2227.2010.02048.x

Ellis, A. (1957). Rational psychotherapy and individual psychology. *Journal of Individual Psychology, 13*, 38–44.

Estrada, R. V., Bosch, R., Nogueira, M., Gómez-Barros, N., Valero, S., Palomar, G., . . . Ramos-Quiroga, J. A. (2013). Psychoeducation for adults with attention deficit hyperactivity disorder vs. cognitive behavioral group therapy: A randomized controlled pilot study. *Journal of Nervous and Mental Disease, 201*, 894–900. http://dx.doi.org/10.1097/NMD.0b013e3182a5c2c5

Evans, S. W., Schultz, B. K., & DeMars, C. E. (2014). High school–based treatment for adolescents with attention-deficit/hyperactivity disorder: Results from a pilot study examining outcomes and dosage. *School Psychology Review, 43*, 185–202.

Fabiano, G. A., Pelham, W. E., Cunningham, C. E., Yu, J., Gangloff, B., Buck, M., . . . Gera, S. (2012). A waitlist-controlled trial of behavioral parent training for fathers of children with ADHD. *Journal of Clinical Child and Adolescent Psychology, 41*, 337–345. http://dx.doi.org/10.1080/15374416.2012.654464

Faigel, H. C. (1995). Attention deficit disorder in college students: Facts, fallacies, and treatment. *Journal of American College Health, 43*, 147–155. http://dx.doi.org/10.1080/07448481.1995.9940467

Faraone, S. V., & Doyle, A. E. (2001). The nature and heritability of attention-deficit/hyperactivity disorder. *Child and Adolescent Psychiatric Clinics of North America, 10*, 299–316, viii–ix.

Favorite, B. (1995). Coaching for adults with ADHD: The missing link between the desire for change and achievement of success. *The ADHD Report, 3*, 11–12.

Feder, K. P., & Majnemer, A. (2007). Handwriting development, competency, and intervention. *Developmental Medicine & Child Neurology, 49*, 312–317. http://dx.doi.org/10.1111/j.1469-8749.2007.00312.x

Field, S., Parker, D. R., Sawilowsky, S., & Rolands, L. (2013). Assessing the impact of ADHD coaching services on university students' learning skills, self-regulation, and well-being. *Journal of Postsecondary Education and Disability, 26*, 67–81. Retrieved from http://ahead.org/uploads/publications/JPED/jped26_1/JPED26_1_FullDocument.pdf#page=69

Fried, R., Petty, C., Faraone, S. V., Hyder, L. L., Day, H., & Biederman, J. (2013). Is ADHD a risk factor for high school dropout? A controlled study. *Journal of Attention Disorders, 18*, 179–185.

Gaddy, S. (2008). Students with ADHD get "ACCESS" to support network. *Disability Compliance for Higher Education, 13*, 1–16. http://dx.doi.org/10.1002/dhe.20007

Gizer, I. R., Ficks, C., & Waldman, I. D. (2009). Candidate gene studies of ADHD: A meta-analytic review. *Human Genetics, 126,* 51–90. doi:10.1007=s00439-009-0694-x http://dx.doi.org/10.1007/s00439-009-0694-x

Goldstein, S. (2005). Coaching as a treatment for ADHD [Editorial]. *Journal of Attention Disorders, 9,* 379–381. http://dx.doi.org/10.1177/1087054705282198

Grenwald-Mayes, G. (2002). Relationship between current quality of life and family of origin dynamics for college students with attention-deficit/hyperactivity disorder. *Journal of Attention Disorders, 5,* 211–222. http://dx.doi.org/10.1177/108705470100500403

Gudjonsson, G. H., Sigurdsson, J. F., Gudmundsdottir, H. B., Sigurjonsdottir, S., & Smari, J. (2010). The relationship between ADHD symptoms in college students and core components of maladaptive personality. *Personality and Individual Differences, 48,* 601–606. http://dx.doi.org/10.1016/j.paid.2009.12.015

Harbour, W. S. (2004). *The 2004 AHEAD survey of higher education disability service providers.* Waltham, MA: Association of Higher Education and Disability.

Harrison, J. R., Bunford, N., Evans, S. W., & Owens, J. S. (2013). Educational accommodations for students with behavioral challenges: A systematic review of the literature. *Review of Educational Research, 83,* 551–597. http://dx.doi.org/10.3102/0034654313497517

Hart, E. L., Lahey, B. B., Loeber, R., Applegate, B., & Frick, P. J. (1995). Developmental change in attention-deficit hyperactivity disorder in boys: A four-year longitudinal study. *Journal of Abnormal Child Psychology, 23,* 729–749. http://dx.doi.org/10.1007/BF01447474

Health Insurance Portability and Accountability Act of 1996. Pub.L. 104–191, 110 Stat. Retrieved from http://www.hhs.gov/ocr/privacy/hipaa/administrative/privacyrule

Hearn, A. (2009). *The processing exercise.* Unpublished manuscript.

Hearn, A., & Levrini, A. (2009). *The juggling exercise.* Unpublished manuscript.

Heiligenstein, E., Guenther, G., Levy, A., Savino, F., & Fulwiler, J. (1999). Psychological and academic functioning in college students with attention deficit hyperactivity disorder. *Journal of American College Health, 47,* 181–185. http://dx.doi.org/10.1080/07448489909595644

Hinshaw, S. P., & Scheffler, R. M. (2014). *The ADHD explosion: Myths, medications, money, and today's push for performance.* New York, NY: Oxford University Press.

Hodgson, K., Hutchinson, A. D., & Denson, L. (2014). Nonpharmacological treatments for ADHD: A meta-analytic review. *Journal of Attention Disorders, 18,* 275–282. http://dx.doi.org/10.1177/1087054712444732

Hoza, B., Gerdes, A. C., Mrug, S., Hinshaw, S. P., Bukowski, W. M., Gold, J. A., . . . Wigal, T. (2005). Peer-assessed outcomes in the multi-modal treatment study of children with attention-deficit hyperactivity disorder. *Journal of the American Academy of Child and Adolescent Psychiatry, 34,* 74–86.

Individuals With Disabilities Education Improvement Act of 2004, 20 U.S.C. §§ 1412(a)(16)(A) (2004). Retrieved from http://idea.ed.gov.proxy.lib.fsu.edu/download/statute.html

Jaska, P., & Ratey, N. (1999, Summer). Therapy and ADD coaching: Similarities, differences, and collaboration. *Focus, 3,* 10–11.

Kamradt, J. M., Ullsperger, J. M., & Nikolas, M. A. (2014). Executive function assessment and adult attention-deficit/hyperactivity disorder: Tasks versus ratings on the Barkley Deficits in Executive Functioning Scale. *Psychological Assessment, 26,* 1095–1105. http://dx.doi.org/10.1037/pas0000006

Kazantzis, N., Deane, F. P., & Ronan, K. R. (2000). Homework assignments in cognitive and behavioral therapy: A meta-analysis. *Clinical Psychology: Science and Practice, 7,* 189–202. http://dx.doi.org/10.1093/clipsy.7.2.189

Kazantzis, N., Lampropoulos, G. K., & Deane, F. P. (2005). A national survey of practicing psychologists' use and attitudes toward homework in psychotherapy. *Journal of Consulting and Clinical Psychology, 73,* 742–748. http://dx.doi.org/10.1037/0022-006X.73.4.742

Kelly, K., & Ramundo, P. (2006). *You mean I'm not stupid, lazy, or crazy?* New York, NY: Scribner.

Kern, R. M., Rasmussen, P. R., Byrd, S. L., & Wittschen, L. K. (1999). Lifestyle, personality, and attention deficit hyperactivity disorder in young adults. *The Journal of Individual Psychology, 55,* 101–116.

Kessler, G. (2014, January 27). Fact checker: Do nine out of 10 new businesses fail, as Rand Paul claims? *The Washington Post.* Retrieved from http://www.washingtonpost.com/blogs/fact-checker/wp/2014/01/27/do-9-out-of-10-new-businesses-fail-as-rand-paul-claims

Kessler, R. C., Adler, L., Barkley, R., Biederman, J., Conners, C. K., Demler, O., . . . Zaslavsky, A. M. (2006). The prevalence and correlates of adult ADHD in the United States: Results from the National Comorbidity Survey Replication. *The American Journal of Psychiatry, 163,* 716–723. http://dx.doi.org/10.1176/appi.ajp.163.4.716

Keyes, M. A., Sharma, A., Elkins, I. J., Iacono, W. G., & McGue, M. (2008). The mental health of U.S. adolescents adopted in infancy. *Archives of Pediatrics & Adolescent Medicine, 162,* 419–425. http://dx.doi.org/10.1001/archpedi.162.5.419

Knouse, L. E., Cooper-Vince, C., Sprich, S., & Safren, S. A. (2008). Recent developments in the psychosocial treatment of adult ADHD. *Expert Review of Neurotherapeutics, 8,* 1537–1548. http://dx.doi.org/10.1586/14737175.8.10.1537

Knouse, L. E., & Safren, S. A. (2010). Current status of cognitive behavioral therapy for adult attention-deficit hyperactivity disorder.

Psychiatric Clinics of North America, 33, 497–509. http://dx.doi.org/10.1016/j.psc.2010.04.001

Kooij, S. J. J., Bejerot, S., Blackwell, A., Caci, H., Casas-Brugué, M., Carpentier, P. J., . . . Asherson, P. (2010). European consensus statement on diagnosis and treatment of adult ADHD: The European Network Adult ADHD. *BMC Psychiatry, 10*, 67. http://dx.doi.org/10.1186/1471-244X-10-67

Kubik, J. A. (2010). Efficacy of ADHD coaching for adults with ADHD. *Journal of Attention Disorders, 13*, 442–453. http://dx.doi.org/10.1177/1087054708329960

Lambert, M. J., & Finch, A. E. (1999). The Outcome Questionnaire. In M. E. Maruish (Ed.), *The use of psychological testing for treatment planning and outcomes assessment* (2nd ed., pp. 831–869). Mahwah, NJ: Erlbaum.

Langmaid, R. A., Papadopoulos, N., Johnson, B. P., Phillips, J. G., & Rinehart, N. J. (2012). Handwriting in children with ADHD. *Journal of Attention Disorders, 18*, 504–510. http://dx.doi.org/10.1177/1087054711434154

Larson, K., Russ, S. A., Kahn, R. S., & Halfon, N. (2011). Patterns of comorbidity, functioning, and service use for US children with ADHD, 2007. *Pediatrics, 127*, 462–470. http://dx.doi.org/10.1542/peds.2010-0165

Lerner, M. D., Mikami, A. Y., & McLeod, B. D. (2011). The alliance in a friendship coaching intervention for parents of children with ADHD. *Behavior Therapy, 42*, 449–461. http://dx.doi.org.proxy.lib.fsu.edu/10.1016/j.beth.2010.11.006

Levrini, A. (2012). *The inspiration toolbox.* Unpublished manuscript.

Levrini, A., & Prevatt, F. (2012). *Succeeding with adult ADHD: Daily strategies to help achieve your goals and manage your life.* Washington, DC: American Psychological Association.

Levrini, A. & Prevatt, F. (2014). *Adult ADHD* [DVD]. Washington, DC: American Psychological Association. Available from http://www.apa.org/pubs/videos/4310917.aspx

Loe, I. M., & Feldman, H. M. (2007). Academic and educational outcomes of children with ADHD. *Journal of Pediatric Psychology, 32*, 643–654.

Lott, D. (1999, May). Drawing boundaries. *Psychology Today.* Retrieved from http://www.psychologytoday.com/articles/199905/drawing-boundaries

Marchetta, N. D., Hurks, P. P., De Sonneville, L. M., Krabbendam, L., & Jolles, J. (2008). Sustained and focused attention deficits in adult ADHD. *Journal of Attention Disorders, 11*, 664–676. http://dx.doi.org/10.1177/1087054707305108

Martin, S. D., & Zirkel, P. A. (2011). Identification disputes for students with attention deficit hyperactivity disorder: An analysis of the case law. *School Psychology Review, 40*, 405–422.

McCleary, L., & Ridley, T. (1999). Parenting adolescents with ADHD: Evaluation of a psychoeducation group. *Patient Education and Counseling, 38,* 3–10. http://dx.doi.org/10.1016/S0738-3991(98)00110-4

McGough, J. J., Smalley, S. L., McCracken, J. T., Yang, M., Del'Homme, M., Lynn, D. E., & Loo, S. (2005). Psychiatric comorbidity in adult attention deficit hyperactivity disorder: Findings from multiplex families. *The American Journal of Psychiatry, 162,* 1621–1627. http://dx.doi.org/10.1176/appi.ajp.162.9.1621

Millan, F. (2014, August). *Tele-psychology best practices.* Paper presented at the Annual Convention of the American Psychological Association, Washington, DC.

Miller-Johnson, S., Coie, J. D., Maumary-Gremaud, A., & Bierman, K., & the Conduct Problems Prevention Research Group. (2002). Peer rejection and aggression and early starter models of conduct disorder. *Journal of Abnormal Child Psychology, 30,* 217–230. http://dx.doi.org/10.1023/A:1015198612049

Mohammadi, M. R., & Akhondzadeh, S. (2007). Pharmacotherapy of attention-deficit/hyperactivity disorder: Nonstimulant medication approaches. *Expert Review of Neurotherapeutics, 7,* 195–201. http://dx.doi.org/10.1586/14737175.7.2.195

Monastra, V. J. (2005). Overcoming the barriers to effective treatment for attention-deficit/hyperactivity disorder: A neuro-educational approach. *International Journal of Psychophysiology, 58,* 71–80. http://dx.doi.org/10.1016/j.ijpsycho.2005.03.010

Monastra, V. J. (2014). *Parenting children with ADHD: Ten lessons that medicine cannot teach* (2nd ed.). Washington, DC: American Psychological Association.

Mongia, M., & Hechtman, L. (2012). Cognitive behavior therapy for adults with attention-deficit/hyperactivity disorder: A review of recent randomized controlled trials. *Current Psychiatry Reports, 14,* 561–567. http://dx.doi.org/10.1007/s11920-012-0303-x

Montano, B. (2004). Diagnosis and treatment of ADHD in adults in primary care. *Journal of Clinical Psychiatry, 65*(Suppl. 3), 18–21.

Montoya, A., Colom, F., & Ferrin, M. (2011). Is psychoeducation for parents and teachers of children and adolescents with ADHD efficacious? A systematic literature review. *European Psychiatry, 26,* 166–175. http://dx.doi.org/10.1016/j.eurpsy.2010.10.005

Morgan, K. (2012, August 2). Smooth transition: Researchers helping freshmen with ADHD succeed in college. *Science Daily.* Retrieved from http://www.sciencedaily.com/releases/2012/08/120802122317.htm?+Brain+News+—+Child+Development)

MTA Cooperative Group. (1999). A 14-month randomized clinical trial of treatment strategies for attention-deficit/hyperactivity disorder. *Archives of General Psychiatry, 56,* 1073–1086. http://dx.doi.org/10.1001/archpsyc.56.12.1073

Murphy, K. (2005). Psychosocial treatments for ADHD in teens and adults: A practice-friendly review. *Journal of Clinical Psychology, 61*, 607–619. http://dx.doi.org/10.1002/jclp.20123

Murphy, K., & Barkley, R. A. (1996). Attention deficit hyperactivity disorder adults: Comorbidities and adaptive impairments. *Comprehensive Psychiatry, 37*, 393–401. http://dx.doi.org/10.1016/S0010-440X(96)90022-X

Murphy, K., Ratey, N., Maynard, S., Sussman, S., & Wright, S. D. (2010). Coaching for ADHD. *Journal of Attention Disorders, 13*, 546–552.

Nadeau, K. G. (1996). *Adventures in fast forward: Life, love and work for the ADD adult*. New York, NY: Brunner-Routledge.

Nadeau, K. G. (1998). Psychotherapy for adults with ADHD: A call to training. *The ADHD Report, 3*, 9–11.

Nigg, J. T. (2012). Future directions in ADHD etiology research. *Journal of Clinical Child and Adolescent Psychology, 41*, 524–533. http://dx.doi.org/10.1080/15374416.2012.686870

Nigg, J. T., Nikolas, M., & Burt, S. A. (2010). Measured gene-by-environment interaction in relation to attention-deficit/hyperactivity disorder. *Journal of the American Academy of Child and Adolescent Psychiatry, 49*, 863–873. http://dx.doi.org/10.1016/j.jaac.2010.01.025

Nikolas, M. A., & Burt, S. A. (2010). Genetic and environmental influences on ADHD symptom dimensions of inattention and hyperactivity: A meta-analysis. *Journal of Abnormal Psychology, 119*, 1–17. http://dx.doi.org/10.1037/a0018010

Nordal, K. C. (2014). ICD implementation: Aim for the moving target. *Monitor on Psychology, 45*, 49. Retrieved from http://www.apa.org/monitor/2014/06/perspectives.aspx

Overbey, G. A., Snell, W. E., Jr., & Callis, K. E. (2011). Subclinical ADHD, stress, and coping in romantic relationships of university students. *Journal of Attention Disorders, 15*, 67–78. http://dx.doi.org/10.1177/1087054709347257

Painter, C., Prevatt, F., & Welles, T. (2008). Career beliefs and job satisfaction in adults with symptoms of attention-deficit/hyperactivity disorder. *Journal of Employment Counseling, 45*, 178–188. http://dx.doi.org/10.1002/j.2161-1920.2008.tb00057.x

Parker, D. R., & Boutelle, K. (2009). Executive function coaching for college students with learning disabilities and ADHD: A new approach for fostering self-determination. *Learning Disabilities Research & Practice, 24*, 204–215. http://dx.doi.org/10.1111/j.1540-5826.2009.00294.x

Parker, D. R., Hoffman, S. F., Sawilowsky, S., & Rolands, L. (2013). Self-control in postsecondary settings: Students' perceptions of ADHD college coaching. *Journal of Attention Disorders, 17*, 215–232. http://dx.doi.org/10.1177/1087054711427561

Paulson, J. F., Buermeyer, C., & Nelson-Gray, R. O. (2005). Social rejection and ADHD in young adults: An analogue experiment. *Journal of Attention Disorders, 8,* 127–135. http://dx.doi.org/10.1177/1087054705277203

Powers, R. L., Marks, D. J., Miller, C. J., Newcorn, J. H., & Halperin, J. M. (2008). Stimulant treatment in children with attention-deficit/hyperactivity disorder moderates adolescent academic outcome. *Journal of Child and Adolescent Psychopharmacology, 18,* 449–459. http://dx.doi.org/10.1089/cap.2008.021

Prevatt, F., Lampropoulos, G. K., Bowles, V., & Garrett, L. (2011). The use of between session assignments in ADHD coaching with college students. *Journal of Attention Disorders, 15,* 18–27. http://dx.doi.org/10.1177/1087054709356181

Prevatt, F., Li, H., Welles, T., Festa-Drehar, D., Yelland, S., & Lee, J. (2011, Spring). The Academic Success Inventory for College Students: Scale development and practical implications for use with students. *Journal of College Admission,* 26–31.

Prevatt, F., Walker, J. V., Baker, L., & Taylor, N. (2010). College students' self-perception of changes in ADHD symptoms over time for *DSM–V* subtype schema. *The ADHD Report, 16,* 9–16. http://dx.doi.org/10.1521/adhd.2010.18.4.9

Prevatt, F., & Yelland, S. (2013). An empirical evaluation of ADHD coaching in college students. *Journal of Attention Disorders.* Advance online publication. http://dx.doi.org/10.1177/1087054713480036

Prevatt, F., & Young, J. L. (2014). Recognizing and treating attention-deficit/hyperactivity disorder in college students. *Journal of College Student Psychotherapy, 28,* 182–200.

Quinn, P. O. (Ed.). (2001). *ADD and the college student: A guide for high school and college students with attention deficit disorder.* Washington, DC: Magination Press.

Quinn, P. O. (2005). Treating adolescent girls and women with ADHD: Gender-specific issues. *Journal of Clinical Psychology, 61,* 579–587. http://dx.doi.org/10.1002/jclp.20121

Rabiner, D. L., Anastopoulos, A. D., Costello, J., Hoyle, R. H., & Swartzwelder, H. S. (2008). Adjustment to college in students with ADHD. *Journal of Attention Disorders, 11,* 689–699. http://dx.doi.org/10.1177/1087054707305106

Raggi, V. L., & Chronis, A. M. (2006). Interventions to address the academic impairment of children and adolescents with ADHD. *Clinical Child and Family Psychology Review, 9,* 85–111. http://dx.doi.org/10.1007/s10567-006-0006-0

Ramsay, J. R., & Rostain, A. L. (2006). Cognitive behavior therapy for college students with attention-deficit/hyperactivity disorder. *Journal of College Student Psychotherapy, 21,* 3–20. http://dx.doi.org/10.1300/J035v21n01_02

Ratey, N. A. (2002). Life coaching for adult ADHD. In S. Goldstein & A. Teeter Ellison (Eds.), *Clinician's guide to adult ADHD: Assessment and intervention* (pp. 261–279). San Diego, CA: Academic Press. http://dx.doi.org/10.1016/B978-012287049-1/50016-5

Reaser, A. (2008). *ADHD coaching and college students* (Doctoral dissertation). Florida State University, Tallahassee. Retrieved from http://diginole.lib.fsu.edu/cgi/viewcontent.cgi?article=4395&context=etd

Reaser, A., Prevatt, F., Petscher, Y., & Proctor, B. (2007). The learning and study strategies of college students with ADHD. *Psychology in the Schools, 44*, 627–638. http://dx.doi.org/10.1002/pits.20252

Rehabilitation Act of 1973, Pub. L. No. 93-112, 93rd Cong., H.R. 8070.

Richman, E. L., Rademacher, K. N., & Maitland, T. L. (2014). Coaching and college success. *Journal of Postsecondary Education and Disability, 27*, 33–50. Retrieved from http://ahead.org/uploads/publications/JPED/JPED27_1/JPED27_1_FullDocument.pdf

Rosenberg, M. (1965). *Society and adolescent self-image*. Princeton, NJ: Princeton University Press.

Safren, S. A., Otto, M. W., Sprich, S., Winett, C. L., Wilens, T. E., & Biederman, J. (2005). Cognitive-behavioral therapy for ADHD in medication-treated adults with continued symptoms. *Behaviour Research and Therapy, 43*, 831–842. http://dx.doi.org/10.1016/j.brat.2004.07.001

Safren, S. A., Perlman, C. A., Sprich, S., & Otto, M. W. (2005). *Mastering your adult ADHD: A cognitive-behavioral treatment program*. New York, NY: Oxford University Press.

Sampson, J. P., Jr., Peterson, G. W., Lenz, J. G., Reardon, R. C., & Saunders, D. E. (1999). *The use and development of the Career Thoughts Inventory*. Retrieved from ERIC database. (ED447362)

Schachar, R. (2014). Genetics of attention deficit hyperactivity disorder (ADHD): Recent updates and future prospects. *Current Developmental Disorders Reports, 1*, 41–49.

Schatz, D. B., & Rostain, A. L. (2006). ADHD with comorbid anxiety: A review of the current literature. *Journal of Attention Disorders, 10*, 141–149. http://dx.doi.org/10.1177/1087054706286698

Schirduan, V., Case, K. I., & Faryniarz, J. (2002). How ADHD students are smart. *The Educational Forum, 66*, 324–328. http://dx.doi.org/10.1080/00131720208984851

Sciberras, E., Mueller, K. L., Efron, D., Bisset, M., Anderson, V., Schilpzand, E. J., . . . Nicholson, J. M. (2014). Language problems in children with ADHD: A community-based study. *Pediatrics, 133*, 793–800. http://dx.doi.org/10.1542/peds.2013-3355

Semrud-Clikeman, M. (2010). The role of inattention and social perception and performance in two subtypes of ADHD. *Archives Clinical Neuropsychology, 25*, 771–780. doi:10.1093/arclin/acq074

Shaw, P., Lerch, J., Greenstein, D., Sharp, W., Clasen, L., Evans, A., . . . Rapoport, J. (2006). Longitudinal mapping of cortical thickness and clinical outcome in children and adolescents with attention-deficit/hyperactivity disorder. *Archives of General Psychiatry, 63,* 540–549. http://dx.doi.org/10.1001/archpsyc.63.5.540

Shifrin, J. G., Proctor, B. E., & Prevatt, F. F. (2010). Work performance differences between college students with and without ADHD. *Journal of Attention Disorders, 13,* 489–496. http://dx.doi.org/10.1177/1087054709332376

Sibley, M. H., Kuriyan, A. B., Evans, S. W., Waxmonsky, J. G., & Smith, B. H. (2014). Pharmacological and psychosocial treatments for adolescents with ADHD: An updated systematic review of the literature. *Clinical Psychology Review, 34,* 218–232. http://dx.doi.org/10.1016/j.cpr.2014.02.001

Sibley, M. H., Pelham, W. E., Mazur, A. N., Ross, J. M., & Biswas, A. (2012). The effect of video-feedback on the social behavior of an adolescent with ADHD. *Journal of Attention Disorders, 16,* 579–588.

Sibley, M. H., Pelham, W. E., Molina, B. S., Gnagy, E. M., Waschbusch, D. A., Biswas, A., . . . Karch, K. M. (2011). The delinquency outcomes of boys with ADHD with and without comorbidity. *Journal of Abnormal Child Psychology, 39,* 21–32. http://dx.doi.org/10.1007/s10802-010-9443-9

Sisk, C. L., & Foster, D. L. (2004). The neural basis of puberty and adolescence. *Nature Neuroscience, 7,* 1040–1047. http://dx.doi.org/10.1038/nn1326

Smith, S. M., Prevatt, F., Diers, S., Marshall, D., Coleman, J., Valler, E., . . . Belle, J. (2014, August). *ADHD coaching with college students: Exploring the processes involved in motivation and goal completion.* Paper presented at the Annual Convention of the American Psychological Association, Washington, DC.

Sobanski, E. (2006). Psychiatric comorbidity in adults with attention-deficit/hyperactivity disorder (ADHD). *European Archives of Psychiatry and Clinical Neuroscience, 256*(1), i26–i31.

Solanto, M. (2013). *Cognitive-behavioral therapy for adult ADHD.* New York, NY: Guilford Press.

Solanto, M. V., Marks, D. J., Wasserstein, J., Mitchell, K., Abikoff, H., Alvir, J. M., & Kofman, M. D. (2010). Efficacy of meta-cognitive therapy for adult ADHD. *The American Journal of Psychiatry, 167,* 958–968. http://dx.doi.org/10.1176/appi.ajp.2009.09081123

Sonuga-Barke, E. J., Daley, D., Thompson, M., Laver-Bradbury, C., & Weeks, A. (2001). Parent-based therapies for preschool attention-deficit/hyperactivity disorder: A randomized, controlled trial with a community sample. *Journal of the American Academy of Child & Adolescent Psychiatry, 40,* 402–408. http://dx.doi.org/10.1097/00004583-200104000-00008

Steinberg, L., Fletcher, A., & Darling, N. (1994). Parental monitoring and peer influences on adolescent substance use. *Pediatrics, 93,* 1060–1064.

Suchy, Y. (2009). Executive functioning: Overview, assessment, and research issues for non-neuropsychologists. *Annals of Behavioral Medicine, 37,* 106–116. http://dx.doi.org/10.1007/s12160-009-9097-4

Surman, C. B. H., Adamson, J. J., Petty, C., Biederman, J., Kenealy, D. C., Levine, M., . . . Faraone, S. V. (2009). Association between attention-deficit/hyperactivity disorder and sleep impairment in adulthood: Evidence from a large controlled study. *Journal of Clinical Psychiatry, 70,* 1523–1529. http://dx.doi.org/10.4088/JCP.08m04514

Swartz, S., Prevatt, F., & Proctor, B. E. (2005). A coaching intervention for college students with attention deficit/hyperactivity disorder. *Psychology in the Schools, 42,* 647–656. http://dx.doi.org/10.1002/pits.20101

Tamm, L., Nakonezny, P. A., & Hughes, C. W. (2012). An open trial of a metacognitive executive function training for young children with ADHD. *Journal of Attention Disorders, 18,* 551–559. http://dx.doi.org/10.1177/1087054712445782

Teeter, P. A. (2000). *Interventions for ADHD: Treatment in developmental context.* New York, NY: Guilford Press.

Thomas, M., Rostain, A., & Prevatt, F. A. (2013). ADHD diagnosis and treatment in young adults and college students. In A. Joffee (Ed.), *Adolescent medicine: State of the art reviews* (pp. 659–680). Elk Grove Village, IL: American Academy of Pediatrics.

Thompson, A. E., Morgan, C., & Urquhart, I. (2003). Children with ADHD transferring to secondary schools: Potential difficulties and solutions. *Clinical Child Psychology and Psychiatry, 8,* 91–103. http://dx.doi.org/10.1177/1359104503008001009

Thompson, A. L., Molina, B. S., Pelham, W., Jr., & Gnagy, E. M. (2007). Risky driving in adolescents and young adults with childhood ADHD. *Journal of Pediatric Psychology, 32,* 745–759. http://dx.doi.org/10.1093/jpepsy/jsm002

Torrente, F., López, P., Alvarez Prado, D., Kichic, R., Cetkovich Bakmas, M., Lischinsky, A., & Manes, F. (2012). Dysfunctional cognitions and their emotional, behavioral, and functional correlates in adults with attention deficit hyperactivity disorder (ADHD): Is the cognitive-behavioral model valid? *Journal of Attention Disorders, 18,* 412–424. http://dx.doi.org/10.1177/1087054712443153

Troller, J. (2010). ADHD: A lifespan perspective. *Journal of Paediatrics and Child Health, 46*(Suppl. 2), 1–6.

Tuckman, A. (2012). *Understand your brain, get more done: The ADHD executive functions workbook.* Plantation, FL: Specialty Press.

Ursiny, T. (2005). *The confidence plan: How to build a stronger you.* Naperville, IL: Sourcebooks.

Wachter, G. (2001, February 23). *HIPAA's privacy rule summarized: What does it mean for telemedicine?* Telemedicine Information Exchange. Retrieved from http://tie.telemed.org/articles/article.asp?path=legal &article=hipaaSummary_gw_tie01.xml

Weinstein, C. E., & Palmer, D. R. (2002). *The Learning and Study Strategies Inventory: User's manual* (2nd ed.). Clearwater, FL: H & H.

Wender, P. H., Wolf, L. E., & Wasserstein, J. (2001). Adults with ADHD. An overview. *Annals of the New York Academy of Sciences, 931*, 1–16. http://dx.doi.org/10.1111/j.1749-6632.2001.tb05770.x

Wente, M. (2014, March 18). Adult ADHD: A prescription for distraction. *The Globe and Mail.* Retrieved from http://www.theglobeandmail.com/globe-debate/a-prescription-for-distraction/article17530313

Wentz, E., Nydén, A., & Krevers, B. (2012). Development of an Internet-based support and coaching model for adolescents and young adults with ADHD and autism spectrum disorders: A pilot study. *European Child & Adolescent Psychiatry, 21*, 611–622. http://dx.doi.org/10.1007/s00787-012-0297-2

Weyandt, L. L. (2005). Executive function in children, adolescents, and adults with attention deficit hyperactivity disorder: Introduction to the special issue. *Developmental Neuropsychology, 27*, 1–10. http://dx.doi.org/10.1207/s15326942dn2701_1

Weyandt, L. L. (2007). *Attention deficit hyperactivity disorder: An ADHD primer* (2nd ed.). Mahwah, NJ: Erlbaum.

Weyandt, L., DuPaul, G. J., Verdi, G., Rossi, J. S., Swentosky, A. J., Vilardo, B. S., . . . Carson, K. S. (2013). The performance of college students with and without ADHD: Neuropsychological, academic, and psychosocial functioning. *Journal of Psychopathology and Behavioral Assessment, 35*, 421–435. http://dx.doi.org/10.1007/s10862-013-9351-8

Wigal, S. B. (2009). Efficacy and safety limitations of attention-deficit hyperactivity disorder pharmacotherapy in children and adults. *CNS Drugs, 23*(Suppl. 1), 21–31. http://dx.doi.org/10.2165/00023210-200923000-00004

Wigal, S. B., Wigal, T., Schuck, S., Brams, M., Williamson, D., Armstrong, R. B., & Starr, H. L. (2011). Academic, behavioral, and cognitive effects of OROS® methylphenidate on older children with attention-deficit/hyperactivity disorder. *Journal of Child and Adolescent Psychopharmacology, 21*, 121–131. Retrieved from http://www.ncbi.nlm.nih.gov/pubmed/21488750.

Wilens, T. E., Faraone, S. V., & Biederman, J. (2004). Attention-deficit/hyperactivity disorder in adults. *JAMA, 292*, 619–623. http://dx.doi.org/10.1001/jama.292.5.619

Willcutt, E. G., Doyle, A. E., Nigg, J. T., Faraone, S. V., & Pennington, B. F. (2005). Validity of the executive function theory of attention-deficit/hyperactivity disorder: A meta-analytic review. *Biological Psychiatry, 57*, 1336–1346. http://dx.doi.org/10.1016/j.biopsych.2005.02.006

Wilmshurst, L., Peele, M., & Wilmshurst, L. (2011). Resilience and well-being in college students with and without a diagnosis of ADHD. *Journal of Attention Disorders, 15*, 11–17. http://dx.doi.org/10.1177/1087054709347261

Wolraich, M. L., Wibbelsman, C. J., Brown, T. E., Evans, S. W., Gotlieb, E. M., Knight, J. R., . . . Wilens, T. (2005). Attention-deficit/hyperactivity disorder among adolescents: A review of the diagnosis, treatment, and clinical implications. *Pediatrics, 115*, 1734–1746. http://dx.doi.org/10.1542/peds.2004-1959

World Health Organization. (2010). *International classification of diseases* (10th rev.). Retrieved from http://www.who.int/classifications/icd/en

Young, S., Bramham, J., Gray, K., & Rose, E. (2008). The experience of receiving a diagnosis and treatment of ADHD in adulthood: A qualitative study of clinically referred patients using interpretative phenomenological analysis. *Journal of Attention Disorders, 11*, 493–503. http://dx.doi.org/10.1177/1087054707305172

Young, S., Gray, K., & Bramham, J. (2009). A phenomenological analysis of the experience of receiving a diagnosis and treatment of ADHD in adulthood: A partner's perspective. *Journal of Attention Disorders, 12*, 299–307. http://dx.doi.org/10.1177/1087054707311659

Zwart, L. M., & Kallemeyn, L. M. (2001). Peer-based coaching for college students with ADHD and learning disabilities. *Journal of Postsecondary Education and Disability, 15*, 1–15.

Index

A
Academic accommodations, 221–222
Academic performance
   of adolescents with ADHD, 12, 13
   and BDEFS score, 66–67
   of children with ADHD, 12
   of college students with ADHD, 14–15
Academic Success Inventory for College
     Students (ASICS), 67–68, 234
   in concluding sessions, 79
   in intake interviews, 63
   for students with executive functioning
     deficits, 172, 173, 176, 177
Accounting software, 122, 125
ACO (ADHD Coaches Organization), 233
ADDitude Magazine, 232
ADHD. *See* Attention-deficit/hyperactivity
     disorder
ADHD Coaches Organization (ACO), 233
ADHD coaching
   counseling vs., 110–111
   metaphors in discussions about, 90–92
   rules for, 50–51
   training programs in, 112
ADHD Coaching Evaluation form, 80
ADHD coaching interventions, 25–31, 33–44.
     See also specific coaching programs
   CBT as foundation for, 26, 34–35
   CBT counseling vs., 29–31
   described, 26
   empirical support for, 26–28

   executive functioning as focus of, 38–40
   procedures used in, 40–43
   psychoeducation as framework for, 35–37
   strategies in. *See* Coaching strategy(-ies)
   suitability of clients for, 40, 191
*ADHD Coaching Tips and Strategies Part I-Psych
     Ed Coaches—Abigail Levrini, PhD* (video),
     235
ADHD Coaching Tips and Strategies Part II (video),
     235
ADHD Life Wheel, 85–88, 179, 180, 186
ADHD Planner, 105
The ADHD Report, 232
The ADHD Workbook for Kids (L. E. Shapiro), 231
Adolescent (case study), 207–225
   academic accommodations in, 221–222
   assessing motivation in, 216–217
   beginning sessions, 210–219
   brainstorming about rewards and conse-
     quences in, 217–218
   Coaching Topics Survey in, 209–213
   creating long-term goals in, 218–219
   creating weekly objectives in, 219–220
   final sessions, 223–224
   initial assessment, 209
   middle sessions, 219–223
   psychoeducation in, 222–223
   reviewing weekly objectives in, 220–221
Adolescents (in general)
   academic performance of, 12
   books on ADHD for, 231

Adolescents (in general) *continued*
   building rapport with, 214, 218
   Coaching Topics Survey for, 209–212
   comorbidities of ADHD for, 20
   disability rights of, 37
   empirical support for coaching with, 26–27
   fun activities in sessions with, 219
   gaining trust of, 208, 214
   goals of coaching for, 30
   impairments due to ADHD for, 12–13
   relationships of parents and, 223–224
   symptoms of ADHD in, 12–13
Adult ADHD (video), 235
The Adult ADHD Toolkit (J. R. Ramsay & A. L. Rostain), 230
Adult Learning Evaluation Center (ALEC), 3, 4, 231
   ADHD Coaching Evaluation form of, 80
   assessment of client's motivation at, 41
   Informed Consent form of, 47, 49
   number of sessions in program at, 43
   precoaching paperwork at, 47, 48
   setting new goals at, 78
   weekly progress notes at, 70–75
Adults. *See also specific case studies*
   beginning sessions with children vs., 131, 147
   books on ADHD for, 229–230
   comorbidities of ADHD for, 20
   disability rights of, 37
   empirical studies of coaching with, 27–28
   endorsement of CTS items by, 136
   goals of coaching for, 30
   improving social skills of, 100
   motivation of, 41–42
   prevalence of ADHD for, 10
   results of ADHD treatments for, 25
   rewards and consequences for, 135
   symptoms of ADHD in, 13–19
Age, behavioral manifestations of ADHD and, 145
AHEAD (Association on Higher Education and Disability), 233
ALEC. *See* Adult Learning Evaluation Center
Alexander, S. J., 20
American Professional Society of ADHD and Related Disorders (ASPARD), 233
American Psychiatric Association, 10, 21
American Psychological Association (APA), 23, 113, 191
Americans With Disabilities Act (2008), 37
Amphetamine, 42
Anastopoulos, A. D., 21
Anxiety. *See also* Young adult with comorbid mood disorders (case study)
   assessing severity of, 146, 148–149
   coaching clients with, 40–41
   coaching during treatments for, 190–191
   as comorbidity of ADHD, 20–21, 196
   metaphors for dealing with, 90
   strategies for dealing with, 201–202

Anxiety disorder, 20
APA. *See* American Psychological Association
Application for services, 48
Applications (apps), 105–107
   for children, 106
   goal-tracking, 202
   mood-tracking, 200–201
   for motivation, 103
   planner, 96–97
   time management and organization, 105–106
ASICS. *See* Academic Success Inventory for College Students
ASPARD (American Professional Society of ADHD and Related Disorders), 233
Assessment, initial. *See* Initial assessment
Association on Higher Education and Disability (AHEAD), 233
Attention Deficit Disorder Association (ADDA), 233
Attention-deficit/hyperactivity disorder (ADHD), 9–24
   comorbidities with, 20–21
   diagnostic criteria for, 21–23
   etiology of, 19, 35–37
   impairment with, 10–19
   prevalence of, 10
   previous diagnosis of, 190
   symptoms of. *See* Symptoms of ADHD
   trends in treatment of, 4
Attention Magazine, 232, 234
Attention Talk Radio, 234
Autism spectrum disorder, 22

B
Barkley Adult ADHD Rating Scale—IV, 48
Barkley, R. A., 13, 15, 17, 18, 38–40, 100, 229–232
Barkley Deficits in Executive Functioning Scale (BDEFS), 39, 48
   for college student with executive functioning deficits, 173, 176
   in concluding sessions, 79
   generating hypotheses based on, 176
   in intake interviews, 63
   setting goals based on, 66
   for students with academic difficulties, 66–67
   for young professional adult, 153, 166
Barriers to meeting objectives, discussing, 77–78, 141, 161–162, 184
BDEFS. *See* Barkley Deficits in Executive Functioning Scale
Beginning coaching sessions. *See* Initial coaching sessions
Behavior(s)
   age and ADHD-related, 145
   reinforcement for anxiety-driven, 202–203
Behavioral control, 118
Behavioral disorders, 19
Behavioral execution, 40
Behavioral interventions, 89

Behavior modification programs, 26
Beliefs, negative, 34
Between-session assignments (BSAs), 68–70
Between-session communications, 30, 71, 76
Biederman, J., 15
Billing, in coaching practices, 121–122
Bipolar disorder, 20
Bluetooth tracking devices, 99
Bodily kinesthetic intelligence, 85
Boundaries
    of competence, 114, 191
    maintaining, with clients, 113
Boys, ADHD symptoms in, 11
Brain, pathways of, 90
Brainstorming, about rewards and consequences, 135–136, 198–199, 217–218
Brown, T. E., 38
BSAs (between-session assignments), 68–70
Buermeyer, C., 17
Business plans, 116
Business structures, 116–117
Byrd, S. L., 17–18

C

Career indecision, adult with. *See* Middle-aged adult (case study)
Career-related goals, 100, 107–108
Career Thoughts Inventory (CTI), 108
CBT. *See* Cognitive behavior therapy
C corporations, 116
Center of Excellence in ADHD and Related Disorders, 232
Centers for Disease Control and Prevention (CDC), 10, 23, 235
Centers for Medicare and Medicaid Services (CMS), 23
CHADD (Children and Adults With Attention-Deficit/Hyperactivity Disorder), 37, 232–234
Chalder, T., 34
Children
    beginning sessions with adults vs., 131, 147
    books on ADHD for, 231
    Coaching Topics Survey for, 54, 64
    comorbidities with ADHD for, 20
    disability rights of, 37
    empirical support for coaching interventions with, 26–27
    fun activities in sessions with, 219
    goals of coaching for, 30
    impairments due to ADHD for, 10–12
    individual coaching with, 207
    motivation of, 41–42
    parents as executive function system for, 174
    prevalence of ADHD for, 10
    results of ADHD interventions for, 26
    symptoms of ADHD in, 10–12
    views of, on therapists, 208–209
Children and Adults With Attention-Deficit/Hyperactivity Disorder (CHADD), 37, 232–234
Chore Pad, 106
Client(s)
    collaboration with, 152, 155
    expectations of, 111–112
    identifying strengths and weaknesses of, 176
    learning styles of, 84–85
    maintaining engagement of, 133–134
    marketing to attract, 118–120
    mental health issues of, 40–41
    monitoring priorities of, 138
    motivation of, 41–42
    suitability of, for ADHD coaching, 40, 191
Client Goals and Objectives form, 56–61
    for college student with executive functioning deficits, 186
    completing, 59–61
    Follow-Up Questions on, 76, 77, 162, 163
    items on, 57–58
    monitoring progress with, 159, 160, 167
    reinforcing plans with, 154
    and setting weekly objectives, 56–59
    for young adult with comorbid mood disorders, 181
Client Symptom Checklist (CSC), 62
    assessing anxiety and depression with, 146, 191, 193
    for college student with executive functioning deficits, 172
    in concluding sessions, 79, 166
    in intake interviews, 63
    for young adult with comorbid mood disorders, 191, 193
Clinics with ADHD specialties, 231–232
CMS (Centers for Medicare and Medicaid Services), 23
Coaches, roles of therapists vs., 110–112
Coaching practices, establishing. *See* Independent coaching practice(s)
Coaching sessions, 33–81. *See also specific types*
    ASICS tool in, 67–68
    between-session assignments, 68–70
    between-session communications, 71, 76
    Client Goals and Objectives form in, 59–61
    creating weekly objectives in, 56–59
    discussing barriers in, 77–78
    discussing successes in, 76–77
    improving executive functioning with, 65–67
    involvement of parents in, 208
    number of, 42–43
    plan for, in progress notes, 73
    preparing for, 47, 48
    setting long-term goals in, 51–56
    setting new goals in, 78
    steps in, 46
    timers for, 96
    weekly progress notes in, 70–75

Coaching strategy(-ies), 78–79, 83–108
    ADHD Life Wheel, 85–88
    for clients with career-related goals, 100
    Cognitive Impulsivity Exercise, 94–95
    for developing social skills, 99–100
    goal-specific, 95–104
    for improving decision making and prioritization, 100–102
    for improving healthy living and life skills, 97–99
    for improving learning and study strategies, 97
    for improving time management, 95–97
    Inspiration Toolbox, 89
    Juggling Exercise, 92–93
    and learning styles of clients, 84–85
    mantras in, 92
    multimodal approach to, 102–104
    Processing Exercise, 93–94
    for psychoeducational phase, 84–95
    using metaphors as, 90–92
Coaching Topics Survey (CTS), 51–54
    in adolescent case study, 209–212
    and ASICS, 177
    for children, 209–210
    for college student with executive functioning deficits, 173, 186
    in concluding sessions, 79
    decision-making-related items on, 100
    educating clients about, 84
    grouping endorsed items on, 136
    healthy living and life skills-related items on, 98–99
    in intake interviews, 63
    learning- and study-related items on, 97
    long-term goals based on, 51–54, 148
    for middle-aged adult, 130, 136
    Parent-Child version of, 54, 64
    in precoaching paperwork, 48
    social skills-related items on, 99
    time management items on, 95
    for young adult with comorbid mood disorders, 192–195
    for young professional adult, 148, 166–167
Cognitive-Behavioral Therapy for Adult ADHD (J. R. Ramsay & A. L. Rostain), 228
Cognitive-Behavioral Therapy for Adult ADHD (M. V. Solanto), 228
Cognitive behavior therapy (CBT)
    ADHD coaching interventions vs., 29–31
    books on, 228
    as foundation for coaching interventions, 26, 34–35
    results of ADHD interventions using, 25–26
    similarities and differences with coaching, 29
Cognitive Impulsivity Exercise, 94–95
Cognitive reframing, 139, 162
Cognitive triad, 112
Collaboration, with clients, 152, 155
College, transition to, 15, 66–67

College students
    ADHD and cognitive ability of, 84–85
    BDEFS for students with academic difficulties, 66–67
    characteristics of academic success for, 67–68
    comorbidities with ADHD for, 20, 21
    disability rights of, 37
    empirical studies of coaching interventions for, 27–28
    long-term goals of, 55
    medication effectiveness for, 42
    prevalence of ADHD for, 10
    symptoms of ADHD in, 13–19
College student with executive functioning deficits (case study), 171–188
    beginning sessions, 173–181
    creating long-term goals in, 180–181
    discussing barriers in, 184
    discussing medication in, 184–186
    final sessions, 186–187
    initial assessment, 172–173
    middle sessions, 181–186
    psychoeducation in, 178–180
    rewards and consequences in, 182–184
Committed relationships, setting goals with clients in, 136
Communications, between-session, 30, 71, 76
Comorbidities, 20–22
Competence, boundaries of, 114, 191
Computer-based planners, 96, 220
Concept maps. *See* Graphic organizers
Concern, areas of (basing goals on), 148
Concluding coaching sessions, 46, 79–80
    in adolescent case study, 223–224
    for college student with executive functioning deficits, 186–187
    for middle-aged adult, 141–142
    for young adult with comorbid mood disorders, 203–204
    for young professional adult, 166–168
Conduct disorder, 11, 20
Confidentiality, 113–114
Consensus of the European Network Adult ADHD, 35
Consent, informed, 47, 49, 114
Consequences
    in adolescent case study, 217–218
    brainstorming about, 135–136, 198–199, 217–218
    for college student with executive functioning deficits, 182–184
    for middle-aged adult, 135–136
    as part of BSAs, 69, 70
    in progress notes, 73
    rewards as motivation vs., 182
    for young adult with comorbid mood disorders, 198–199
    for young professional adult, 158–166

Control, behavioral and financial, 118
Cooperatives, 116
Cooper-Vince, C., 30
Coping mechanisms, 147
Copper, Jeff, 234
Corporations, 116
Costello, J., 21
Counseling, ADHD coaching vs., 110–111
Cozi (app), 105
CPT (Current Procedural Terminology), 122
Credit card payments, 121
CSC. *See* Client Symptom Checklist
CTI (Career Thoughts Inventory), 108
CTS. *See* Coaching Topics Survey
Current ADHD Symptoms Scale, 63, 79
Current Procedural Terminology (CPT), 122

D
Daily life functioning
    coaching strategies to improve, 98–99
    impairment in, 18–19
    young adult with difficulties in. *See* Young professional adult (case study)
Datexx Smart Cube Timer, 105
Decision making, improving, 100–102
Decision-Making Form, 100–101
Deep breathing exercises, 99
DeMars, C. E., 27
Depression, 20. *See also* Young adult with comorbid mood disorders (case study)
    and ADHD, 17, 20–21, 196
    assessing severity of, 146, 148–149
    coaching during interventions for, 190–191
    coaching interventions for clients with, 40–41
    strategies for dealing with, 201–202
Diagnostic and Statistical Manual of Mental Disorders (DSM–5), 4, 9, 18, 20–23
Disability rights, 37
Disruptive mood dysregulation disorder, 20
Dittner, A. J., 34
DSM–5. *See Diagnostic and Statistical Manual of Mental Disorders*

E
Eco therapy, 102, 103
Edge Foundation, 235
EF (executive functioning), 38–40. *See also* Executive functioning deficits
Eisenhower, Dwight D., 101
Eisenhower Matrix, 101–103, 150–151
Eisenhower Principle, 101, 102
Electronic health records, 122, 125
Emotional status, reflection on, 201
Empirical support
    for ADHD coaching interventions, 26–28
    for psychoeducation, 37
Employment difficulties, 15–16
Engagement, client, 133–134

Enjoyment, of objective-related activities, 60
Epic Win, 106
Estrada, R. V., 37
E-therapy, 113
Ethical issues, for independent practices, 112–115
"Ethical Principles of Psychologists and Code of Conduct," 113–115, 191
Ethical standards, 112
Etiology, of ADHD, 19, 35
Evaluation, of coaching by client, 80
Evans, S. W., 27
Evernote, 106
Evernote Peek, 106
Executive functioning (EF), 38–40
Executive functioning deficits. *See also* College student with executive functioning deficits (case study)
    and academic impairment, 15
    and ADHD symptoms, 38–39
    of college students, 174
    definition of, 38
    etiology of, 39
    measuring, 39–40
    understanding, 65–67
Exercise, physical, 99, 139
Expectations, clients', 111–112
Expertise, 158
Externalizing behaviors, 18
External motivation, 69, 184
Extinction burst, 203

F
Fabiano, G. A., 27
Faigel, H. C., 15
Failure, concept of, 162
Family issues, adolescent with. *See* Adolescent (case study)
Family members, 207. *See also* Parents
Faraone, S. V., 15
Favorite, B., 30
Feedback, 79, 80
Fees, coaching, 121
Field, S., 27–28
Fin, Fur, and Feather Bureau of Investigation, 236
Final coaching sessions. *See* Concluding coaching sessions
Financial control, 118
Financial objectives, clients with, 139
Fischer, M., 13, 18
Fletcher, K., 13
Florida State University, 4, 231
Florida State University Career Center, 108
Focus, maintaining, 156–157
Follow-Up Questions (Client Goals and Objectives form), 76, 77, 162, 163
Free association, 157
Friendship Coaching groups, 27

G

Gender differences, in ADHD symptoms, 11–12, 14
Genetic factors
  in ADHD, 19
  in executive functioning deficits, 39
Girls, ADHD symptoms in, 11–12
Goals. *See also* Client Goals and Objectives form; Long-term goals
  BDEFS as basis for, 66
  career-related, 100, 107–108
  in CBT vs. ADHD coaching, 30
  measurable, 54–55
  overarching, 59–60
  process-based, 55
  realistic, 55
  setting new, 78
  strategies for meeting specific, 95–104
  time-sensitive, 55
Goals and Objectives form. *See* Client Goals and Objectives form
Goal-tracking apps, 202
Graphic organizers, 97, 98, 107
"Green" settings, coaching in, 102, 103
Group coaching, 28, 118
Gudjonsson, G. H., 18
Gudmundsdottir, H. B., 18
GuideStar, 117

H

Harrison, A. G., 20
Health Insurance Portability and Accountability Act (HIPAA), 23, 49, 112–113, 166
Healthy living, 97–99
Heritability, of ADHD, 19
High-functioning adults, 147
Hinshaw, S. P., 10
HIPAA. *See* Health Insurance Portability and Accountability Act
Homework assignments, 68–70
Hoyle, R. H., 21
Hughes, C. W., 27
Hyperactivity (hyperactive symptoms)
  of college students and adults, 13–14
  in *DSM–5*, 21–22
Hyperactivity-impulsivity type of ADHD, 11
Hyperverbal (term), 137

I

ICD. See International Classification of Diseases
IEPs (individualized education plans), 222
Impairment(s), 10–19
  academic, 14–15
  for adolescents with ADHD, 12–13
  for children with ADHD, 10–12
  for college students and adults with ADHD, 14–19
  in daily life-functioning, 18–19
  in employment, 15–16
  in executive functioning. *See* Executive functioning deficits
  in interpersonal relationships, 16–18
Important activities (on Eisenhower Matrix), 102
Impulsivity (impulsive symptoms)
  cognitive impulsivity, 94–95
  for college students and adults, 13–14, 16–18
  in *DSM–5*, 21–22
  and maintaining focus with clients, 156–157
Inattention (inattentive symptoms)
  for college students and adults, 14, 16
  in *DSM–5*, 21
Inattentive type of ADHD, 11
Incentives
  clients who do not use, 182
  as part of BSAs, 69, 70
  in progress notes, 73
Independent coaching practice(s), 109–125
  assessing readiness to begin, 115–116
  business plans for, 116
  business-related issues for, 115–123
  business structures for, 116–117
  ethical issues for, 112–115
  fees, billing, and insurance reimbursement in, 121–123
  marketing by, 118–121
  and role of coach vs. therapist, 110–112
  solo vs. group, 118
Individualization, of coaching strategies, 83
Individualized coaching, 27–28
Individualized education plans (IEPs), 222
Individuals With Disabilities Education Improvement Act (2004), 37
Information-sharing platforms, 113
Informed consent, 47, 49, 114
Informed Consent forms, 47, 49
Initial assessment
  in adolescent case study, 209
  of client's mental health issues, 40–41
  of client's motivation, 41–42
  for college student with executive functioning deficits, 172–173
  for middle-aged adult, 130
  of suitability for ADHD coaching, 40
  for young adult with comorbid mood disorders, 192
  for young professional adult, 146–147
Initial coaching sessions, 45–64
  in adolescent case study, 210–219
  with adults vs. children, 131, 147
  Client Goals and Objectives form in, 56–61
  for college student with executive functioning deficits, 173–181
  creating weekly objectives in, 56–59
  intake interviews in, 49–50, 63–64
  for middle-aged adult, 131–137
  preparing for, 47, 48
  and rules of coaching, 50–51

setting long-term goals in, 51–56
for young adult with comorbid mood disorders, 196–200
for young professional adult, 147–153
In-network providers, 122
Inspiration Toolbox, 89, 92, 141, 198
Insurance panels, 122
Intake interviews, 49–50, 63–64
Intelligence, types of, 85
Internal motivation, 69, 184, 197–198
Internal Revenue Service (IRS), 118
International Classification of Diseases (*ICD*), 4, 9, 21
International Classification of Diseases, 9th Edition—Clinical Modification (*ICD–9–CM*), 22
International Classification of Diseases, 10th Edition—Clinical Modification (*ICD–10–CM*), 22, 23
International Coaches Federation, 234
Interpersonal intelligence, 85
Interpersonal relationships
of college students and adults with ADHD, 16–18
objectives related to improving, 139
Interviews, 49–50, 63–64, 120
Intrapersonal intelligence, 85
iReward Chart, 106
IRS (Internal Revenue Service), 118

J
Journal of Attention Disorders (*JAD*), 232–233
Journals, ADHD, 232–233
Juggling Exercise, 92–93, 222–223

K
Kallemeyn, L. M., 28
Kern, R. M., 17–18
Kinesthetic learners, 85
Inspiration Toolbox for, 89
Juggling Exercise for, 92–93
Knouse, L. E., 30
Krevers, B., 27
Kubick, J. A., 26, 28

L
Learning
adolescent with difficulties in. *See* Adolescent (case study)
coaching based on clients' style of, 84–85
strategies for improving, 97
Learning and Study Strategies Inventory, 28
Leonard, Thomas, 234
Lerner, M. D., 27
Levrini, A., 105, 229–230, 235
Life skills
deficits in, 18–19
strategies for improving, 97–99
Limited liability companies (LLCs), 116, 117
Linear thinking, 132

Long-term goals
in adolescent case study, 218–219
and BSAs, 70
collaborating with clients on, 152
of college student with executive functioning deficits, 180–181
creating, 51–56
defined, 51
metaphors in discussions of, 90
of middle-aged adult, 136–137
in progress notes, 72
of young adult with comorbid mood disorders, 199–200
of young professional adult, 150–153
Lott, D., 113
Lumosity, 107

M
Maitland, T. L., 28
Mantras, 92
Marketing, 118–121, 125
Marriage satisfaction, 17
Married clients, goal setting with, 136
Mastering Your Adult ADHD (S. A. Safren et al.), 228
McLeod B. D., 27
Measurable goals, 54–55
Medication management, 139
Medications, ADHD
discussions with clients about, 42, 90, 184–186
metaphors for activity of, 90
prevalence of, 10
Meditation Oasis, 106
Memory aids, 107
Memory difficulties, 71
Men, ADHD symptoms of, 14
Mental health functioning
of adults with ADHD, 18–19
assessing, 40–41
of middle-aged adult, 134–135
of young professional adult, 148–150
Metaphors, 90–92
Middle-aged adult (case study), 129–143
assessing mental health functioning and motivation in, 134–135
beginning sessions, 131–137
brainstorming about rewards and consequences in, 135–136
creating long-term goals in, 136–137
creating weekly objectives in, 138
CTS in, 136
final sessions, 141–142
initial assessment, 130
middle sessions, 137–141
reviewing weekly objectives in, 138–141
Middle coaching sessions, 46, 76–78
in adolescent case study, 219–223
for college student with executive functioning deficits, 181–186

Middle coaching sessions *continued*
  discussing barriers in, 77–78
  discussing successes in, 76–77
  for middle-aged adult, 137–141
  setting new goals in, 78
  for young adult with comorbid mood disorders, 200–203
  for young professional adult, 153–166
Mikami, A. Y., 27
The Mindfulness Prescription for Adult ADHD (L. Zylowska), 230
Mind maps. *See* Graphic organizers
Minors, informed consent form, 49. *See also* Adolescents (in general); Children
Monastra, V. J., 231
Mood disorders. *See* Anxiety; Depression
Mood swings, 17
Moodtracker.com, 106
Mood-tracking apps, 200–201
More Attention, Less Deficit (A. Tuckman), 230
Motivation
  in adolescent case study, 216–217
  apps for, 103
  assessing clients', 41–42
  and between-session communications, 71, 76
  in clients with ADHD, 30
  in coaching, 50
  to complete weekly objectives, 60
  and executive functioning deficits of clients, 67
  external, 69, 184
  internal, 69, 184, 197–198
  of middle-aged adult, 134–135
  and rewards vs. consequences, 182
  and stress, 148–149
  for young professional adult, 148–150
Mount Sinai School of Medicine, 232
Multimodal approach to coaching strategies, 102–104
Murphy, K., 15, 16, 20, 30, 34, 35, 38
Musical intelligence, 85
My Next Move, 108

N
Nadeau, K. G., 16, 17
Nakonezny, P. A., 27
National Center for O*Net Development, 108
National Institute of Mental Health, 236
National Institute of Mental Health Multimodal Treatment of ADHD Study, 25
National Resource Center on ADHD, 234, 236
Naturalist intelligence, 85
NCHS (U.S. National Center for Health Statistics), 23
Negative messages, for people with ADHD, 20
Negative thoughts and beliefs, 34
Nelson-Gray, R. O., 17
Neurodevelopmental disorder, ADHD as, 19
Nigg, J. T., 19

Nonprofit organizations, 117
Nutrition, 139, 185–186
Nydén, A., 27

O
Objectives, weekly
  in adolescent case study, 219–221
  BSAs based on, 69
  on Client Goals and Objectives form, 56–61
  creating, 56–59, 138, 153–155, 200–201, 219–220
  in discussions of successes and barriers, 76–78
  ease of completing, 162, 163
  for middle-aged adult, 138–141
  motivation and enjoyment of, 60
  primary importance of accomplishing, 161
  in progress notes, 72, 73
  quantity and quality of completion of, 162, 163
  refining, 155–158, 201–203
  reviewing, 138–141, 220–221
  for young adult with comorbid mood disorders, 200–203
  for young professional adult, 153–158
Obstacles, to meeting objectives, 72, 73, 156
Online tools, 107–108, 117. *See also* Applications (apps)
Online video sharing, 119
Oppositional-defiant disorder, 11, 20
Otto, M. W., 228
Outcome Questionnaire—45 (OQ-45)
  assessing anxiety and depression with, 146
  for college student with executive functioning deficits, 172, 186
  in concluding sessions, 79
  in intake interviews, 63
  in precoaching paperwork, 48
  for young professional adult, 146, 167
Out-of-network providers, 122
Overarching goals, 59–60

P
Painter, C., 16
Paper-and-pencil planners, 96, 220
Paperwork, precoaching, 47, 48
Parent-Child version of Coaching Topics Survey, 54, 64
Parenting Children With ADHD (V. J. Monastra), 231
Parents
  adolescent clients' relationships with, 223–224
  books on ADHD for, 230–231
  coaching requests from, 41–42
  completion of CTS by, 209, 212, 213
  as executive function system for children, 174
  informing, of adolescent clients' objectives, 219–220
  involvement of, in coaching interventions, 27
  involvement of, in coaching sessions, 208

Parker, D. R., 27–28
Partnerships, 116
Paulson, J. F., 17
Perlman, C. A., 228
Planner Plus, 105
Planners (organizers, calendars), 59, 96–97, 105, 220
Planning difficulties, 153–154
Podcasts, 120
Precoaching paperwork, 47, 48, 176
Prevalence rates, of ADHD, 10
Prevatt, F., 16, 28, 229–230, 235
Printed marketing materials, 120–121
Priorities of clients, monitoring, 138
Prioritization, 100–102, 156
Problem solving
  in coaching, 50, 51
  to create BSAs, 69
  guiding clients in, 157–158
  progress notes as blueprint for, 71
Process-based goals, 55
Processing Exercise, 93–94
Proctor, B. E., 16, 28
Professional directories, 120
Professional referral networks, 119
Progress notes, weekly, 70–75
  format and purpose of, 70–71
  sample, 74–75
  template and instructions for creating, 72–73
  for young professional adult, 164–166
Psych Ed Coaches, 3–4
  common long-term goals at, 55
  number of sessions in program at, 43
  setting new goals at, 78
Psychoeducation
  about disability rights, 37
  about etiology of ADHD, 35–37
  in adolescent case study, 222–223
  for college student with executive functioning deficits, 175, 178–180
  empirical support for, 37
  as framework for coaching interventions, 35–37
  in initial sessions, 50
  strategies for, 84–95
Psychopharmacological interventions, 25
Psychosocial impairment, 11
Psychosocial interventions, 25–26
Psychostimulants, 13, 42, 185

Q
Quinn, P. O., 11

R
Rabiner, D. L., 21
Rademacher, K. N., 28
Radio shows, ADHD, 234
Ramsay, J. R., 228, 230
Rapport, with adolescent clients, 214, 218

Rasmussen, P. R., 17–18
Ratey, N. A., 30
Reading disorders, 12
Realistic goals, 55
Receipts, coaching session, 122, 123
Referral networks, 119
Rehabilitation Act, 221–222
Reinforcement, of anxiety-driven behavior, 202–203
Relationships
  of adolescent clients with parents, 223–224
  between businesses and workers, 118
  of college students and adults with ADHD, 16–18
  improving, 139
  setting goals with clients in committed, 136
Relaxation exercises, 99
Reminders, 159
Rewards
  in adolescent case study, 217–218
  brainstorming about, 135–136, 198–199, 217–218
  for college student with executive functioning deficits, 182–184
  for middle-aged adult, 135–136
  motivation and consequences vs., 182
  for young adult with comorbid mood disorders, 198–199
  for young professional adult, 158–166
RIASEC environments, 108
Richman, E. L., 28
Rimes, K. A., 34
Rituals, 99
Rolands, L., 27–28
Rosenberg Self-Esteem Scale
  for college student with executive functioning deficits, 172, 173, 186
  in concluding sessions, 79
  in intake interviews, 63
  in precoaching paperwork, 48
  for young professional adult, 146, 167
Rostain, A. L., 228, 230
Routines, 99
Russell, A. J., 34

S
Safren, S. A., 30, 228
Sawilowsky, S., 27–28
Scheffler, R. M., 10
School-based accountability laws, 10
Schultz, B. K., 27
S corporations, 116
SDS (Self-Directed Search), 107–108
Search engines, web presence in, 120
Section 504 accommodations, 221–222
Self-Directed Search (SDS), 107–108
Self-esteem, 71
Self-regulation, 40
Sequential thinking, 93–94, 156

Shapiro, L. E., 231
Shifrin, J. G., 16
Sigurdsson, J. F., 18
Sigurjonsdottir, S., 18
Skitch, 106
Smallish, L., 13
Smari, J., 18
Social cues, 16–17
Social media, practice's presence in, 119
Social skills, 99–100, 139
Solanto, M. V., 228
Sole proprietorships, 116, 117
Solo coaching practices, 118
Spatial intelligence, 85
Specified ADHD, 22
Spouses of clients
  coaching requests from, 41–42
  goal setting with, 136
Sprich, S., 30, 228
Strategizing sessions, 164
Strengths, identifying clients', 176
Stress, as motivator, 148–149
Study strategies, 97
Substance use and abuse, 132–133
Succeeding With Adult ADHD (A. Levrini & F. Prevatt), 229–230
Success(es)
  academic, 67–68
  discussions of, 76–77, 141, 161
  in progress notes, 72
Swartz, S., 28
Swartzwelder, H. S., 21
Symptoms of ADHD, 10–14
  age and behavioral manifestations of, 145
  checklist for. *See* Client Symptom Checklist (CSC)
  client's previous strategies for addressing, 133
  Current ADHD Symptoms Scale, 63, 79
  and executive functioning deficits, 38–39

T
Taking Charge of Adult ADHD (R. A. Barkley), 229–231
Tamm, L., 27
TaskCurrent, 106
Tasks, breaking down, 155
TaskTimer, 106
Test anxiety, 15
Testimonials, 114, 115
Theoretical framework, for ADHD coaching, 34–35, 65
Therapists
  children's views of, 208–209
  roles of coaches vs., 110–112
Thinking
  linear, 132
  sequential, 93–94, 156
Thoughts, negative, 34
Tile App, 107

Time management, 95–97
Timers, 95–96, 104–105
Time-sensitive goals, 55
Time Timer, 104–105
Total Recall, 107
Training programs, 112
Trust, with adolescent clients, 208, 214
Tuckman, A., 230
211 call centers, 117

U
Understand Your Brain, Get More Done (A. Tuckman), 230
University of Pennsylvania School of Medicine Adult ADHD Treatment and Research Program, 232
Unspecified ADHD, 22
Unstuck, getting, 107, 139
Urgent activities (on Eisenhower Matrix), 102
U.S. Department of Education, 221, 222
U.S. Department of Labor, 108
U.S. National Center for Health Statistics (NCHS), 23

V
Videos, 119, 235
VSee program, 49

W
Watchminder, 107
Weaknesses, identifying clients', 176
Web Clipper, 106
Webinars, 120
WEBMD, 236
Websites, 119–120, 235–236
Weekly objectives. *See* Objectives, weekly
Weekly progress notes. *See* Progress notes, weekly
Welles, T., 16
Wentz, E., 27
Weyandt, L., 15, 18, 20, 38
"What Influences ADHD?" fact sheet, 35–36
Wilens, T. E., 15
Willpower, 184
Wittschen, L. K., 17–18
Women, ADHD symptoms for, 14
Work performance, 15–16
World Health Organization, 21
Writing, 96
Wunderlist, 105

Y
Yelland, S., 28
Young adult with comorbid mood disorders (case study), 189–205
  beginning sessions, 196–200
  brainstorming about rewards and consequences in, 198–199
  creating long-term goals in, 199–200

creating weekly objectives in, 200–201
CTS in, 192–195
final sessions, 203–204
initial assessment, 192
middle sessions, 200–203
refining objectives in, 201–203
Young professional adult (case study), 145–169
    assessing mental health functioning and motivation in, 148–150
    beginning sessions, 147–153
    creating long-term goals in, 150–153
    creating weekly objectives in, 153–155
    final sessions, 166–168
    initial assessment, 146–147
    middle sessions, 153–166
    refining objectives in, 155–158
    rewards and consequences in, 158–166

Z

Zwart, L. M., 28

About the Authors

Frances Prevatt, PhD, is a professor in the Department of Educational Psychology and Learning Systems at Florida State University. She is also executive director of the Adult Learning Evaluation Center (ALEC), where thousands of college students have been evaluated and treated for attention-deficit/hyperactivity disorder (ADHD) and learning disabilities. She is the author of two previous books and more than 75 publications in the field of educational psychology. She coauthored (with Abigail Levrini) the best-selling book, *Succeeding With Adult ADHD: Daily Strategies to Help You Achieve Your Goals and Manage Your Life* (2012), and appeared in a video on treating adults using ADHD Coaching (2013). Dr. Prevatt is on the professional advisory board of the National Resource Center on ADHD.

Abigail Levrini, PhD, is a licensed clinical psychologist and owner of Psych Ed Coaches, a private practice specializing in in-person and remote ADHD coaching for individuals and families. She has published several scientific articles on ADHD (including her 2008 dissertation, *ADHD Coaching and College Students*, under her unmarried name "Reaser") and presented her coaching model in professional settings throughout the country. She is a sought-after expert on the subject of ADHD, having been interviewed for articles on popular websites such as WebMD and Psych Central, and she has conducted numerous ADHD-based webcasts and workshops for major companies and associations. Dr. Levrini is also coauthor (with Frances Prevatt) of the best-selling book *Succeeding With Adult ADHD: Daily Strategies to Help You Achieve Your Goals and Manage Your Life* (2012).